CYCLING
SOJOURNER

Ellee Thalheimer

Into Action Publications
2012

CYCLING SOJOURNER
A Guide to the Best Multi-Day Bicycle Tours in Oregon

by Ellee Thalheimer

Published by
Into Action Publications
4110 SE Hawthorne Blvd #109
Portland, OR 97214
http://cyclingsojourner.com
ISBN 978-1-934620-18-2
First Edition, 2012

Edited by Lucy Burningham
Cover by Laura Cary
Design by Joe Biel
Maps by Jeff Smith
Fonts by Ian Lynam

ACKNOWLEDGMENTS

Joe Partridge, thanks for being the pinnacle of support who dealt with my extended absences, gave up weekends helping me research, took on all household tasks while I went into my writer hole for months and labored over the history sections in many chapters. You make me the luckiest woman in the world.
I couldn't have asked for a better editor or friend in **Lucy Burningham**. Thanks for being there every step of the way, even for the non-sexy, grunt work.
Joe Biel, your talent, generosity and super powers humble.
Jeff Smith, map whiz, thanks for your weekends, aptitude and courage to try something new.
Laura Cary, thanks for believing in this project and giving it your time and talent.
Elly Blue, thanks for scheming our takeover of the world and endless inspiration.
Contributors, thanks for your sheer love of the bicycle and time spent crafting your words for my readers. Steph Routh, Alex Phillips, Lynn Penner-Ash, Joel Grover, Brian Wilson, Bill Heimann, Dan Little, Barbie Borst, Donnie Kolb and Troy Nave.

THANKS TO

Cycle Oregon for making this book possible with your support.
Travel Oregon and **Kristin Dahl** for supporting this project and being huge bike tourism advocates.
Jerry Norquist for route consults and believing in this project.
Keith Ketterling and **Bart Eberwein** for being enthusiastic advocates for the book. (And to Keith for the IPAs.)
Alex Phillips for helping me foster great ideas from the get-go and for all your hard work on the Scenic Bikeways program.
Donnie Kolb and **Lindsay Kandra** for expert advice.
Stephanie Edman, Pete Kellers, Joe Partridge, Tori Bortman, Laura Prisbe, Susan Sterne and **Barbie Borst** for accepting the adventure of bike touring with me (and being tolerant of my research).
Diane Wilson and the **Yes Yogis** for keeping me sane and grounding me into what's most important.
All the **fabulous Oregonians** along the way for your hospitality, friendly words and good laughs.

INTRODUCTION

It may sound creepy, but I've been thinking about you for years. As I've traipsed all over this fine state with my bicycle—from mountain passes to wine country—I've been sussing out the best multi-day tours in Oregon just for you. Whether you are a hedonistically inclined cyclist or a gravel grinder seeking epic adventure, I've got your back.

It wasn't hard to find world-class tours for almost everyone. The variety of cycle-scapes in this state feels a bit gluttonous: alkaline deserts, vineyards, cowboy country, painted hills, volcanoes, alpine lakes, humongous old-growth forests, lava fields, coastline and calderas. And the cycle-loving cities in between make the riding all the more sweet.

No matter where you choose to ride, bike touring usually inspires an adventure. My Oregon cycling adventures have landed me in the back of the pick-up truck driven by a one-eyed, old man named "Junior." I've spent the night in a shed at a rural goat cheese fromagerie. A coal miner taught me how to shoot a gun. I've sipped Pinot with renowned winemakers and perused Wild West art in a tiny town called Joseph. My life is all the richer, and my legs all the stronger, for these experiences.

I hope this book—with its routes, logistical details, tips and insider information—makes it easy to take the leap and embark on your own cycling sojourn. Who knows what the road may hold. Yikes, I'm excited for you.
cowbells

P.S. Adventuring by bike can recalibrate your perspective on life and your connection to the world. Even though you may feel every stupendous emotion and unsavory mood while pedaling mile after mile through evergreen forests or cracked deserts, in the end, you might discover a satisfied calm and find yourself closer to being the person you want to be. In those moments, a loaded bicycle is a true mechanism of freedom.

MY APPROACH

Planning a tour from the ground up takes a lot of time. I've tried to do the grunt work so you can just make a couple of calls, grab your gear and head out into Oregon, one of the most fantastic places to ride in the country. Basically, I've created my fantasy guidebook which neither skimps on cool details that cycle tourists want nor reads like an appliance manual. This book is entirely opinionated and slanted to my value system. Word.

The Gist

First and foremost, I prioritize route, riding, safety and logistical information. While I expect my readers to be wary cyclists who are responsible for themselves (I don't warn you about every cattle grate or hole in the pavement), I try to give you a heads up about pertinent things like narrow tunnels, lack of water, good pie, etc.

Out of the Saddle

Because I know you are a creative and apt adventurer, I simply point you to camping, lodging, eating and drinking spots that I dig, which you can take or leave. So you know, I'm drawn to locally-owned, bike-friendly businesses that are run by affable folks.

For camping, I like both naturally beautiful campgrounds and sites close to town; I try to list both when possible. I don't mention or map out every existing campground but do give you numerous choices along every route. For lodging, I list an array of cost options when possible, keeping in mind campers needing to dry out for the night and high rollers. Most lodging listings are within easy walking distance of town centers. For DIY lodging, especially if you are traveling with a number of people, I suggest **VRBO. com** (Vacation Rentals By Owner), a fabulous resource for rentals all over Oregon. If you want to go shoe-string and/or have a more extroverted personality, **Warmshowers.org** is an amazing, reciprocity-fueled resource that connects cycle tourists to local folks who will house you for the night for free.

For eating—and I'm really fond of eating—I like restaurants that use local, sustainable, organic ingredients to make delicious meals. I like homemade food. I like quirky places with attitude and local flavor. I like beer. I love wine. I always mention conventional and health food grocery stores (and farmers markets) for resupply.

Money

The tours are rated according to required purse size. **Small** ($25-50 per day) suggests you can camp most days and cook your own food (see Bike Camping on a Shoestring, page 7). **Medium** ($50-100 per day) usually means lower end motels and a meal or two out daily. **Bulging** ($100-300 or more) is all about luxury accommodations and upscale restaurants. Cost ratings don't take into consideration travel expenses to or from the tour. Though I don't go into specific costs the Chow Down listings, I will mention if a place is upscale (the cheapest entrée running more than $15). I'll also mention if a spot is really economical (entrees between $4-6).

Local Wisdom

Oregon is the home of amazing cyclists, adventurers and personalities. Throughout the book, many of these people have generously written guest sections, so you can be as inspired by them as I am.

Other Bits

Throughout the chapters, you'll see sections and side notes about history, environment, mountain biking, wine tasting and other interesting, relevant topics. I also mention opportunities for extracurricular activities like hiking, picnicking, fishing, museums, etc. If there is a yoga studio in a destination town, I let you know in case you want to catch a class.

* DISCLAIMER

OREGON LOVES CYCLING

With Portland on the active transportation forefront, and Eugene, Ashland, Bend and Corvallis close on her heels, Oregon has evolved into a bikecentric state. Outside the cities and beyond transportation initiatives, Oregonian's cycling enthusiasm doesn't waver. With top-quality mountain biking (see Trade in your Slicks, page 76), road riding and cyclo-cross racing, Oregon has a well-rounded bike-crazy portfolio. All over the state you'll find bike advocacy groups, cycling clubs, trail proponents and quirky people like zoo bombers (who fly down the Oregon Zoo hill on kiddie bikes), bike polo players and birthday-suit participants of the World Naked Bike Ride. No wonder so many cyclists want to visit.

In collusion with the Oregon Department of Transportation, Cycle Oregon, Travel Oregon and **Oregon State Parks and Recreation** (see Scenic Bikeways, below) help develop Oregon's progressive cycling infrastructure.

Cycle Oregon (www.cycleoregon.com) is a non-profit that organizes two annual multi-day bike rides and is dedicated to transforming individuals and communities through bicycling. Their fund gives over $100,000 to projects that preserve and protect Oregon's rural communities.

Travel Oregon (www.traveloregon.com), the state's tourism commission, has taken initiative in developing a bike tourism strategy. They've created RideOregonRide.com, providing resources, including user-suggested mountain bike trails and cycling routes that highlight some of Oregon's most beautiful places.

SCENIC BIKEWAYS:
OREGON DID IT FIRST

by Alex Phillips, bicycle recreation coordinator for the
State of Oregon www.oregonscenicbikeways.org

The Oregon Scenic Bikeways Program is designed to provide nuts and bolts information about high-quality cycling routes that inspire people to experience Oregon's natural beauty and cultural heritage by bicycle. These routes also offer economic and social benefits to the state's communities, residents and visitors. Oregon is the first state to officially designate Scenic Bikeways and is currently promoting 600 miles of some of the best road biking in the state.

Online resources provide maps, cue sheets and suggested itineraries with logistical information about campgrounds, restrooms and water stops on route. This information makes planning an afternoon bike ride or a multi-day bike camping trip easy.

Cycle Oregon first conceived of the idea of state designated Scenic Bikeways and encouraged Oregon Parks and Recreation Department to lead the program. With cycling growing in popularity, it made perfect sense. After clocking many hours collaborating with partners at Cycle Oregon, Travel Oregon and the Oregon Department of Transportation, this innovative program is now a reality.

SHOESTRING BIKE CAMPING
by Steph Routh, executive director of the
Willamette Pedestrian Coalition

If you've priced touring gear recently, you may agree that there seems to be no ceiling to the cost of equipment. The following is not an exploration of the ceiling, but rather about learning to love the floor, thanks to some DIY tips and tricks from clever friends who have perfected the art of shoestring bike camping.

First, the basics: A bicycle, spare tubes, bike lights, first aid kit, pump, multi-tool, water bottles, patch kit, map, change of socks and extra underwear should be on every trip. You may find yourself sad if you don't have these items. Duct tape, zip ties, rubber bands and airplane clips also come in delectably handy at strange times.

Riding clothes: I generally ride in knee-length

skirts because they feel more fun and breezy, they're much cheaper than bike shorts, and I already own them. Skirts also pack down really well.

Gloves: Sure, you can spend $100 on gloves that may or may not be waterproof, or you can use large dishwasher gloves over thin liner gloves.

Arm warmers: These things are great! If you have a few knee-length wool socks that you're not using anymore, cut off the toes and a little of the heels. Instant arm warmers!

Tent: Tyvek or a plastic tarp can be a great ground cloth or jerry-rigged into a tent using cord, tent stakes and a few well-placed grommets. Used tents are cheap and easy to find, as well.

Stove: I prefer the trail mix and cold food camping method, but the coolest stove I've ever seen was John Kangas', which was made out of two soda cans with a tire spoke bent into a pot stand (you can also use a bent wire hanger). www.dailymotion.com/video/x69z0b_how-to-make-a-soda-can-stove_school.

A note about packing: Have at least one bike rack. A bike pannier or two (or 3-4) to hang on your rack(s) is my preferred choice, but others have employed garbage bags and milk crates with aplomb. Bungee cords, old spare tubes or a cargo net are versatile and useful. Inside your bag, Ziploc bags can separate your stuff (bathroom, spices, cords, etc.) and make life simple.

There are a few luxury items I have come to love over the years. Cycling booties (my fella uses neoprene socks) keep feet warm(er). Chemical hand warmers are marvelous on cold days. Finally, a generator hub and generator bike lights are an incredible investment that I can't praise enough.

If you're a little nervous about pedaling solo, join Cycle Wild for a weekend bike camping trip. Cycle Wild is a marvelous group based in Portland that is dedicated to connecting people with nature via the bicycle. They organize trips for the sheer love of it, and it shows. Check out their camping/touring schedule and gear lists (www.cyclewild.org).

YOUR BIKE

If you are a cyclist, then you probably have a bike you can take on a tour. You can use a carbon road bike or heavy steel commuter without braze-ons (which allow you to attach a rack) by using a trailer.

You can use rigid mountain bikes with slick tires. Cyclocross bikes, folding bikes and recumbents will do. Touring-specific bikes, especially ones with couplers for airplane travel, are nice but not necessary. I recommend an easy gear ratio, a professional bike fit and a safety check from your local bike shop with emphasis on the cables, housings, brake pads, chain and wheel true. If you know bike geeks, they will LOVE to talk with you about this topic. For more info, check out the reference section (page 11).

CARRYING YOUR STUFF

Panniers and trailers are the most common totes for touring. I'm a pannier girl, and I loves me some handlebar bag. Trailer people swear by them. Joel Grover (page 76) tours with a cargo bike. Check out the reference section (page 11) for opinions and ideas galore.

Panniers: Bags that are designed to clip onto bike racks. Two can be mounted over the rear wheel and two more can be mounted in the front on the fork. They fasten securely to the bike and can create a balanced load. Front panniers take some getting used to, as they can affect handling. This effect is minimized on touring-specific bikes.

Handlebar Bag: I heart my handlebar bag. It provides easy access for everything from cell phones and snacks to a light extra layer and a photo of your sweetheart. Many have clear plastic covers on top that can hold maps or cue sheets.

Saddle bags: These bags fit cutely under your saddle and provide easy access to flat repair paraphernalia and a multi-tool. Hawt.

Trailers: A great option for a bicycle without rack mounts (braze-ons). There are many different types of trailers: single-wheel or two-wheel chassis, dry bag or plastic box storage container. All trailers require an attachment point mounted on the frame. Trailers carry a large load without the handling issues that can come with heavily-loaded panniers. Downsides include possible fishtailing (from swinging back and forth while descending at high speed), complications with braking and more hassle traveling to and from the start of a tour.

Things I like: Compression sacks for squishing clothes down, bungees for extra pannier support or strapping stuff on, and DIY straps that let you

carry your panniers over one shoulder and turn your handlebar bag into a purse.

Packing: There are as many approaches as there are cycle tourists. Some methods are very dogmatic and disciplined. On the other hand, I've seen my friend Barbara throw all her crap into either pannier and go down the road, easy cheesy. For more packing advice, see the reference section.

TRAVELING WITH A BIKE

The days of **flying with a bike** for free or cheaply are just about over. There are still a couple of airlines (like Frontier and Southwest) that make it financially feasible. But more likely, you will be charged hundreds of dollars each way to fly with your bike. The International Bicycle Fund website (www.ibike.org/encouragement.travel/bagregs.htm) gives you the rundown on individual airlines' bike policies. If you don't have a folding bike or couplers (which allow a bike to be packed small enough to be counted as regular luggage) and aren't flying internationally, consider **shipping your bike** to a local bike shop at your start point. In many cases, shipping will be cheaper and less of a hassle. More shipping advice: www.adventurecycling.org/features/shippingbikecases.cfm.

The majority of bus lines, some trains and all airlines require you to **box your bike**. It's a pain, but eventually you get quick at assembly and disassembly, and it's not that big a deal. If you begin and end your tour in one spot, I recommend a using a hard bike case. If not, bike shops can usually give you a cardboard bike box. Here's Adventure Cycling Association's advice on bike boxing: www.adventurecycling.org/features/boxingbike.cfm.

Ride Oregon Ride (www.rideoregonride.com/resources/traveling-with-your-bike) has Oregon-specific bike travel advice and points outs helpful resources related to travelling locally with your bike.

YOU

The party is over if you feel like doo doo. The sluggish, nothing-in-the-world-matters, crab apple feeling resulting from not eating is called bonking; also known as being *hangry*. Once you bonk, it's hard to bounce back, so I advise constant noshing—for the sake of you and your riding partner. **Eat bits of food along the way** *before* you are hungry. **Drink water**; if you don't, you'll feel crappy. Dehydration can be dangerous, leaving you more susceptible to unsavory things like heat exhaustion. Getting bike-tour compatible **travel insurance** is always a smart move. I suggest **being well acquainted with your bike and gear** before your tour. I also advise **paying attention to what your body tells you**. Stretching or **practicing yoga** on a bike tour will make your body and mind happier.

REFERENCE

Good online resources that address the how-tos of bike touring:

Path Less Pedaled (www.pathlesspedaled.com) For inspiration and a gear guide.

Traveling Two (www.travellingtwo.com) Nuts and bolts of cycle touring.

Adventure Cycling Association (www.adventurecycling.org) The "How-To" page is helpful.

Ray Thomas (www.stc-law.com/bicycle.html) A bicycle law expert lays out Oregon's rules of the road and provides "Pedal Power," a free, downloadable legal guide for cyclists.

Bicycle Safe (www.bicyclesafe.com) Detailed safety advice.

Track My Tour (www.trackmytour.com) Lets family and friends track your route, photos and musings.

MotionX (www.gps.motionx.com) GPS app that navigates and records routes.

PICKING A RIDING PARTNER

In the past, I've been a little too cavalier in picking a touring partner. I would go with anyone willing to embark on an adventure. It worked beautifully in most cases, but not all cases. And those exceptional cases were, uh, painful.

Going on tour with someone means you will be around them all the time: for most meals and sleeping near them. You will be tired and hungry with them, therefore, artifice (a major source of social lubrication) will likely fall away. Touring can even be hard on dear friendships, but your relationship will be the stronger for it in the end. Romantic relationships will be tested, but, on the other hand, touring is one of the most romantic things ever. You will experience immense joy with your partner(s) and a sense of accomplishment. Sometimes you will have to work as a team. At the end, bonds of friendship and love can be tighter than you ever imagined. Or, in a worst-case scenario, you won't talk much anymore.

Here are some questions to ask yourself before you plan a tour with someone:
• Does the person annoy you more than other friends?
• Does the person have good communication skills?
• Does the person sport a negative attitude?
• Does the person take responsibility when at fault?
• Are they a team player? Does the person help you out

when you need it and let you help when he/she does?

Now ask yourself the same questions and warn your partner if necessary.

Here are some things you might want to discuss before you leave:

• Tell tour buddies how you act when you're frustrated or sugar-low so they can identify what is going on. Talk about the best ways to deal with that situation.

• Agree to talk about frustrations and to do it in a constructive way.

• Talk about expectations for the tours and needs (alone time, riding styles, how close you are going to ride to each other, etc.).

RIDING ACROSS THE CULTURAL DIVIDE

While riding your bike through the gaucho-land of Argentina's Pampa, of course you'd be wide-eyed trying to comprehend and understand another culture. However, subtle cultural differences happen closer to home. Even just riding over the West Hills from NW Portland, I notice slight changes in how people talk to each other, different types of political signs in front yards and other kinds of food and atmospheres in restaurants.

Venturing just little ways out from our homes widens our perception about how people live their lives. Out on tour, people you meet might have an irresistible curiosity about where you're going, how far you've come and how many miles per day you ride. That inquisitiveness helps them open up to answering questions about themselves. Two people from different cultures connect and learn about each other; the world becomes a better place. Who would have thought a Schwinn could do so much?

~CONTENTS~

Bonus Ride

Visit www.cyclingsojourner.com to download a free extra ride. **Get Out of Town! Vernonia Loop** is a two-day tour from Portland that takes you through timber country and on one of the coolest rails-to-trails in the state, the Banks-Vernonia Trail.

ARRIVING / LEAVING PORTLAND

Portland is Oregon's major transportation hub, and while traveling with a bike is never as simple as with a backpack, Portland has more bike transportation infrastructure than most places.

Airplane

Portland International Airport (PDX, www.portofportland.com) is ready for cycle tourists. On its website, they provide a bike map of the multi-use path that connects the airport to the city. They also have secure bike parking, a bike assembly and repair station, and tool check-out. If you don't want to ride into town, you can take the **MAX Red Line** (www.trimet.org) right into the city; it has designated spots for bikes. Get on the light rail car labeled with a blue bike.

Bus

Greyhound (www.greyhound.com, 800-231-2222, 550 NW 6th Ave) has a station downtown with statewide and national connections. **Trimet** (www.trimet.org) has an extensive, widely used inter-city bus network. There are two bike racks on the front of most buses.

Train

From Portland, **Amtrak** (www.amtrak.com, 800-872-7245, 800 NW 6th Ave) trains go to Vancouver, BC, L.A., and Chicago. The **MAX** (www.trimet.org) light rail can take you and your bike around the city and outlying areas.

PDX by Bike: Portland's resource for bicycle tourism

PDX by Bike founders Elly Blue and Meghan Sinnott are two moguls in Portland's bike culture scene. In 2011 they created PDX by Bike, a website and printed guide zine that orients travelers, transplants, and timid cyclists to Portland with tips and observations.

"We prime you for Portland bike culture, demystify some of the cycling infrastructure, help you choose between fun bike events and share a bit of history and terminology," Meghan explains. "We also provide custom itineraries so that you can experience events and places in Portland according to your individual needs and desires. Our hope is to empower people to discover Portland on their own two wheels."

For more information, check out their website (www.pdxbybike.com) or buy a pocket-sized guide by the same name, which is available for purchase online, at bike shops around town and at Powell's City of Books (a destination they highly recommend).

Portland
Pop. 566,000
Elevation 50 ft.

My soul hurts knowing I won't be able to do justice to Portland with my coverage (due to a space deficit). Though I mention some of my favorite places around town, I'm really just giving you the bare bones of what you need to know to have a little fun, eat well, drink well and prosper (by bike).

BikePortland.org is a nationally recognized news source for all things bike in Portland. If you want to catch up on the latest and greatest, check it out.

LODGING
Most of Portland's nicer options are downtown, from fancy boutique hotels to corporate chains. A number of lower-end motels are far out in the notably seedy SE 82nd zone. There are no great options for

camping in the city. My favorite part of town is close-in Eastside and North Portland, where there are scant lodging choices, but lots of divine restaurants and cool things to do.

Friendly Bike Guest House
(www.friendlybikeguesthouse.com, 503-799-2615, 4039 N Williams, room $76, semi-private twin $45, bunk $36) Equipped with a mechanic stand and indoor bike lock-up, this hostel uniquely caters to bicycle tourists. Pretty awesome.

Portland Hawthorne Hostel
(www.portlandhostel.org, 503-447-3031, 3031 SE Hawthorne Blvd, Portland, OR, $20-24 dorm beds, $48-55 private rooms, non-HI members add $3, discounts for cycle tourists $5) A cycle tourist hub, this hostel offers cycle tourists discounts, and its website gives bike directions to arrive. The building has a living roof, and the hostel hosts a potluck brunch every Sunday.

Bluebird Guesthouse
(www.bluebirdguesthouse.com, 503-238-4333, 3517 SE Division Street, Portland, OR, $60-105) A slight upgrade from the less private Hawthorne Hostel, the Bluebird is adorable and situated in a fabulous location. Indoor bike storage.

CHOW DOWN
There are so many mind-blowing restaurants in this town. Portlanders are a spoiled population of foodies. Here is the tiniest slice of the P-town culinary circus.

Food Carts (www.foodcartsportland.com) Portland is a hot bed of food carts. Hundreds of carts are spread out city-wide in various clusters. Vendors sell fresh, fast, cheap and darned near gourmet food.

¿Por Qué No? (www.porquenotacos.com, lunch and dinner) With a location on SE Hawthorne (503-954-3138, 4635 SE Hawthorne Blvd) and on N Mississippi (503-467-4149, 3524 N Mississippi), these Mexican eateries have bike parking out front and a delicious menu of sustainably-sourced dishes. Hello, Brian's Bowl. Mmm.

Hopworks BikeBar (www.hopworksbeer.com, 503-287-6258, 3947 N Williams Ave, Sun-Thurs 11am-11pm, Fri-Sat till 12am) Right a on a bike thoroughfare, this bar displays 40 bike frames built by local builders and has stationary bikes that generate electricity for the building. The beer is organic, and the bar sources its food ingredients locally. So. Freaking. Portland.

Toro Bravo (www.torobravopdx.com, 503-281-4464, 120 NE Russell St, 5-10pm, Sat-Sun till 11pm) This exceptional, high-end restaurant serves renowned tapas. Be prepared to wait. The owner is cycle happy. Bike parking.

Farmers Markets

(www.portlandfarmersmarket.org) In the summer, you can find a local farmers market most any day of the week. Every quadrant (and N Portland) has one.

New Seasons Market

(www.newseasonmarket.com) is a locally owned health food store with locations in SE, NE and N Portland.

Pastaworks (www.pastaworks.com) is a high-end, European-style grocer in SE and N Portland with the most fantastic cheese and wine selection.

Fred Meyer (www.fredmeyer.com) is a conventional grocery store with multiple locations around town.

BIKE SHOPS

If you toss a wrench, you'll hit a bike shop in Portland. Here are just a few recommendations.

River City Bicycles (www.rivercitybicycles.com, 503-233-5973, 706 SE MLK Blvd, Mon-Fri 10am-7pm, Sat till 5pm, Sun 12-5pm) Excellent, centrally-located shop. These are my people.

Sellwood Cycle Repair

(www.sellwoodcycle.com, 503-233-9392,

7953 SE 13th Ave, Tues-Sat 10am-6pm) I love this place for repairs. The dear owner Erik is like a cycling Bodhisattva. Located in Southeast's Sellwood neighborhood.

Western Bikeworks

(www.westernbikeworks.com/visit-store, 503-342-9985, 1015 NW 17th, Mon-Fri 10am-7pm, Sat 8am-6pm, Sun 8am-5pm) Huge, comprehensive bike shop in NW.

Coventry Cycles (www.coventrycycle.com, 503-230-7723, 2025 SE Hawthorne Blvd, Tues-Sat 10am-6pm, except Thurs till 7pm) The place for recumbents.

Community Cycling Center

(www.communitycyclingcenter.org, 503-287-8786, 1700 NE Alberta, 10am-6pm) A non-profit that has a bike shop in NE Portland which does repairs and sells new and used parts. This organization is the beneficiary of a portion of the profits from this book. Their mission is to broaden access to bicycling and its benefits, and their vision is to build a vibrant community where people of all backgrounds use bicycles to stay healthy and connected.

YOGA

Exhale (www.exhalepdx.com, 503-545-8312, 4940 NE 16th Ave, drop-in $7-12) A variety of classes all days. Teacher Nicole Swanson rocks.

Yes Yoga Coop (www.yesyogapdx.com, 407 NE 12th Ave, 2nd floor, drop-in $10) Advanced Hatha practice classes.

HOSPITAL

Providence Portland Medical Center

(www.providence.org, 503-215-1111, 4805 NE Glisan St) 24/7 emergency care.

∼TOUR OF TERROIR∽

Willamette Valley Wine Country

**Four days and three nights
Sherwood to the Hillsboro MAX station
128.8 miles total**

THE SKINNY

PRICE POINT: This tour is most easily done with a **medium to bulging purse**. It's appallingly easy to spend a lot of money in wine country because of the fabulous restaurants and lodging options, not to mention the wine tastings and tempting bottles. It is possible to spend a moderate amount of money, but for a budget traveler, it's more difficult because of limited camping. But a budget tour can be done.

DIFFICULTY RATING: 4.4 Though this ride has lots of flat terrain and modest mileage, there are a couple of factors that could be challenging for a beginner. On Day 2 you either have to ride a gravel road for 3.6 miles (which takes bike handling skills) or a busy road (with substantial shoulder). There is a small stretch of busy road (with shoulder) on Day 3.

JAW-DROP FACTOR: 5 Though there are some lovely pastoral landscapes and valley views, the libations of the land draw us here.

STAND OUT CAMPING: Camping options are slim, but **Champoeg State Park** (page 29), which is about 7.4 miles from Newberg, is a favorite of Portlanders.

STAND OUT LODGING: I have to give it up for **Hotel Oregon** (Day 2, page 34). In a land of high-priced accommodations, Hotel Oregon gives you a reasonable alternative with tons of sass.

AVERAGE TEMP IN FEBRUARY: Low 35, high 51 degrees

AVERAGE TEMP IN AUGUST: Low 52, high 83 degrees

This tour is indulgent. If you aren't interested in freeing your inner hedonist and totally opening yourself to the flavors and experience of wine, then you will miss half the fun. When pedaling through wine country, you have the opportunity to explore the subtle and ancient art of winemaking. It doesn't matter how little or much you know about wine at the start; the journey is about savoring and delighting in whatever you experience.

Swirl cycling into the wine country mix and double your hedonism, double your fun. Crossing paths with a couple of SUV limos going to and from wineries was imminently satisfying for me. Even though the passengers probably thought they were doing wine country in ultimate style, I was having a 10-times richer experience. What a shame to be jumping in and out of a moving box. You'd miss the pungent loam, sunshine, endorphin highs, raging appetites

Fist Bump!

- The **surprisingly short bus ride** from Portland to the beautiful borderlands of Willamette Valley wine country (Day 1, page 27)
- The **short, steep climb to Penner-Ash Wine Cellars** (Day 1, page 28), a beautiful winery owned by bike lovers
- The **rooftop bar at Hotel Oregon** (Day 2 and 3, page 34) in McMinnville
- The restaurant **Thistle** (Day 2 and 3, page 35) in McMinnville
- **Willamette Valley Wine Center** (Day 2 and 3, page 35) in McMinnville
- **The Blue Goat** restaurant (Day 3, page 45) in Amity
- Cycling **Masonville Rd and Youngberg Hill Rd** (Day 3, page 36)
- The food and wine in little **Carlton** (Day 4, page 42: Stop and sip)
- The view from **Sokol Blosser** (Day 2, page 33), **Amity Vineyards** (Day 3, page 36) and **Willakenzie Estates** (Day 4, page 42)
- **Tastings** at all the wineries I mention (all days)

and interactions with the hard-working people who help create the increasingly famous libations from this region.

This bike tour stalks the most decadent wine and food of the valley and chooses the most splendid way to arrive. Though the *terroir* of the valley isn't as dramatic or remote as some of other tours in the book, the stage is sweetly set for cycling. Low-traffic roads roll past vast fields of neatly rowed vines garnished by roses, the odd alpaca farm, groves of fragrant trees and a horizon punctuated with undulating hills of manicured vines.

Due to low-mileage days, rolling terrain and many opportunities to stop, this beginner/intermediate ride is perfect for getting wary partners out on a bike and intoxicating them with the touring experience. Plus, there are lavish inns and hotels out here, so if you are into splurging on a super special and/or capital R for *romantico* tour, this is the perfect place. And you can fashion it into a weekend-length jaunt from Portland. Cheers!

Put on Your Tasting Beret

Wet juicy slurps are totally acceptable sounds to make while sipping Pinot Noir in the Willamette Valley wine country. A luscious slurp is best followed by a visit to your inner thesaurus. Go ahead, say whatever description the wine brings to mind: a shy blush of rose, fluffed with crushed pomegranate seeds, bursting at its tannic seams, operatic on the front end, brings a chocolate sword to a cherry fight, whatever. Embrace the free form fun of wine culture. This isn't the time to feel intimidated or pretentious. Remember, no matter what, your palate is right.

HISTORY TIDBITS

Oregon's wine industry didn't exist 40 years ago. Conventional wisdom and expert opinion proclaimed that Oregon was too cold and wet to grow good grapes. It was thought that Sauvignon and Merlot grapes, which were successful in California, would do poorly if planted too far north.

The fact that we enjoy locally grown, world class Pinot Noir is due in large part to someone who chose not to accept what wine experts said. David Lett, a graduate of the Viticulture Program at UC Davis, spent time in Napa Valley and in the Burgundy region of France, and he had a vision.

Lett took a risk and planted grapes native to Burgundy—Pinot Noir and Pinot Gris—outside Dundee in 1965. The weather and grapes were a perfect match; the vines (and the risk Lett took) bore fruit. In 1979 and 1980, his Pinot Noir wines won a prestigious wine competition in France. The potential to produce great wines in the chilly, damp Willamette Valley was revealed to the world, and Lett became known as "Papa Pinot."

Lett was a pioneer in another way; he was dedicated to organic farming and the preservation of land for viticulture use. The Lett family's Eyrie Vineyards has always embraced natural, sustainable and organic methods of growing grapes and making wine. Lett believed the quality of the soil should come through in the wine, so he strove to preserve the soil itself. Until 2008, when Lett passed away, he worked to preserve land for wine production, sometimes strategically opposing commercial and residential development.

Even though he wasn't a native Oregonian, David Lett came to represent what is best about the state as a slightly contrary, risk-taking anti-authoritarian and lover of truly great wines.

ENVIRONMENT

People talk dirt out here all the time. So let me give you a crash course. Knowing about soil is important because different dirt can produce dramatically different wines.

Many wineries produce single-vineyard labels (sometimes from a specific area of that one vineyard), which means the grapes in that bottle all come from the same acreage; those wines can be pricier, but they capture the purity of the soil characteristics.

Conversely, folks also like to blend pinot noir grapes from numerous vineyards in the Willamette Valley to create unique blends; those bottles, labeled as a winery's "Willamette Valley Pinot Noir," are less expensive, and I find them delicious.

It's fun to try single-vineyard labels side by side with Willamette Valley Pinot Noirs. It's also interesting to compare "horizontals:" single-vineyard bottles from the same estate that come from different sections of the vineyard with variant soils.

There are three main soil super-stars in the Willamette Valley: Jory, Willakenzie and Loess. They were fashioned, respectively, by volcanoes, the sea and wind. That's pretty cool.

Jory, the most prominent type of soil, is a volcanic, basalt-based soil high in clay, iron and nutrient content. It's well-draining and is found above 300 ft. The color originates from iron oxide that's changed

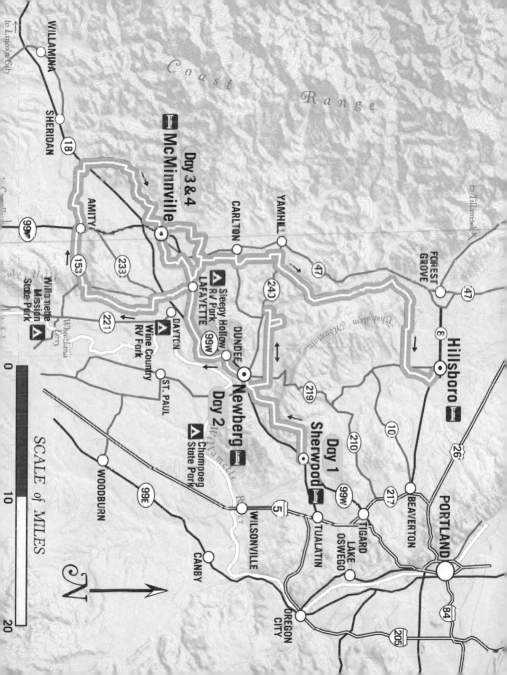

the dark grey parent soil to a rust red hue. Wines produced from Jory soil tend to have minerality, red fruit flavors and earthiness.

Willakenzie, which is more labor intensive for the wine maker, is a loose, sedimentary soil that is dry and powder-like. This dirt originates from an ancient marine sea floor from around 15 million years ago. It has a high quartz content and is a rich, brown color. Wines produced on Willakenzie soil tend to be more structured and dark, with black fruit and chocolate undertones. These wines improve with age.

Loess, which strikes me as the most romantic of the soils, is glacial sediment that was wrenched from its home and dramatically blown onto the north-facing hillsides of Chehalem Mountains by violent windstorms. This windblown, silty loam is the rarest, shallowest and youngest (its one-way ticket to the Willamette Valley happened between one million and 50,000 years ago) of the soils. The Loess soil creates wines with brighter acidity, which are fine and lighter in color.

Side note: this chapter lists tastings rooms in and routes passing through each of the six American Viticulture Areas (AVAs) of the Willamette Valley: Chehalem Mountains and Ribbon Ridge (Day 1), Dundee Hills (Day 2), McMinnville and Eola-Amity Hills (Day 3) and Yamhill-Carlton (Day 4). Each AVA creates a characteristic wine profile that results from specific geological features, like soils, hills and elevations.

What does it mean to be a sustainable vineyard?

Lots of wineries say they are "sustainable," but what does that actually mean? Well, there are various certifications that let consumers know about the environmental practices of a vineyard. It seems like the **Oregon Certified Sustainable Wine** (www.ocsw.org) is one of the top commendations. The organization certifies using an independent third party and requires a combination of the following certifications:

• **LIVE** (Low Input Viniculture and Enology, www.liveinc.org) is a non-profit that uses a scoring system which certifies a winery according to sustainable viticulture practices.

• **Demeter Biodynamic** (www.demeter-usa.org) is a certification that requires a vineyard to be more than just organic. Being biodynamic necessitates that the farm act as a self-contained, self-sustaining organism by, for example, using compost instead of fertilizers and using cover crops to regenerate the soil.

• **USDA Organic** (www.usda.gov) means the grape growing process at a vineyard meets the organic standards of the Department of Agriculture.

• **Salmon Safe** (www.salmonsafe.org) certification requires proper management of water run-off from hillside vineyards and enhancement of native biodiversity on vineyard sites.

• **Food Alliance** (www.foodalliance.org)

certification indicates that a vineyard has safe and fair working conditions, minimized pesticide use, conservation methods in regard to soil and water, and protections of biodiversity.

• **LEED** (Leadership in Energy and Environmental Design, www.usgbc.org) certification suggests the structures on a vineyard meet green construction, design, operation and maintenance standards.

There are only 21 vineyards that have obtained the Oregon Certified Sustainable Wine certification. Ten of those wineries are mentioned in this chapter.

RIDING SEASON

You can ride this tour year round, which is awesome. The nicest time weather wise to ride would be May through September, but that is also the peak season for tourism (tourists driving around in cars and tasting wine). During the summer, advance reservations for lodging are important, especially on weekends. If you could find a sunny couple of days in the spring, fall or even winter, that might be ideal. Alternatively, mid-week during the summer won't be as busy.

WEATHER

Summers in wine country are gorgeous, with a fair amount of sun, highs averaging in the 70s and 80s, and some occasional hot days. Winter is mild with a fair amount of rain and temperatures that hover in the 40s and 50s.

ARRIVING / LEAVING

See Portland's Arriving / Leaving section (page 14).

ARRIVING FROM PORTLAND
Bus

From downtown, you can take **TriMet's No. 12 bus** (www.trimet.org; 503-238-7133, 50 mins, $2.40) to Sherwood at the SW Langer and Sherwood Plaza stop, the beginning of the ride. Starting at 5:30am, the 12 bus runs till 1:47am every 10-50 minutes; it runs every 15 minutes or so during non-vampire hours. Sundays it runs less frequently. Check the schedule online or call. There are only two bike racks per bus, so avoid rush hours.

Bike

One way or another, you'll have to ride through some portion of schwaggy traffic to get to Sherwood. You can minimize that headache significantly by finding zig-zaggy back-road alternatives in SW Portland with the City of Portland's **free bike map** (www.portlandonline.com/transportation under "Getting Around Portland," 503-823-5185). That won't get you all the way, but Google Maps (bike option) will help with the rest. Riding down SW Barbur Ave to Sherwood isn't sexy, but it has a bike lane.

RETURNING TO PORTLAND
Light Rail

It's super easy to catch the **Hillsboro Blue Line MAX** (www.trimet.org, 503-238-7433, to Portland 50-60 minutes, $2.40) for a ride back to Portland on Day 4. The MAX runs every 7-30 minutes from Hillsboro, more during rush hour and less on weekends, from 5:35am till 10:47pm (later on weekends). Check the schedule online or call. There are a couple of designated spots on a MAX train for bikes and a symbol of a bike on entrances closest to the racks. Avoid rush hours.

USEFUL WEBSITES
Chehalem Valley Chamber of Commerce
www.chehalemvalley.org
Discover Oregon Wine
www.oregonwine.org
Willamette Valley Visitor's Association
www.oregonwinecountry.org
Willamette Valley Wineries
www.willamettewines.com
Willamette Mobile Wine Tour
willamette.mobilewinetour.com; includes hours and contact info for wineries in the Willamette Valley, as well as a free downloadable app for smart phones that gives you turn-by-turn directions to different wineries.

LODGING
Holy moly, prices can be high in this part of Oregon. The nicer bed and breakfasts and the Allison Inn and Spa near Newberg can run between $250-500 per night. There are also fine options for Best Western-satisfied plebeians. On summer weekends and holidays, it's best to book in advance. Because there are so many lodging options in this area, I didn't mark every one on the map. If you want more choices, other lodging can be found on the websites I recommend in this chapter.

CAMPING
It is possible to camp on this tour. You can stay at the prettiest choice, Champoeg State Park (page 29), on the first night and at one of two RV Parks (page 34) near McMinnville on Days 2 and 3. But camping isn't as easy on this tour, as the tour centers around eating and drinking in towns, far from good campsites. ¡Ole!

FOOD AND DRINK
You will have the opportunity to taste some of the best Pinot Noirs in the world. Additionally, there are top-notch restaurants along the way that focus on delightful wine pairings, cocktails and seasonal Pacific Northwest cuisine. You can spend as much money as you want. Alternatively, there are more moderately priced eateries and grocery stores each day for those on a tighter budget. As most of the wineries don't sell food, bring food during the day. See How Not to Get Drunk (page 25).

STOP AND SIP
I highlighted certain wineries for a combination of reasons: my enjoyment of their wines, reputation, sustainability standards and proximity to bike-friendly roads. There are only 21 vineyards that have obtained the Oregon Certified Sustainable Wine (see Environment, page 22) status. Ten of those wineries are mentioned in this chapter. I chose to feature about three wineries per day, because two or three tastings is the cap beyond which everything becomes a Pinot blur. But you can visit more with the help of a wine country map;

see Maps (see below). If you are willing to ride gravel, a whole other world of vineyards opens to you.

HYDRATION

You aren't in the boondocks by any stretch of the imagination. But don't let that fact lull you into hydration complacency, especially if you are doing a wine tasting or three. See "How Not to Get Drunk" (below).

MAPS
Willamette Valley Wineries Association
(www.willamettewines.com, 503-646-2985, PO Box 25162, Portland) prints a free map of the wine country, which is not as useful for road navigation as it is for general winery locations and information. These are available at establishments all over the valley. The WVWA also has that map online and a smart phone app that will give you exact directions from one winery to the next. For a detailed lay of the land, the **Benchmark Oregon Atlas** (www.benchmarkmaps.com, 541-772-6965, $22.95) covers the route.

TIPS AND HEADS UP
• Fancier hotels and B&Bs provide "tasting tickets" for certain partner wineries that allow you to taste for free.
• It's not unusual to try three pinot noirs on one tasting menu. Chardonnay is also a fave in these parts.
• Most wineries let you bring and eat lunch on their lovely premises if you buy a bottle of wine or pay for a tasting.
• Wine bottles in paper bags can sometimes fit into flexible water bottle holders, but that system gets risky on bumpy roads.

Alternatively, use your pannier or a bungee to jerry-rig a bottle on your rack.
• Lots of wineries ship orders, depending on the destination. In some states, shipping wine is illegal.
• Be warned that a number of the wineries are perched on hills (which you will have to climb in order to reach their libations). On the plus side, you work on your fitness, will be hungry at the end of the day and usually earn fantastic views of the valley and vineyards. The con: you have to climb a steep hill.
• See the "How Not to Get Drunk" box (below).
• North Valley Rd, on Day 1, doesn't have shoulders and can be sketchy during the higher traffic times, like summer weekends.
• Be aware (as always) of cars—and maybe a bit more defensive—during the late afternoons when wine tasters are returning from their adventures.

CELL COVERAGE
No worries.

How Not to Get Drunk (Don't Get Drunk)
It's hard enough to stay on top of eating and drinking on a regular tour. However, on a tour where you are doing tastings at one to three wineries per day, and maybe having a glass of wine with lunch, it is uber-super-dooper important to drink more water than usual and eat food regularly. Fatty foods like cheese and nuts will be helpful, not to mention

tasty and easy to stash in your bag. Even better, combine fatty foods with carbohydrates: sandwiches, cheese and crackers, etc. Salads and fruit won't do much to ground you.

As most of the wineries don't offer food, bring your own. Tasting rooms usually encourage it, and may even have a verandah for noshing. There are fabulous places to get picnics to-go, like **Farm to Fork in Dundee** (Day 2, page 33), **The Horse Radish in Carlton** (Day 4, page 42) or indulgent, high-end grocery stores like **Red Hills Market in Dundee** (Day 2, page 33) and **Harvest Fresh in McMinnville** (Day 3 & 4, page 35). Along the route, I also note good restaurants for lunch in the "Stop and Eat" sections.

Another great way to avoid getting tipsy? Split a tasting with your friend... just ask your pourer. Also, wineries are equipped with buckets where you can spit wine or pour leftovers from tastings. You don't have to drink at all.

You're putting yourself and others at risk when you ride drunk, an act that's just as serious as driving drunk. It's not worth it. If you want to get saucy, cheers! But indulge within a walkable distance from your hotel at one the fabulous wine bars, tasting rooms or restaurants in McMinnville or Newberg, not at a rural winery.

HOSPITALS

Providence Newberg Medical Center (www.oregon.providence.org, 503-537-1555, 1001 Providence Dr, Newberg) 24/7 emergency care.

Tuality Healthcare (www.tuality.org, 503-681-1860, 335 SE 8th Ave, Hillsboro) 24/7 emergency care.

Legacy Meridian Park Medical Center (www.legacyhealth.org, 503-692-1212, 19300 SW 65th Ave, Tualatin) 24/7 emergency care.

EXTRACURRICULAR ACTIVITIES

Eating and drinking.

MORE TOUR!

It's easy to connect to Pacific City on the **Oregon Coast** tour (see page 52) via the Nestucca River Rd west of Hillsboro. To download a two day loop to Vernonia from Portland, visit: www.cyclingsojourner.com

COST OPTIONS

People say that the Willamette Valley is what Napa Valley used to be before the touristplosion and price mega-jack. There is some mini price-jacking happening, however, as prices here are higher than in Portland.

Budget camping tour: Day 1, Champoeg State Park (page 29); Day 2, Sleepy Hollow RV Park (page 34).

High falootin' credit card camping: Day 1, Allison Inn and Spa (page 28); Day 2, 3rd Street Flats (page 34).

Swish and Swill: How to get the most out of your wine tasting

by Lynn Penner-Ash, co-owner of Penner-Ash Wine Cellars and avid cyclist

• Don't wear perfume, cologne or lipstick. You will alter the tasting experience.

• Pick up the wine glass up by the stem not the bowl. You don't want to increase the wine's temperature beyond the ideal tasting temp.

• Examine the wine in the glass; look for color appropriate to the age of the wine. A young white wine should not be dark yellow or brown. A young red wine should have a bright red hue and not be brick in color.

• Gently swirl the glass to release the aroma and then take a sniff. Think about the aromas: do they remind you of fresh or dried fruits? Red or black fruits? Is the wine intriguing enough to make you want a taste?

• Now take a sip. Not a gulp, but a sip. Put enough wine into your mouth so you can gently aerate the wine and feel all the flavors and textures. Often flavors are felt in the nasal cavities. Be sure to swish the wine throughout your mouth and allow all your taste buds to enjoy the wine. Different tasters have unique sensitivities in various areas of their mouth.

• Spitting is acceptable and encouraged. After spitting, think about the finish of the wine and the lingering flavors. It should draw you back in and make you want to take a bottle home.

• Buy a bottle and bring it home. A great day can be shared and enjoyed again with a glass of a special wine from a day out in Oregon wine country!

*Note that Lynn's winery, Penner-Ash Wine Cellars, rewards cyclists for climbing the hill to the winery with a complimentary tasting.

DAY ONE
Sherwood to Newberg
23.4 miles
Elevation Climbed 2,800 ft.

An hour after I boarded the No. 12 bus in downtown Portland, I was standing less than a quarter of a mile from rolling, tree-lined back roads in the borderlands of Willamette Valley wine country. I didn't realize how easy it was to leave the strip-mallish outskirts of Portland and arrive at the pretty edge of wine country. As the route wound along the back way to Newberg, Dr. Seussesque alpacas grazed

roadside, country quiet settled in and hallmark vineyard rows began to grace the hills.

Once in Newberg, you can drop your bags at your hotel and head out to North Valley Rd, an area Dave Paige, winemaker at Adelsheim Vineyard, proclaims as containing a cluster of "true Pinot Noir geeks." Wineries serving decadent libations sprinkle the 16-mile loop west of Newberg, with smaller, offshoot roads, like Dopp and Caulkins, as the cycling highlights.

STOP AND SIP
Adelsheim Vineyard
(www.adelsheim.com, 503-538-3652, 16800 NE Calkins Ln, 11am-4pm, tours by appt, tasting $15) This sustainable, low-yield vineyard prefers no cleats on their cherry floors, but they don't mind you taking off your shoes. You're lucky if Cindy is your pourer. OCSW certified.

Bergström Wines
(www.bergstromwines.com, 503-554-0468, 18215 NE Calkins Lane, 11am-4pm, tasting $15) Super friendly people! The winery's patio overlooking the hills is an excellent place to lean back, take in the *terroir* and taste wine.

Penner-Ash Wine Cellars
(www.pennerash.com, 503-554-5545, 15771 NE Ribbon Ridge Rd, Wed-Sun 11am-5pm, tastings free to cyclists!) Though you have to climb a very narrow, steep road to get here, the view is worth it. And cyclists who climb the hill get a complimentary tasting (and a cheer let out). The winery's sustainable, three-tier gravity system is fascinating and creates a lovely result. OCSW certified.

RIDING TIPS AND HEADS UP
• You can skip dropping your bags in Newberg and do the loop fully loaded by taking Bell Rd straight to North Valley Rd. Newberg, however, holds your only lunch options.
• North Valley Rd has no shoulder and can have some ornery drivers. Be very cautious. A number of cyclists have been hit on this road.

Newberg
Pop. 22,830
Elevation 175 ft.

USEFUL WEBSITES
Newberg Downtown Coalition
www.newbergdowntown.org

LODGING
Allison Inn and Spa
(www.theallison.com, 503-554-2525, 2525 Allison Ln, $305-550) Ultra-luxury, super spa. Unless you pack some nicer duds, you may feel out of place (or invisible), but this is an incredibly indulgent spot with the high-end Jory Restaurant (get happy hour truffle fries!). It's 2.5 miles from the town center.
Lions Gate B&B
(www.distinctivedestination.net, 503-476-2211, 401 N Howard St, $150-200) A couple cost tiers below the Allison, you

still get an upscale and more personalized B&B experience. It's an easy walk to downtown.

Best Western Newberg Inn

(www.bestwestern.com, 503-537-3000, 2211 Portland Rd, $80) One of the numerous lower-end hotels off of Hwy 99. It's a longer, but doable, walk to downtown.

CAMPING
Champoeg State Park

(www.oregonstateparks.org, 503-678-1251, reservations 800-551-6949, 8239 Champoeg Rd NE, St. Paul, cabins $36-43, yurts $35-41, tent site $19, hiker/biker tent site per person $5) Located 7.5 miles southeast of Newberg, this verdant campground has specific cycle tourist sites and is equipped with showers, laundry and sweet multi use trails.

CHOW DOWN

On or near the main drag on 1st St, you'll also find a variety of restaurants: Chinese, Thai and Mexican.

Coffee Cat

(www.coffeecatcoffeehouse.com, 503-538-2580, 107 S College St, Mon-Fri 7am-7pm, Sat 7:30am-7pm, Sun 7:30am-5pm) This is a cozy, artsy place to grab a strong cup of coffee and a pastry.

Recipe (www.recipenewbergor.com, 503-487-6853, 115 N Washington St, Tues-Thurs 11:30am-9pm, Fri-Sat till 10pm) This is my choice for a nice dinner in Newberg with local "slow food" tailored for wine, a casual farmhouse atmosphere and a communal table option. The three-course prix fixe dinner menu ($25) is easy on the pocketbook. Lunch prices range from $11-17 per entree.

Newberg Natural Foods (503-538-9311, 308 W Sheridan St, Tues-Sat 9:30am-5:30pm) Mostly supplements, but they do have bulk food.

Newberg Farmers Market (mike@ newbergdowntown.org, 503-537-1010, 415 E Sheridan St, late May-Sept, Tues 1:30-6pm) Good choice for fresh, local snacks.

Wine Country

Nap's Thriftway

(www.napssupermarket.com, 503-538-8286, 112 E 1st St, 24 hours) Conventional store near downtown.

WINE TASTING IN TOWN

These are just a few of the possible venues. For a map that shows more, go to the Newberg Downtown Coalition website (www.newbergdowntown.org).

Chehalem Winery

(www.chehalemwines.com, 503-538-4700, 106 S Center St, 11am-5pm, tasting per person $15) With many accolades, this winery specializes in Pinot Noir and Pinot Gris. OCSW certified.

Fox Farm Wine Bar

(www.foxfarmvineyards.com, 503-538-8466, 12am-8pm) This tasting room offers its own wines as well as wines from eight other boutique vineyards in the area.

BIKE SHOP

Newberg Bicycle Shoppe (503-538-8850, 500 E 1st St, Mon-Fri, 10am-5pm, Sat 10am-6pm) This shop has the basics, plus a service department. It seems like

casual bikes are more their thing than road cycling.

YOGA
First Street Yoga

(www.firststreetyoga.com, 503-554-5485, 516 E First St, drop-in $15) The downtown yoga studio has classes all days but Thursdays and Sundays.

DAY TWO
Newberg to McMinnville
24 miles
Elevation Climbed 1,000 ft.

Very soon after leaving Newberg, back roads will channel you into Dundee, an epicenter of wine country action where you can dawdle about tasting rooms, wine bars and delicious restaurants to your heart's content. Or as much as having 21.5 more miles will allow.

After Dundee, the route dives into rural farm country, which is fabulous for the bucolic scenery and low-traffic but also includes 3.6 miles of gravel road. Gravel roads fluctuate in graveliness, depending on use and maintenance throughout the year. When I rode the route, SE Edwards was really doable and Crawford Ln got a little more gravelicious. If you are a beginner with shaky bike handling skills, you might opt to take the shoulder of busy Hwy 99, the only other alternative.

The gravel back roads spit you out you out at the base of a paved climb to the Sokol Blosser winery, where sumptuous

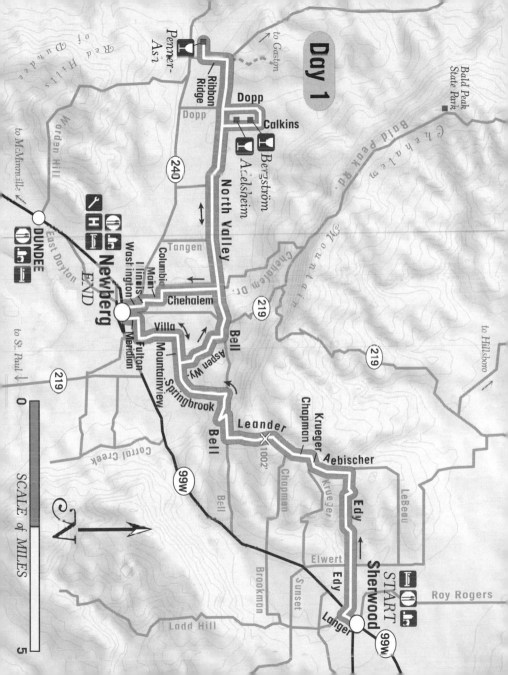

Wine Country

Day One
Sherwood to Newberg

0	•	From the Sherwood Plaza No. 12 bus stop, continue straight on SW Langer
.2	☞	SW Sherwood Blvd
.3		Onto Edy Rd
3.3		SW Aebischer Rd
4.1	☞	SW Kruger Rd
4.3		SW Chapman Rd
5	☞	Leander Dr
6.1	☞	Bell Rd
6.6		Bell Rd
7.4		Continuing to the North Valley loop ride
or		Springbrook Rd to Newberg
8.8		NE North Valley Rd
12.9	☞	NE Caulkins Ln
13.5	•	Adelsheim Vineyards
14.3	•	Bergström Wines
15.6		NE Dopp Rd
17.3		NE North Valley Rd
or ☞		To Penner-Ash Wine Cellars (about 2 miles off route)
20.9	☞	NE Chehalem Dr
22.1		Columbia Dr
22.3	☞	N Main St
22.8		E Illinois St
22.9	☞	N Washington St
23.3		E 1st St
23.4	•	Newberg Bicycle Shoppe

SHERWOOD to NEWBERG — ELEVATION (ft.) vs MILES

wines conspire with a lush patio looking over the Pinot-laden valley to create an indulgent experience. It's a perfect stop for a picnic; if you buy wine, you can cop a squat.

On the home stretch via quiet roads to McMinnville, the Stoller Winery might tempt you with a final tasting. Keep in mind there will be many opportunities to tempt your palate with food and wine in McMinnville; the town's adorable main street (3rd St) has top-notch restaurants and tasting rooms.

RIDING TIPS

• For more information about the area, check out the Dundee Hills Winegrowers Association website (www.dundeehills.org).
• There is always traffic congestion in Dundee.
• Note to gravel riders: Worden Hill Rd and Archery Summit Rd are steep but have many fine wineries.

STOP AND SIP

Argyle Winery (www.argylewinery.com, 503-538-8520, 691 Hwy 99W, 11am-5pm, tasting $10) A long-time Oregon Pinot Noir and sparkling wine producer, this winery continues to rake in the accolades. It's located right near the Red Hill Market in downtown Dundee. OCSW certified.

Sokol Blosser (www.sokolblosser.com, 503-864-2282, 5000 Sokol Blosser Ln, 10am-4pm, tasting $5-15) You'll have to climb about a mile on a long paved hill to get there, but the view, wine and grounds are fine recompense. OCSW certified.

Stoller Vineyards

(www.stollervineyards.com, 503-864-3404, 16161 NE McDougall Rd, 11am-5pm, tasting $10) This vineyard honors the environment with multi-faceted sustainable practices, and their grapes are sought after across the valley. OCSW certified.

STOP AND EAT

Red Hills Market

(www.redhillsmarket.com, 971-832-8414, 115 SW 7th St, Dundee, 7am-8pm) Beyond the kudos they get for the bocce ball court, the local, seasonal picnic fare screams wine country. Don't expect low grocery store prices, however.

Tina's (www.tinasdundee.com, 503-538-8880, 760 Hwy 99W, Dundee, Tues-Fri 11:30am-2pm, 5pm-close) Recommended to me by the most trusted of foodies, Tina's crafts delicious cuisine with organic food from local sources. Lunch entrees cost $11-14.

Farm to Fork

(www.innatredhills.com/restaurant; 503-538-7970, 1401 N Hwy 99, Dundee, hours variable) Looking for breakfast or brunch right outside of Newberg? Bam, here you go. A constantly changing seasonal menu is on the pricier side.

HEADS UP

There is some gravel today unless you opt to ride a stretch of shoulder on busy Hwy

99. Hwy 47 (mile 14.8) and Westside Rd (mile 17.3) lack shoulder.

McMinnville
Pop. 31,700
Elevation 160 ft

USEFUL WEBSITES
McMinnville Chamber of Commerce
www.mcminnville.org
McMinnville AVA
www.mcminnvilleava.org

EVENTS OF NOTE
SIP – McMinnville Wine and Food Festival—In March, local winemakers and chefs strut their stuff.

LODGING
For tighter budgets, there are also a couple of lower-priced motels close-ish to downtown near Hwy 99.
Hotel Oregon (www.mcmenamins.com/hoteloregon, 503-472-8427, 310 NE Evans St, $60-145) Definitely the hippest AND best value in town. With a fabulous rooftop bar, murals all over the place and a location as central as it gets, this would be my choice in McMinnville, even if the cheaper rooms have shared baths. Likey.
3rd Street Flats (www.thirdstreetflats.com, 503-857-6248, 219 NE Cowl St, $165-240) These European-style flat rentals are styled-out, have kitchens and are near downtown.
A Tuscan Estate (www.a-tuscanestate.com, 503-434-9016,

809 NE Evans St, $140-235) This place reminds me of a true-to-form, typical wine country bed and breakfast, equipped with four-poster beds in a Colonial home. It stands out because it's close to downtown.

CAMPING
Willamette Wine Country RV Park (www.willamettewinecountryrvpark.com, 503-864-2233, 16205 SE Kreder Rd, Dayton, tent site $32) This RV Park in Dayton will permit tent camping but won't waive the whopping RV hook-up rate for tent camper. *Expensivo!* But they do have a heated pool and a fitness center (just what you need after a day of riding).
Sleepy Hollow RV Park (503-864-3740, 775 E 3rd St, Lafayette, tent site $15) This isn't the most scenic option, but it's cheap. The park is 9.5 miles from McMinnville via back roads; taking Hwy 99, it's 5.5 miles away.

CHOW DOWN
Mexican, Thai and pizza are also downtown.
Wildwood Cafe (503-435-1454, 319 N

Baker St, 7am-2pm) People recommend Wildwood's rival, the Crescent Cafe, but there always seems to be an hour wait when I'm there. The kitschy, tongue-in-cheek decor at the Wildwood Cafe entertains as much as the hardy, tasty breakfast fare fills the belly.

Golden Valley Brewery
(www.goldenvalleybrewery.com, 503-472-2739, 980 NE 4th St, Sun-Thurs 11am-10pm, Fri-Sat till 11pm) If you want to take a break from Pinot Noir, here's your chance for some local brew and salt-of-the-earth pub food.

La Rambla (www.laramblaonthird.com, 503-435-2126, 238 NE 3rd St, Mon-Thurs 11:30 am-2:30pm and 4-9pm, Fri til 10; Sat and Sun open 11:30am-10pm; Tues-Wed closed in low season) Delicious, Northwest-inspired Spanish cuisine. It was here that I first tried a Patricia Green wine. That means it will always be a special place for me. Upscale prices are in line with the food's quality.

Thistle (www.thistlerestaurant.com, 503-472-9623, 228 NE Evans St, Tues-Thurs 5:30-10pm, Fri-Sat till 11pm) This place rocks. If I wanted to splurge on a wine country dinner, I would go here. The atmosphere is more farmhouse-cozy with hip undertones than pretentious, but the locally-sourced food, wine and service are impeccable.

Harvest Fresh Grocery and Deli
(www.harvestfresh.com, 503-472-5740, 251 NE 3rd St, Mon-Fri 8am-8pm, Sat 8am-7pm, Sun 10am-7pm) McMinnville's

natural food store with a snazzy deli.

McMinnville Public Market
(www.mcminnvillepublicmarket.com, 503-550-3812, 755 NE Alpine St, Saturdays 10am-3pm) McMinnville's chefs, produce purveyors and artists flaunt their wares.

WinCo Foods (www.wincofoods.com, 503-434-5858, 2585 NE Hwy 99, 24 hours) Conventional grocery store.

TASTING ROOMS IN TOWN
Willamette Valley Wine Center
(www.wvv.com/visit/wine_center, 503-883-9012, 300 NE 3rd St, Sun-Fri 10am-6pm, Sat 10am-6pm) I loved the informative exhibits and AVA maps on the wall. The center offers a complimentary tasting, and you have the opportunity to try wines from a variety of vineyards besides Willamette Valley Vineyard, which is OCSW certified.

Twelve (www.twelvewine.com, 503-435-1212, 581 NE 3rd St, Wed-Sun 12-6pm, shortened winter hours) This newer, up-and-coming vineyard experiments with

whole cluster fermentation. One might even call the winery's approach "hip."

BIKE SHOP
Tommy's Bicycle Shop
(www.tommysbicycle.net, 503-472-2010, 624 NE 3rd St, Mon-Fri 10am-6pm, Sat till 5pm) The shop is conveniently located downtown.

YOGA
4 Elements Yoga Shop and Studio
(www.4eyoga.com, 503-687-1750, 424 NE 4th St, drop-in 15) Right in downtown, this studio has a variety of classes seven days per week.

DAY THREE
McMinnville Day Ride
41.2 miles
Elevation Climbed 1,250 ft.

Leaving your panniers on the hotel room floor and closing the door behind you can be a very satisfying way to start a ride, so enjoy.

After you conquer the short stint of Hwy 99 before Lafayette (mile 11.2), you mostly cruise deserted countryside roads on your way to Amity. In Amity, you have a choice: you can climb a steep gravel road for a mile to Amity Vineyards, which rewards you with a spectacular view and great wine, or you can visit Coelho Winery right in town, which has Portuguese-inspired wines along with Pinot Noir. Or do both.

The second half of the ride is my favorite. The route becomes more pastoral and wooded. You'll pass both Maysara Winery, whose driveway is easy to ride, and Youngberg Hill Winery, whose "driveway" is a paved mile of upward grade. I will say that the climb to Youngberg is worth it; their old-world, sustainable approach yields delicious results.

STOP AND SIP
Amity Vineyards (www.amityvineyards. com, 503-835-2362, 18150 Amity Vineyards Rd SE, Oct-May 12-5pm, June-Sep 11am-6pm, tasting $8) From Amity, this vineyard is 1.5 miles away, about a mile of which is a heck of a gravel road climb. The view and the wines make you feel better at the top. Tasting fees are waived with purchase. OCSW certified.
Coelho Winery (www.coelhowinery. com, 503-835-9305, 111 5th St, 11am-5pm, tasting $15) This winery's delicious Portuguese-inspired wines came as a pleasant surprise and a diversion from the winery norm. It was a boon that we

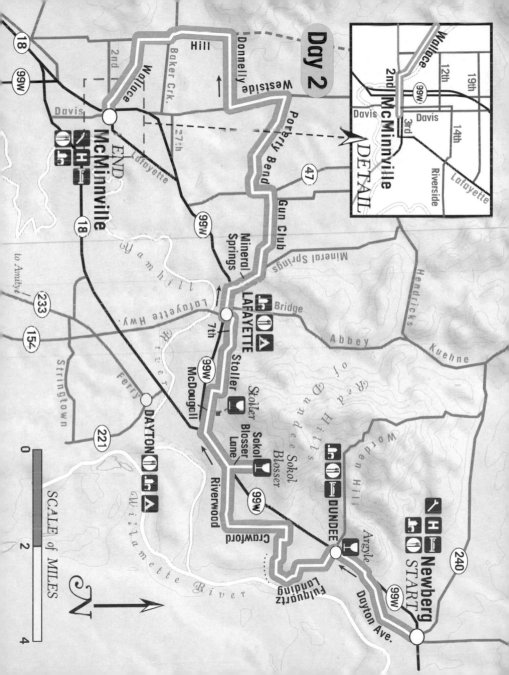

Day 2

DETAIL

McMinnville

SCALE of MILES

0
2
4

N

Day Two
Newberg to McMinnville

0	•	From Newberg Bicycle Shoppe, go south on S Howard St
.1	☞ / ↘	E 2nd St / S Blaine St
.2	☞ / ↘	E 3rd St / Dayton Ave
1.9	↘	Hwy 99
2.5	•	Dundee • Red Hills Market, Argyle Tasting Room
2.8	↘	SE 10th St
3.1	☞	SE Edwards Dr (gravel)
5.5	↘	NE Crawford Ln
6.7	☞	NE Riverwood Dr (pavement)
7.9	↘	Hwy 99
8	•	Sokol Blosser (about a mile to tasting room)
8.2	☞	NE McDougall Rd
9.6	•	Stoller Vineyards
9.7	☞ / ↘	Stoller Road / Unmarked road
11.2	↘	Becomes 7th St • Lafayette
11.5	✔	Continuing on unsigned 7th Street
11.8	↘	Washington St
12	☞	3rd St, becomes 99W
12.3	☞	Mineral Springs Rd
13.1	↘	Gun Club Rd
14.8	↘	Hwy 47
15.1	☞	NW Poverty Bend Rd
17.3	↘	Westside Rd
18.5	☞	NW Donnelly Ln
20.1	↘	NW Hill Rd
21.2	↘	Baker Creek Rd
21.5	☞	Hill Rd
22.2	↘	Wallace Rd
23.6	↘	NW 2nd St
24	↘ / •	NE Davis St / Hotel Oregon

NEWBERG to McMinnville — ELEVATION (ft.) — Newberg — Lafayette — McMinnville — 200 100 — MILES — 0 — 10 — 20

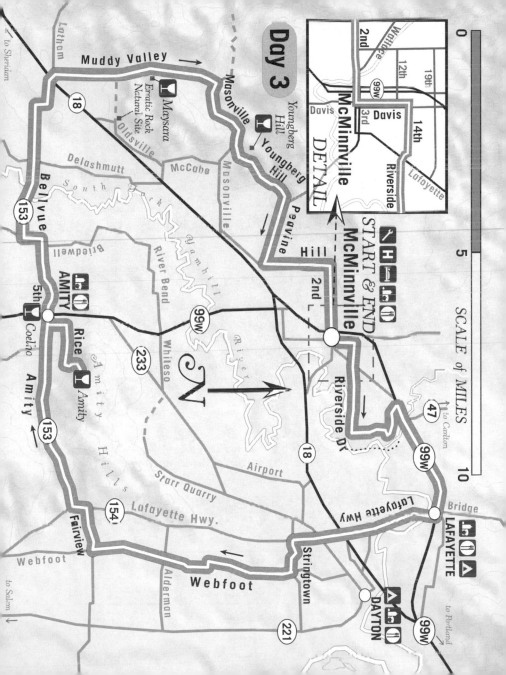

Day Three
Day ride from McMinnville

0	•	From Hotel Oregon, head north on NE Evans St
.5	☞	NE 14th St
1.1		Cross NE Lafayette Ave, becomes NE Riverside Dr (bike lane)
2.6	⬎	Continue on NE Riverside Dr to the left
4.3	☞ / ☞	Unsigned road/unsigned but obvious Hwy 99
7.3	☞	Madison St, becomes Lafayette Hwy (no shoulder, though less traffic) • Lafayette
9.5		Cross Hwy 18
10		Cross Hwy 233
	or ⬎	To Dayton, the Joel Palmer House, Block House Cafe
10.7	⬎	Stringtown Rd
11.5	☞	Webfoot Rd
14.5	•	Adorable house
15.6	•	Haur of the Dauen Winery
16.3	☞	Fairview Rd
17.3	⬎	To 'Amity,' unsigned Lafayette Hwy
17.5	☞	To 'Amity,' unsigned Hwy 153
22.2	☞	Trade street • Amity
22.4	⬎ / •	5th st, becomes Bellveue Hwy; Cohelo Winery
	or	Following signs to Amity Winery (1.5 mile horrible, steep road)
28.6		Cross Hwy 18 • Bellveue; road curves and becomes SW Muddy Valley Rd
30.7	•	Mayasara Vineyards
32.6	☞	Masonville Rd
34.4	⬎	Youngberg Hill Rd
35.1	•	Youngberg Hill Winery (one mile climb)
36.2	✔	At stop sign at intersection of Peavine and Youngberg Hill Rds
37.9	⬎	Hill Rd S
39.5	☞	NW 2nd St
41.2	⬎ / •	NE Evans St/ Hotel Oregon

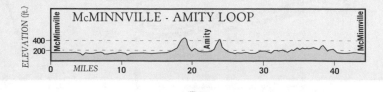

brought blue cheese to nibble with these heavier wines. A nice alternative if you aren't into the Amity Vineyards climb.

Mayasara (www.maysara.com, 503-843-1234, 15765 Muddy Valley Rd, Mon-Sat 12-5pm, tasting $7) Locally and critically acclaimed, this winery embraces a "biodynamic" approach to wine making.

Youngberg Hill Winery

(www.youngberghill.com, 503-472-2727, 10660 SW Youngberg Hill Rd, 11am-5pm, tasting $10) This vineyard uses a traditionalist approach and offers a variety of single-vineyard (see Environment, page 20) Pinot Noirs. On summer weekends, there might be a chance they're booked for private events. OCSW certified.

STOP AND EAT

Block House Cafe (mile 10, www.theblockhousecafe.com, 503-864-8412, 302 Ferry St, Dayton, Tues-Thurs 9am-7pm, Fri-Sat 7am-7pm, Sun 9am-2pm) You won't leave hungry from this budget-friendly greasy spoon. They have famous cinnamon roll pancakes.

Joel Palmer House (mile 10, www.joelpalmerhouse.com, 503-864-2995, 600 Ferry St, Dayton,Tues-Sat 5-9pm) An acclaimed, upscale restaurant with a mushroom fetish. Only open for dinner.

RIDING TIPS

• Check out the Eola-Amity Hills AVA website (www.eolaamityhills.com) for more info about the Amity area.

• A significant portion of this ride is flat, through open valleys. Headwinds are a distinct possibility.

• Hwy 153 (mile 17.5) doesn't have a shoulder, but traffic isn't bad.

• On the Bellvue Hwy, you'll pass a local swimming swim spot in a river.

DAY FOUR

McMinnville to the Hillsboro MAX Station
40.2 miles
Elevation Climbed 1,600 ft.

Today you ride the country roads of the Yamhill-Carlton AVA while weaving your merry way to the Hillsboro MAX Station. Hopefully you have room in your pannier for a bottle or two.

Even though Old McMinnville Rd and Yamhill Rd are a bit rough, their lack of traffic and rural character were a highlight for me. These roads bring you right by Carlton, a tiny town with the super-chic Carlton Winemaker's Studio:

a collective of local wineries that lets you taste an assortment of the region's noble rot. Despite its size, Carlton also has delectable lunch options. See Stop and Eat (below).

The route skirts the Chehalem Mountains on the way north over rolling hills, which are covered with a patchwork of vineyards, farms and forests. On the way, you pass Willakenzie Estates. The short but steep grunt to the tasting room is worth it. The glassed-in, high-ceiling building allows for expansive views over the manicured vineyards and the picnic benches outside are a fabulous place for lunch.

The traffic doesn't really pick up too much until several miles outside of Hillsboro. A good way to self-soothe after the end of your incredible wine country tour is to head to Syun Izakaya (page 45) in Hillsboro, a traditional sushi restaurant that will make for a happy postscript.

STOP AND SIP
Carlton Winemakers Studio
(www.winemakersstudio.com, 503-852-6100, 801 N Scott St, 11am-5pm, tasting $10-15) It's a bit trippy to walk into a hip, upcycled wine studio located in the rural hamlet of Carlton. This innovative studio is shared by 10 small-batch wineries, which are featured in the tasting room on a rotating basis.

Willakenzie Winery
(www.willakenzie.com, 503-662-3280, 19143 NE Laughlin Rd, May-Oct 11am-5pm, off season till 4pm, tasting $15) With best in environmental and business practices, the philanthropic French-American couple who own Willakenzie creates a fabulous wine. We rode past the cyclist husband and Frenchman, Bernard Lacroute, on the way out. He was very encouraging and enthusiastic about the fact that we climbed the gigantor (but paved) hill to get the winery. OCSW certified.

Day Four
McMinnville to the Hillsboro MAX Station

0	•	From Hotel Oregon go west on NE 3rd St
.1	☞	NE Baker St
2	↰	NE 4th St, becomes NW Park Dr
.5	☞	NW Wallace Rd
1.9	☞	NW Hill Rd
2.5	↰	Baker Creek Rd
2.8	☞	Hill Rd N
3.9	☞	Donnelly Ln
5.5	↰	Westside Rd
6.7	☞	Poverty Bend Rd
8.9	↰	Unsigned Hwy 47
9.2	☞	Gun Club Rd
9.3	↰	Old McMinnville Hwy
12.1	☞	Hendricks Rd
	Or ↰	To Carlton (Carlton Winemakers Studio, Horse Radish)
12.8	↰	Johnson Rd
13.2	↰	Yamhill Rd
14.9	🚦	Through stop sign
15.5	•	Turn off to Sejoure Lavendar Farm and Yamhill Vineyards B&B
16.5	☞	Hwy 240
17.2	↰	Laughlin Rd
19	•	Willakenzie Estates (.4 miles to tasting room)
20.8	↰	NE Spring Hill Rd
21.8	🚦	NE Spring Hill Rd
28.2	☞	SW Fern Hill Rd
30.4	☞	SW Blossoming Fern Hill Rd
32.6	☞	Golf Course Rd
32.8	↰	SW Tongue Ln
35.8	☞	Hwy 219
36.1	↰	SW Grabel Rd
36.4	↰	Minter Bridge Rd
38.8	↰	SE 21st Ave
39.3	↰	SE Maple St
39.5	☞	SE 18th Ave
39.7	↰	SE Oak St
40	☞	SE 12th Ave
40.2	•	Hillsboro MAX Station

STOP AND EAT

Cuvée (www.cuveedining.com, 503-852-6555, 214 W Main St, Wed-Sat 5:30-9pm, Sun 5-8pm, Wed-Sun 12-3pm during the summer) Upscale country French cuisine in the in the rural Oregon town of Carlton. Oo la la.

The Horse Radish

(www.thehorseradish.com, 503-852-6656, 211 W Main St, Mon-Thurs 12-4pm, Fri-Sat 12-10pm, Sun 1-5pm) Wine and cheese bar in Carlton. They had me at wine and cheese. You can order picnics here as well.

Blue Goat (www.amitybluegoat.com, 503-835-5170, 506 S Trade St, Wed, Thurs, Sun 11:30am-9, Fri-Sat till 10, shortened winter hours) The wood-fired oven creates decadent dishes at the Blue Goat in Amity. The menu is decked out with local, sustainable ingredients. Shortened winter hours.

Syun Izakaya (503-640-3131, 209 NE Lincoln St, Mon 11am-9pm, Tues-Wed 11am-2pm and 5pm-10pm, Thurs-Sat

12-10pm, Sun 4-10pm) Ragingly fantastic sushi in downtown Hillsboro. So delish. While you're there, try some of the Saké One that's made just down the road in Forest Grove.

RIDING TIPS

• Old McMinnville Hwy (mile 9.3) and Yamhill Rd (mile 13.2) are actually paved, in a chunky kind of way, but in small sections there is gravel on top of the surface.

• Blooming Fern Hill Rd (mile 30.4) is freeze-in-your-pedals steep.

• Crossing busy Hwy 219 (mile 35.8) isn't ideal. Careful does it.

• Check out the Yamhill Valley Visitor's Association website (travelyamhillvalley.org) for detailed info on this area.

◁OREGON COAST◁

"Did Someone Get the Number of that Logging Truck?"

Six days and five nights
Astoria to Brookings
365 miles total

THE SKINNY

PRICE POINT: You could do this tour with a **small to bulging purse**. All the way down the coast, you can eat in restaurants and stay in moderate to high-end lodging. Similarly, you could grocery store-graze and camp every night.

DIFFICULTY RATING: 7.5 You'll experience a hearty portion of climbing, and a calm mind is needed for the gnarly sections of Hwy 101.

JAW-DROP FACTOR: 8.2 Between the undeveloped coastline and the forests of the Coast Range, the scenery is spectacular.

STAND OUT CAMPING: This is a super hard choice because so many coast campgrounds rock. Fort Stevens State Park (page 53) wins for its great beach, lookout tower and lake for swimming.

STAND OUT LODGING: Wild Spring Guest Habitat (page 64), a luxury, eco-friendly splurge.

AVERAGE TEMP IN FEBRUARY: Low 40, high 53 degrees

AVERAGE TEMP IN AUGUST: Low 52, high 67 degrees

Fist Bump!
- **Oregon State Parks**. Love'em. (All days)
- **Miami River Rd** (Day 2, page 57)
- **Manzanita**, adorable beach town (Day 1, page 54)
- **Three Capes Scenic Route** (Day 2, page 57)
- **Pelican Brewery** (Day 2, page 58)
- **Otter Crest Loop Rd** (Day 3, page 61)
- **Seven Devils Rd** outside North Bend (Day 5, page 64)
- Slurping oysters at **Pacific Seafood Restaurant** (Day 2, page 57) in Bay City and **Tony's Crab Shack** (Day 5, page 64) in Bandon

The Oregon coast seduces cyclists from around the world with its rugged shores, expansive beaches and deep forests. Yet, while the coast embraces cyclists as a part of her touristscape, she doesn't totally understand what they need (like low-traffic roads; hold the thousands of logging trucks and RVs, please.)

I understand why you want to cycle the coast. I've cycle toured the entire coast once, and pieces of it numerous times, even with the understanding the Highway 101 is crapalicious, traffic-wise. The mind-blowing scenery is awfully enticing. Plus, the sections of the route that divert away from Hwy 101 reach epic levels of spectacular.

But know that you are signing up for some gnarly traffic, some non-existent shoulders and RVs that don't know how large they really are. If you want remote, ideal roads for cycling with awesome (non-coastal) landscapes, look to other tours in this book. If you have your eye on the coastal prize, and are willing to put up with a little exhaust lung, read on.

This chapter outlines a sweet coastal itinerary so you can grab your bike and go. Because there are so many lodging and eating options along the way, I don't mention many places to eat or stay outside of destination towns or place them on maps, as I do for other tours in remote areas. If you plan to riff off this itinerary, see the Maps section (inside page 51) for helpful info.

HISTORY TIDBITS

Before the arrival of European explorers and settlers, Native American tribes survived on the natural resources. When settlers started to encroach, things quickly turned sour. The discovery of gold in river estuaries, which were traditional Native American settlement locations, rapidly brought conflict. Disease, hunger, war and murder weakened then broke the tribes. Today, the small groups of Native American descendants are working to preserve what is left of their cultural history.

The marine life and forest that had been central to the Native American way of life also motivated the modern development of the fishing and timber industries. The small towns that serviced these industries prospered between 1930 and 1980. But a failure to manage natural resources sustainably led to their depletion.

With the big trees cut and the big fish gone, businesses closed, people moved away and the area suffered. Currently, coastal industries include small-scale fishing, agriculture and tourism, with the occasional artist sprinkled throughout.

Oregon Legislature, You Got it Right This Time

The Oregon Beach Bill (1967) was a significant piece of legislation that helped save public access to all the beaches along the Oregon coast. This bill clarified that a strip of land between the ocean and the line of vegetation is either owned by the State of Oregon or held as a public easement. This means the public has access to all Oregon beaches, even if powerful development interests want otherwise.

ENVIRONMENT

The rolling hills, dense forests and grand ocean vistas are why you come here. But every so often, you'll see where gravel mining and deforestation have scarred the landscape.

Oregonians haven't always done the best job of maintaining and sustaining the natural environment of the coast. Old

Oregon Coast

growth timber was clear cut. Hills and buttes were carved our for gravel. These actions had an immediate positive effect: some people made a bunch of money. Longer-term effects are the erosion of hills and mountains and hazardous runoff from mining operations that sully rivers and estuaries.

Currently, better environmental protections are in place. But clear cutting is still legal in some places, and the gravel mines are still operation in some counties.

We all use paper, and some of the roads we ride are made of the gravel from those mines. Resources have a cost. On the coast, we see the toll.

RIDING SEASON

The high tourist season revs up around April and is in full swing June through Labor Day. Of course, those months are the best times for weather, but traffic-wise they are the worst. Thousands of cyclists ride the coast during the summer anyway. Others chance the weather and go in the off-season. September is my bet for the lowest traffic and the best weather.

WEATHER

Coastal weather is mild year round. Outside of the summer, it's really soggy, which makes temperatures in the 50s seem more penetrating. In summer, there are some warm days but coastal inhabitants rarely go without a nice, thick sweater because chilly, overcast days are a distinct possibility, even in August. Fog is common in the morning and winds can be very strong. Riding south is good choice for avoiding headwinds, but it's likely you'll still encounter them at some point.

ARRIVING / LEAVING ASTORIA

In Astoria, Bikes and Beyond (page 53) is accustomed to receiving bikes shipped from all over. If you are flying to PDX, shipping your bike there may be the easiest and cheapest way.

Car

Hertz Car Rental (www.hertz.com, 800-654-3131, 1110 SE FlightlineDr, one-way $239) is one of two rental places in Astoria, and the only one allowing one-way trips (which are pricy). **U-Haul** (www.uhaul.com, 800-789-3638, two-day rental from Portland starting at $179) also has drop-off locations in Astoria.

Bus

North West Point (www.northwest-point.com, 541-484-4100, two hours and 50 mins, $18) This bus runs twice a day to and from Portland. From Portland, buses leave at 9pm and 6pm, arriving at the Shell Station mini-mart near downtown Astoria. If you leave from the downtown Greyhound Station (550 NW 6th Ave) in Portland, you're less likely to be charged or hassled for your bike, as opposed to the stop at the Portland Amtrak Station. Usually only three bikes can fit and no tandems. Buses going to Portland leave at 8:30am and 6pm.

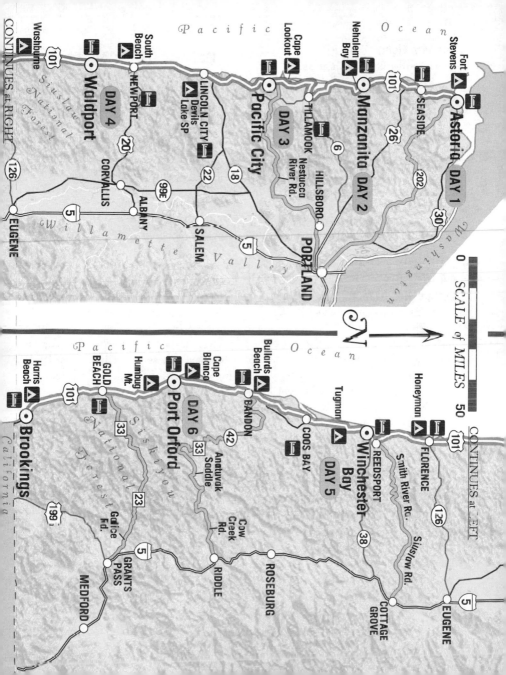

Northern Lights

(www.northernlightstowncar.com, 877-355-9195, two hours, $185) A shuttle service from the Portland airport. The company's Suburbans can fit four bikes and four people.

Bike

There are five recommendable connector roads from the valley/I-5 corridor to the coast. These connectors are marked on the overall chapter map (page 49). The best way to cycle to Astoria from Portland is on the Scappoose-Birkenfeld route.

ARRIVING / LEAVING BROOKINGS

Escape Hatch Sports and Cycle Shop

(page 68) in Brookings will pack your bike and ship it.

Car

The fastest way between Portland/the I-5 corridor and Brookings is Hwy 199, which runs from Grants Pass to Crescent City, CA. No car rental agencies have one-way car rentals to Brookings. U-Haul (www.uhaul.com, 800-789-3638, three-day rental from Portland starting at $228) has drop-off locations.

Bus

Greyhound Bus (www.greyhound.com, 800-231-2222, from Portland, 13.5 hours, $74-84) Service to Brookings. Bike box required and bike fees may apply.

Curry Public Transport

(www.currypublictransit.org, 800-921-2871, $6 bike fee, $20) Connects Brookings to North Bend. Each bus has

Rails-to-Trails between Portland and Astoria?

As this book is being written, **Cycle Oregon** (www.cycleoregon.com) is funding an exploration of the possibilities of making the deserted railway between the two cities into a multi-use trail. I'm rooting for it!

two bike racks on front.

Southwest Point Bus (www.southwestpoint.com, 888-900-2609, 10 hours, $50) Connects Brookings to the Klamath Falls Amtrak Station. Each bus has two bike racks on front. No bike fees.

Bike

The best way to head east by bike from the Brookings area, while staying within Oregon (as opposed to heading farther south and crossing over in California), is from Gold Beach (see overall chapter map, page 49).

USEFUL WEBSITES

Oregon Coast Visitors Association

www.visittheoregoncoast.com

LODGING

As a significant tourist destination, the coast is equipped with lots of lodging. There are fewer high-end options, with a fair number of mid-level hotels and B&Bs. However, mid-level on a weekend in high season usually means well over $100 per night. I like to use VRBO.com (Vacation Rentals By Owner) for renting houses on the coast; prices can be cheaper than a hotel. Also, warmshowers.org, a site that connects cycle tourists with hosts, is a good resource.

CAMPING

The Oregon coast has fantastic camping and state parks. It has been a state priority (see History section, page 47) to keep our beaches public. Fabulous and plentiful campgrounds are a result.

FOOD AND DRINK

Seafood: buy it fresh and cook it up. Lots of restaurants will fry or overcook seafood, but occasionally you'll find an eatery that knows how to do it right. I mention a couple in this chapter. The cuisine of the coast mostly is the cuisine of Middle America: hamburgers, pizza, fish-and-chips, pasta.

HYDRATION

Though the coast route is sprinkled with towns, it's always good to be prepared with 20-30 hilly miles worth of water. As you get farther south, there's more distance between services.

MAPS

The Oregon Department of Transportation distributes the **Oregon Coast Bike Route map** (www.oregon.gov/ODOT/HWY/ BIKEPED/docs/oregon_coast_bike_ route_map.pdf, 503-986-3556, free), an excellent and suggested supplement to this chapter. It shows all campgrounds with details about amenities in case you want to divert from the given itinerary. The map also shows where the roads lack shoulders, bike shop locations and close-up maps for urban areas or tricky intersections. You can download it online, request a copy or pick it up at any tourist or visitor resource on the coast.

Also, the **City of Portland** (www. portlandonline.com) provides detailed maps for two of the five recommended routes from Portland to the coast: Portland to Astoria and Portland to Pacific City via the Nestucca River Rd.

The Adventure Cycling Association (www.adventurecycling.org, 800-755-2453, $14.95) also puts out a detailed cycling map of the Oregon Coast.

GENERAL RIDING TIPS AND HEADS UP

• Hwy 101 has nasty traffic in places and, sometimes, no shoulder. Watch out for logging trucks and RVs (see "Who Sucks the Most," page 52), and wear obnoxiously bright clothes.

• There are two tunnels on route that are equipped with light systems you can activate to let motorists know you're cycling in the tunnel.

• Watch out for gusting winds when crossing bridges.

• Wait out thick morning fog.

• There are tons of awesome parks. Picnicking advised.

• In Astoria, we ran into an inordinate amount of folks tweaking on drugs.

CELL COVERAGE

Though you usually get coverage in the coastal towns, cell service can be spotty in the remote in-between.

Oregon Coast

HOSPITALS
Columbia Memorial Hospital
(www.columbiamemorialhospital.com, 503-325-4321, 2111 Exchange St, Astoria) 24/7 emergency care.

Adventist Health (www.tcgh.com, 503-842-4444, 1000 3rd St, Tillamook) 24/7 emergency care.

Samaritan Pacific Communities Hospital
(www.samhealth.org, 541-265-2244, 930 SW Abbey St, Newport) 24/7 emergency care.

Lower Umpqua Hospital
(www.lowerumpquahospital.com, 541-271-2171, 600 Ranch Rd, Reedsport) 24/7 emergency care.

Curry General Hospital
(www.curryhealthnetwork.com, 541-247-3000, 94220 4th St, Gold Beach) 24/7 emergency care.

MORE TOUR!
On the overall map of this tour, the five cycle-worthy connectors are noted so you can navigate to inland tours. The **Willamette Valley Scenic Bikeway** (see page 7) connects Champoeg Park, near Portland, to Eugene and could be part of a loop.

COST OPTIONS:
Budget camping tour: Day 1, Nehalem Bay State Park (Page 54); Day 2, Whalen Island County Park (Page 58); Day 3, Beachside State Park (Page 61); Day 4, Umpqua Lighthouse State Park (Page 63); Day 5, Cape Blanco State Park (Page 67); Day 6, Harris Beach State Park (Page 68).

High falootin' credit card camping: Day 1, Hotel Elliot (page 53); Day 2, Sunset Surf Motel (page 54); Day 3, Craftsman B&B (page 58); Day 4, Cliff House B&B (page 62); Day 5, WildSpring Guest Habitat (page 64); Day 6, Ocean Suites Motel (page 68).

Astoria
Pop. 9,740
Elevation 18 ft.

USEFUL WEBSITES
Astoria Chamber of Commerce
www.oldoregon.com
Astoria Tourist Website
www.astoriaoregon.com

LODGING
There are a number of low-budget hotels near downtown.

Rose River Inn B&B (www.roseriverinn.com, 503-325-7175, 1510 Franklin Ave, $95-150) Diverging from traditional doily-

Who Sucks the Most: Logging Trucks vs RVs
There are excellent, courteous drivers (love you!) and bad drivers, but either way, logging trucks and RVs are the scariest for cyclists. There have been a number of bike accidents on the coast. You have to be extra wary and know that you're riding dangerous road on certain sections of Hwy 101. Some RVs and logging trucks don't have perspective on how much room to give cyclists. Some are just A-holes. Be careful out there.

like B&B decor, David and Pam Armstrong have a more grounded approach. There's bike storage inside.

Hotel Elliott (www.hotelelliot.com, 503-325-2222, 357 12th St, low season $139-249, high season $179-289) Probably one of the most fashionable places in town, the hotel mixes old-fashioned, modern and trendy.

CAMPING
Fort Stevens State Park (www.oregonstateparks.org, 800-551-6949, reservations 800-452-5687, 100 Peter Iredale Rd, Hammond, cabin $62-85, yurt $41, tent site $21, hiker/biker tent site per person $6) This historic park has awesome multi-use trails and Coffenbury Lake, which has two swimming areas. It's located on a beautiful ocean beach, and there are showers and lower cost hiker/biker sites. The park is 9.6 miles from downtown Astoria across Youngs Bay and 6.5 miles from the tour route.

CHOW DOWN
Blue Scorcher Bakery and Cafe (www.bluescorcher.com, 503-338-7473, 1493 Duane St, 8am-5pm) Here you'll find some of the most delicious food in Astoria. Focusing on seasonal, local and organic items, this cafe makes it fresh. Friendly to gluten-free and vegetarian diets.
Columbian Cafe (www.columbianvoodoo.com, 503-325-2233, 1114 Marine Dr, Wed-Fri 8am-2pm, Sat-Sun 9am-2pm, Thurs and Sun 5-9pm, Fri 6-10pm, Sat 5-10pm) Specializing in fresh seafood and vegetarian fare, this cafe also has a hefty dose of personality.
Astoria Coopertive (www.astoriacoop.org, 503-325-0027, 1355 Exchange St 9am-7pm) Expensive organic food market.
Sunday Market(www.astoriasundaymarket.com, 503-325-1010, Commercial St and 12th St, May-Oct Sundays 10am-3pm) Astoria takes its market seriously with music, fresh produce and art.
Safeway (www.safeway.com, 503-338-2960, 3250 Leif Erikson Dr, 6 1am) Conventional grocery store.

BIKE SHOPS
Bikes and Beyond (www.bikesandbeyond.com, 503-325-2961, 1089 Marine Dr, Mon-Fri 9am-6pm, Sat 10am-6pm, Sun 11am-5pm, shortened winter hours) Astoria's bike shop will ship and receive bikes with a $50 assembly cost or a $10 service charge. Call to notify them that you are sending a bike and have it arrive a week before you do.

YOGA
Yoga Namaste (www.yoganam.com, 503-440-9761, 342 10th St, drop-in $15) Classes Monday, Wednesday, Friday and Saturday.

DAY ONE
Astoria to Manzanita
44.8 miles
Elevation Climbed 3,400 ft.

Pretty soon after you leave the outskirts of Astoria, you'll hit tree-lined Fort Clatsop Rd. At the Fort Clatsop Visitors Center, there is a replica of the historic fort where

Oregon Coast

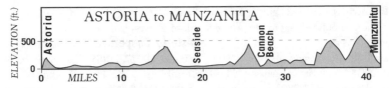

the Lewis and Clark Expedition wintered in 1805. The quiet back way to Seaside is rolling and curvy without very much traffic; it's the cycling highlight of the day.

The route avoids Seaside and cuts through **Cannon Beach**, a great place for lunch and checking out local art galleries. There is always very slow moving car traffic in Cannon Beach, but you will cruise by.

Over the course of this day, there are about 16 miles of riding on Hwy 101. It's not awesome, but at the end of the day you reach Manzanita, one of the most adorable towns on the Oregon coast.

HEADS UP

At mile 36.8, there is a tunnel. Put on your blinkies and activate the light that warns motorists you are in the tunnel.

Manzanita
Pop. 620
Elevation 111 ft.

LODGING

Sunset Surf Motel (www.sunsetsurfocean. com, 800-243-8035, 248 Ocean Rd, high season $89-169, low season discounts) Though this hotel doesn't have a lot of frills or updates, they offer clean rooms at reasonable coast rates and are right on the

ocean. Plus, the heated pool is open in the summer.

Sand Dune Motel

(www.sandune-inn-manzanita.com, 888-368-5163, 428 Dorcas Ln, low season $60-100, high season $110-185) A short walk from the beach, this simple, casual inn is another budget option. Complete with books, movies and games.

Coast Cabins (www.coastcabins.com, 800-435-1269, 635 Laneda Ave, high season $245-379, low seasons discounts) Pure luxury. Pure comfort. I hope you have a high credit card limit.

CAMPING
Nehalem Bay State Park

(www.oregonstateparks.com, 503-368-5154, reservations 800-452-5687, 9500 Sandpiper Ln, yurt $36, hiker/biker tent site per person $5) Three miles south of Manzanita, you'll find the campground and yurts nestled into trees right by the beach dunes. Potable water and showers. Two-mile multi-use trail.

CHOW DOWN

On the main street, Laneda Ave, you'll find Mexican, Italian and pub fare.

Bread and Ocean

(www.breadandocean.com, 154 Laneda Ave, 503-368-5823, Wed-Sun 7:30am-

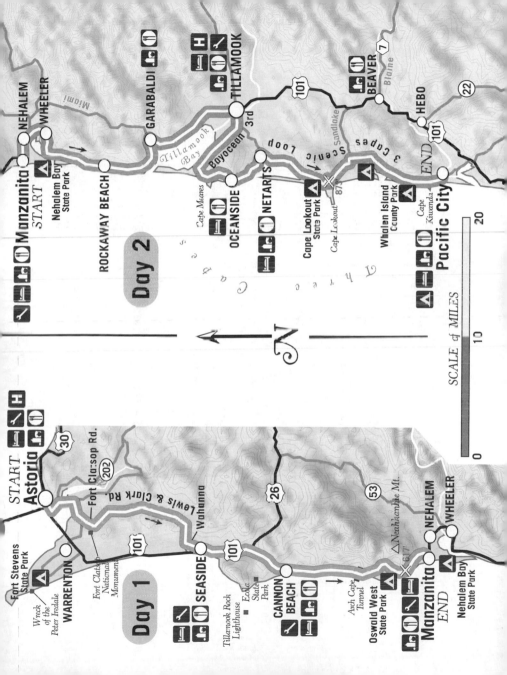

Day One

Astoria to Manzanita

0	•	From the Blue Scorcher head N on Duane St
.3		7th St
.4	☜	Bond St
1	☜	At light, Marine Dr
1.7	☜	At roundabout, second exit (not bridge) to 202 E
3.1	☜	Hwy 101, to 'Seaside'
3.5	•	Bridge, wonky sidewalk
4.7	☜	Following Hwy 101
6.9		Fort Clatsop Rd, to 'visitor center'
7.3		Fort Clatsop National Historic Park
12.7		Road gets rougher
13.2	merge	Unsigned Lewis and Clark Rd
20.2	•	Unsigned Wahanna Rd
20.9	☜	Turning left on Ocean Ave brings you to Seaside
22.7		Unsigned Hwy 101
28.9	☜	To 'Ecola State Park'
29.3		Turnoff to Ecola State Park
29.6	☜	3rd St, becomes Hemlock St
32.5	☜	Hwy 101, to 'Arch Cape'
36.8	•	Tunnel, activate lights
37.1	•	End tunnel
44.3	☜	To 'Manzanita'
44.5	☜	Pine Ave
44.6	☜	Laneda Ave
44.8	•	Manzanita

Day Two

Manzanita to Pacific City

0	•	From Manzanita, head to Hwy 101
.3		Hwy 101
1.1	•	Nehalem Bay State Park
2.2	☜	Hwy 101 • Nehalem
3.7	☜	Hwy 53
4.7	•	Mohler
5.1	☜	Foley Rd, becomes Miami River Rd
17.8		Hwy 101
20.9		Pacific Seafood Restaurant, Bay City
26.5	☜	1st Street, to 'Cape Meares,' • Trask Mountain Cycle
27	☜	Hwy 131, to Three Capes Scenic Route'
28.4	☜	Bayocean Rd, Three Capes Scenic Rte
33.8	☜	Cape Meares Loop, to 'Three Capes Scenic Rte'
35.8	•	Cape Meares State Park
38.3	or ☜	unsigned Netarts-Oceanside Hwy W
		To Oceanside
40.8	☜	Netarts Bay Rd • Netarts
42.2		Following Three Capes Scenic Route
45.6	•	Crazy compound
52.2	☜	To 'Sand Lake Recreation Area'
53.2	•	Sand Lake convenience store
55.8	•	To Clay Myers State Park and Whalen Island County Park
60.2	•	Pelican Brewery, Pacific City

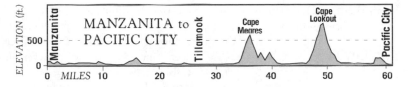

2pm) I loved the sandwiches and baked goods here, so much so that I ignored the service with hipster 'tude. Cash or check only.

Little Apple Grocery and Deli (www. manzanitadeli.com, 503-368-5362, 1931 Laneda Ave, Mon-Fri 7am-9pm, Sat-Sun 7am-11pm) A block away from this market, Mother Nature's Natural Food has pure, organic (expensive as hell) goodness. At the Little Apple you'll still find some organic/natural products, but for less. Plus, there's a deli and conventional grocery items.

Manzanita Farmers Market (www. manzanitafarmersmarket.com, 503-368-3339, June-Sept, Fri 5-8pm) Food, art and community.

BIKE SHOPS

Manzanita Bikes and Boards (www. manzanitabikesandboards.com, 503-368-3337, 170 Laneda Ave, open March-October, Mon-Sun various hours) This rental shop can help you out with basics.

YOGA

Longevity (www.longevitymanzanita.com, 503-368-3800, 123 Laneda Ave, drop-in $10-15) The yoga studio has a class or two every day of the week.

DAY TWO
Manzanita to Pacific City
60.2 miles
Elevation Climbed 4,000 ft.

Goody! You'll ride one of my favorite roads of the northern coast today: Miami River Rd. It threads along valley surrounded by forested knolls. You'll pass grazing horses, broken-down barns and a gurgling river.

After Miami River Rd dumps you back on Hwy 101, you can soon console yourself with juicy raw oysters or a steaming bowl of cioppino at Bay City's **Pacific Seafood restaurant** right by the water at mile 20.9. If you are camping and want to buy some fresh fish to cook for dinner, this place will wrap the catch in ice.

After enduring about nine miles of Hwy 101 (with some seriously gnar traffic), you turn off onto the famous Three Capes Scenic Route from Tillamook. A narrow road leads you around the southern edge of Tillamook Bay and provides the iconic oceans vistas that inspire postcards. Then a steep road cuts inland into the heart of lavishly forested Cape Meares State Park. On the whooshing descent to Netarts Bay, the ocean pops in and out of view.

Eventually you hit Pacific City, home

of Pelican Brewery. This place is a good excuse to stop here for the night.

Pacific City
Pop. 1,060
Elevation 10 ft.

USEFUL WEBSITES
Pacific City Visitor Guide
www.pacificcity.org

LODGING
There are several other options in town.
The Inn at Pacific City
(www.innatpacificcity.com, 503-965-6366, 35215 Brooten Rd, high season $89-99, low season $49-59) This simple hotel is a low-budget option. Five blocks from the ocean.
Craftsman B&B (www.craftsmanbb.com, 503-965-4574, 35255 4th St, high season $130-170, low season $110-150) I'm not usually a fan of B&Bs but this one looks stinking awesome. Remodeled in 2005, the owners really went for Craftsman-era charm. And succeeded. Reasonable prices for the coast considering you get a home-cooked breakfast.

CAMPING
If you want to camp in a gorgeous natural setting, stay at Whalen Island County Park 4.5 miles north of Pacific City.
Camp Kiwanda RV Park
(www.capekiwandarvresort.com, 503-965-6230, 33305 Cape Kiwanda Dr, sleeping cabin $55-75, tent site 22-27) 10 sites. Right across from Pelican Brewery,

you won't be getting away from it all. But the sites are on the back perimeter of the property next to a grove of trees. Sleeping cabins are super basic. Reservations available.
Woods County Campground (www.co.tillamook.or.us/gov/parks, 503-965-5001, hiker/bike tent site per person $5) Seven sites. Near the southern part of town right on the Nestucca River, this little campground is a more secluded than the Camp Kiwanda RV Park and in a natural setting. Reservations available. Closed Oct-April.

CHOW DOWN
Stimulus Espresso (www.stimuluscafe.com, 503-965-4661, 33105 Cape Kiwanda Dr, 6am-6pm) With locally made pastries and Stumptown Coffee, you can't go wrong. Across from Pelican Brewery.
Pelican Brewery (www.pelicanbrewery.com, 503-965-7007, 33180 Cape Kiwanda Dr, Sun-Thurs 8am-10pm, Fri-Sat 8am-11pm) The Pelican is an institution, but it's a righteous one. Right on the ocean, this local brewery likes to pair their food with their brew. I love sitting on the outdoor patio in the summer.
Cape Kiwanda Market Place (www.capekiwandarvresort.com, 503-965-6230, 33305 Cape Kiwanda Dr, Sun-Thurs 8am-9pm, Fri-Sat 8am-10pm) I always get smoked oysters here and would get the fresh seafood any day. They have basic groceries, a surprising wine selection and a deli.

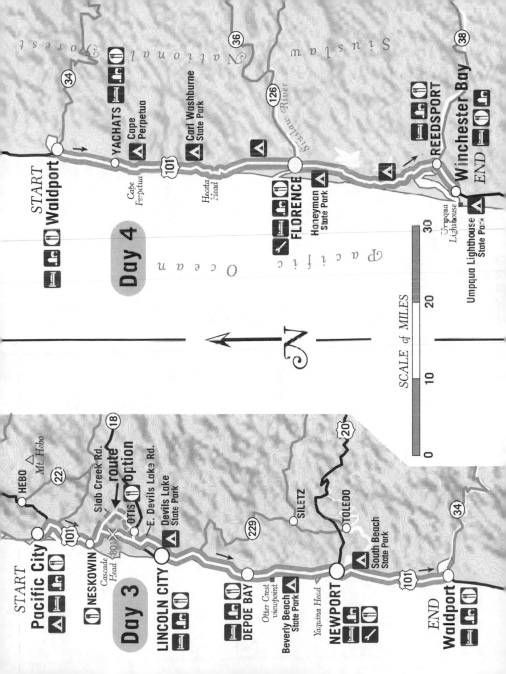

Day 4

START
Waldport

YACHATS

Cape
Perpetua

Cape
Perpetua

Carl Washburne
State Park

Hecata
Head

FLORENCE

Honeyman
State Park

REEDSPORT

Winchester Bay

END

Umpqua
Lighthouse

Umpqua Lighthouse
State Park

Siuslaw National Forest

Siuslaw River

Pacific Ocean

34

36

126

38

101

Day 3

START
Pacific City

HEBO
Mt. Hebo

NESKOWIN

Cascade
Head

Slab Creek Rd.

route
option

OTIS

E. Devils Lake Rd.

Devils Lake
State Park

LINCOLN CITY

DEPOE BAY

Otter Crest
viewpoint

Beverly Beach
State Park

Yaquina Head

SILETZ

TOLEDO

NEWPORT

South Beach
State Park

END
Waldport

22

18

101

229

20

34

SCALE of MILES

0   10   20   30

Oregon Coast

Day Three
Pacific City to Waldport

Mile	Directions	
0	From the Pelican Brewery, head south	•
.9	To 'Three Capes Scenic Route'	
1.1	To 'Three Capes Scenic Route'	
3.8	Hwy 101, to 'Neskowin'	•
10.5	Neskowin	
19	E Devils Lake Rd	
22.4	E Devils Lake State Park	
23.4	Cross Hwy 101 (or left onto 101) 23.6	•
23.7	At stop sign	
24.4	11th St, becomes SW coast Ave	
25.3	SW 24th dr, becomes SW Anchor Ave	
34.4	Hwy 101	
35.2	Boiler Bay – Good picnic spot	•
37.9	Depoe Bay	
39.8	To 'Otter Crest Loop'	
42	To 'Otter Crest Loop'	
42.6	Hwy 101	
47	Beverly Beach State Park	
48.1	NW Oceanview Dr, becomes NW Spring St	
49.1	NW 8th St / NW Coast St, Newport	
50	W Olive St	
50.4	Unsigned road, to 'Oregon Coast Cycling Route'	
52.5	At stop sign / to 'Waldport'	•
59.6	Use bridge's narrow pedestrian lane	•
65	South Beach State Park	•
	Seal Rock	•
	Waldport Visitor Center	•

Day Four
Waldport to Winchester Bay

Mile	Directions	
3.4	Beachside State Park	•
4.6	Tillicum Beach Park	•
7.5	Yachats	•
22.6	Tunnel, activate light that warns for bicyclists	•
22.8	End Tunnel	
23.5	Sea Lion Caves	
24.6	Wicked view	
29.2	Twin Lakes Store	•
32.3	Florence	•
35.2	Bridge with narrow pedestrian sidewalk (with obstacles)	
37.8	Honeyman Campground	•
38.9	Dunes City	
48.1	Tahkenitch Campground	•
53.7	Gardiner	
55.4	Bridge	•
56.2	Reedsport	•
60.3	Winchester Bay	•

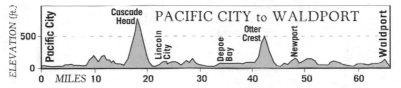

PACIFIC CITY to WALDPORT

ELEVATION (ft.) — Pacific City — Cascade Head — Lincoln City — Depoe Bay — Otter Crest — Newport — Waldport

500

0

0 MILES 10 · 20 · 30 · 40 · 50 · 60

DAY THREE
Pacific City to Waldport
65 miles
Elevation Climbed 4,500 ft.

The four-mile Otter Crest Loop Rd is a highlight of the whole coast bike route. With one way, south flowing car traffic, the other half of the road is dedicated to bikes and foot traffic. The narrow road clings to sheer cliffs, with forest to one side and waves crashing far below on the other.

On the negative side, almost a third of the day is spent riding on Hwy 101, and it sucks. I try to guide the route off Hwy 101 as much as possible. Speedy, thick traffic and strip malls are a couple of the things you will endure; we had carloads of teenagers and yahoos haranguing us as we rode along.

The small town of Waldport is located

on a classic stretch of beautiful Oregon coast near Alsea Bay, which is known for crabbing. There are several lodging options in this wonky little coastal town. If you are camping, grab grub in Waldport then head to Beachside State Park, 3.4 miles south of town, for a fine ocean-side campground.

RIDING TIPS AND HEADS UP
• Newport (mile 48.1) has an awesome bike shop, **Bike Newport** (www.bikenewport. net, 541-265-9917, 150 NW 6th, Mon-Sat 10am-6pm) that caters to and supports cycle tourists passing through. They even have showers and a place upstairs for you to wait out the rain.

Waldport
Pop. 2,040
Elevation 11 ft.

LODGING
America Inn & Suites
(www.americainnandsuiteswaldport.com, 541-563-3249, 190 SW Coast Hwy, $69-93, winter discounts) This is a simple, budget-friendly option right in town.
Cliff House B&B (www.cliffhouseoregon. com, 541-563-2506, 1450 Adahi Rd, $125-225) Probably the nicest lodging in town. The rooms have views, and the house has a large deck and hot tub.

WALDPORT to WINCHESTER BAY

ELEVATION (ft.) — Waldport — Heceta Head — Florence — Reedsport — Winchester Bay

500

0

MILES 0 10 20 30 40 50 60

Oregon Coast

CAMPING

Alsea River RV Park and Marina (www.alseariverrvpark.com, 877-770-6137, 3911 Alsea Hwy, tent site $17) Five sites. A quaint little RV park with tent sites by the river. Showers and laundry.

Beachside State Park
(www.oregonstateparks.org, 541-563-3220, reservations 800-452-5687, 5960 SW Pacific Coast Hwy, yurt $40 tent site $17-21, hiker/biker per person $6) 42 sites. If you're camping, blow through Waldport to grab some groceries. This campground is pretty styled out: right by the beach, not too big, with campsites under the trees. Shower facilites.

CHOW DOWN

Grand Central Pizza (www.grand-central-pizza.com, 541-563-3232, 245 SW Hwy 101, 11am-9pm, shortened winter hours) This pizza joint has stellar Pacific Northwest brews on tap.

Rays Food Place (www.gorays.com, 541-563-3542, 580 NE Broadway St, 7am-10pm) Conventional grocery store.

DAY FOUR
Waldport to Winchester Bay
60.3 miles
Elevation Climbed 5,000 ft.

Now you're officially into the southern half of the coast, where Hwy 101 quiets down a bit. Don't expect serenity, but the traffic situation improves, especially after Florence (mile 32.3).

Even though you are on Hwy 101 all day, some of the scenery makes you feel like you're in a Peter Jackson film. As you climb and descend, you duck in and out of thick forest canopies while ocean views rock your world. The ocean flanks your right side as waves crash and suck on the clambering rocks of the tidal zone. To your left, the thick-trunked evergreens of the Coast Range crowd together. Sometimes you cruise through scrubby coastal environments where stunted trees look like they're bracing themselves for a tidal wave.

In the little town of Winchester Bay, you can pick up fresh baked treats at the Windy Bay Bakery then head up to the sweet Marie Lake campground in Umpqua Lighthouse State Park. There are a handful of lodging options and places to grab a bite in town.

RIDING TIPS AND HEADS UP
• You can avoid a couple of miles of Hwy 101 near Florence if you take Oak St and Kingswood St, which parallel the highway. At mile 22.2, there is a tunnel. Put on your blinkies and activate the light that warns motorists you are in the tunnel.

Winchester Bay
Pop. 500
Elevation 17 ft.

USEFUL WEBSITES
Winchester Bay Merchants Association
www.winchesterbay.org

LODGING
There isn't a ton of variety in town.
Winchester Bay Inn
(www.winbayinn.com, 541-271-4871, 390 Broadway Ave, $56-120) Some rooms have harbor views.
Salmon Harbor Landing Motel
(www.salmonharborlanding.com, 541-271-3742, 265 8th St, $55-70, low season discounts) Another budget option.

CAMPING
Windy Cove Campground
(www.co.douglas.or.us, 541-271-5634, Salmon Harbor Marina, tent site $15) 29 sites, eight reservable with $10 reservation fee. Showers. Right by Oak Rock County

Park and Winchester Bay. A quarter of a mile from the Windy Bay Bakery and other services.
Umpqua Lighthouse State Park
(www.oregonstateparks.org, 541-759-3604, reservations 800-452-5687, 460 Lighthouse Rd, yurt $56-76, sleeping cabin $39, tent site $15-19, hiker/biker tent site per person $5) 24 sites. The campground surrounds pretty Lake Marie, which has a short hiking trail. I dig this woodsy campground, with its hiker/biker component. Showers. 2.2 miles out of town.

CHOW DOWN
There's also a pizzeria and steak and seafood place in town. A couple of small grocery markets, like the Winchester Bay Market and the Pelican Plaza Market, are right off of Hwy 101.
Windy Bay Bakery
(www.windybaybakery.com, 541-234-4989, 75318 Hwy 101, Mon-Sat 9am-6pm, Sun 10am-5pm) Sourdough cinnamon rolls on the weekends and a couple of gluten-free options, not to mention Pacific Northwest wines and sandwiches for savory cravings.
Unger's Bay Fish-n-Chips
(www.ungersbayfishnchips.com, 541-271-4955, Ork Rock Rd (off Salmon Harbor Dr), Sun-Thurs 11am-8pm, Fri-Sat 11am-9pm, shortened winter hours) Sweet location right on a dock. If you're into fish (or scallops or oysters) and chips, I vote this place.

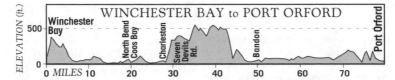

DAY FIVE
Winchester Bay to Port Orford
58.7 miles
Elevation Climbed 5,800 ft.

As the population becomes sparser heading farther south, the forests seem to thicken. With the busier parts of Hwy 101 behind you, the sparkling inlets, iconic bridges and ridiculous ocean views can be enjoyed all the more.

One of the most spectacular portions of this tour is the detour from North Bend to Bandon, which goes through dense coastal forests with secluded ocean vistas. You'll experience some climbing, no doubt, but you leave the 101 hullabaloo far behind. At mile 30.5, you can take a 5.5-mile side trip to the spectacular Cape Arago. Sunset Bay State Park is on route. At mile 34.7, you pass South Slough National Estuarine Sanctuary Visitor Center, which has hiking trails and info about estuaries and coastal watersheds.

The route passes by Bandon's cute tourist area on 1st St. We loved our oyster-slurping stop at **Tony's Crab Shack** (mile 46.4, www.tonyscrabshack.com, 541-347-2875, 155 1st St, sun-up to sun-down), a tiny lean-to right on the water that also sells freshly caught seafood.

Two wacky things you'll see today:

Game Park Safari (home to exotic animals) and a creepily realistic Jesus on a cross on Beach Loop Dr.

Your day ends in Port Orford, part fishing village and part haven for artists, where you can stay at high-end WildSpring Guest Habitat and check out art galleries.

RIDING TIP
• Just north of North Bend, take East Bay Dr around Coos Bay for a longer and more scenic route.

Port Orford
Pop. 1,200
Elevation 66 ft.

USEFUL WEBSITES
City of Port Orford
www.enjoyportorford.com

LODGING
Port Orford has its fair share of B&Bs and vacation rentals.
WildSpring Guest Habitat (www.wildspring.com, 866-333-9453, 92978 Cemetery Loop, $238-308, low season discount) Spa-lovin' enviro-buffs will do a little dance for this place. The sumptuously decorated cabins are nestled into the forest. There's a gorgeous hot tub overlooking the ocean, and massage therapists are available. Buffet breakfast included.

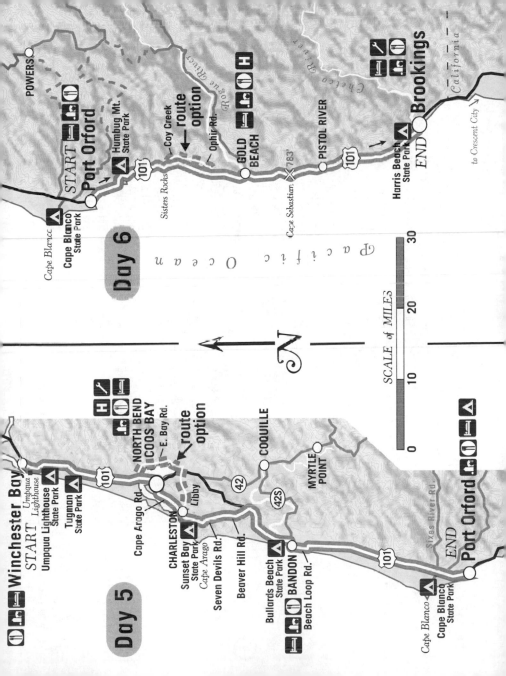

Day 6

POWERS

START
Port Orford

Cape Blanco
Cape Blanco
State Park

Humbug Mt.
State Park

101

Sisters Rocks

Coy Creek
**route
option**

Ophir Rd.

Rogue River

**GOLD
BEACH**

783'
Cape Sebastian

PISTOL RIVER

101

Chetco River

Brookings

Harris Beach
State Park
END

California

to Crescent City

P a c i f i c   O c e a n

SCALE of MILES

0   10   20   30

N

Day 5

Winchester Bay
START
Umpqua Lighthouse
Umpqua Lighthouse
State Park

Tugman
State Park

101

Cape Arago Rd.

**NORTH BEND
COOS BAY**
E. Bay Rd.
**route
option**

Libby

CHARLESTON
Sunset Bay
State Park
Cape Arago

Seven Devils Rd.

Beaver Hill Rd.

42

COQUILLE

42S

MYRTLE
POINT

Bullards Beach
State Park
BANDON
Beach Loop Rd.

101

Cape Blanco
Cape Blanco
State Park

Sixes River Rd.

END
Port Orford

Oregon Coast

Day Five
Winchester Bay to Port Orford

Mile	Cue
0	From the Sourdough Bakery, take 8th St towards water
.1	Beach Blvd
.2	Stop sign, unsigned Salmon Harbor Dr
1.3	Lighthouse Rd
2.2	Umpqua Lighthouse State Park
2.6	Stop sign, unsigned Lighthouse Road
3	Unsigned Hwy 101
7.3	Hugman State Park
19.6	Bridge, activate lights
21.5	Virginia Ave, to 'State Parks' • North Bend
22.3	Broadway Ave
22.9	17th St, turns into Lakeshore Dr
24.8	Taylor Ave, becomes N Marple
25.4	Newmark Ave / S Empire Blvd, to 'Oregon Coast Bike Route'
	or
30.5	To 'Seven Devils Rd'
34.7	To Cape Arago State Park (beautiful) South Slough National Estuarine Sanctuary visitor center
36.9	Becomes W Beaver Hill Rd
41.3	Whiskey Run Lane, to 'Seven Devil Rd'
43.8	Seven Devils Rd
35.7	Seven Devils Rd, at stop sign
41.6	Hwy 101
42	Weiss Estates Lane
42.5	Fahy Rd
43.1	At stop sign/ onto East Fahy Rd crossing Hwy 101
43.5	North Bank Rd
44	Hwy 101, to 'Bandon'
44.2	Bridge with sketchy metal portion
44.8	Riverside Dr
46.4	1st St, cute eateries in Bandon, becomes Edison Ave
47	4th St SW becomes Ocean Dr, becomes 7th Ave SW, becomes Beach Loop Dr
52	Hwy 101
62.2	Langolis
71.1	Turn off to Cape Blanco State Park
74.9	Port Orford, Paradise Café

Day Six
Port Orford to Brookings

Mile	Cue
0	Paradise Café
6.5	Humbug Mountain State Park
16.6	Turnoff to Ophir and quieter back road with less ocean view.
23.8	Old Coast Rd
27.7	To 'Gold Beach' over bridge
29	Harbor Way
29.3	Moore St
29.4	Airport Way
29.8	S jetty Dr
30.7	Hwy 101
46	Boardman State Park
57.8	Harris Beach State Park
59.8	Brookings

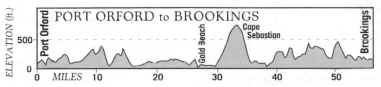

Shoreline Motel (541-332-2903, 206 6th St) or the **Battle Rock Hotel** (541-332-7331, 136 W 6th St) are budget choices right in town. The Battle Rock has ocean views.

CAMPING
Port Orford RV Village (www.portorfordrv.com, 541-332-1041, 2855 Port Orford Loop Rd, $10-15) There's a tent area for bike tourists under large fir trees.

Cape Blanco State Park
(www.oregonstatepark.com, 541-332-6774, reservations 800-452-5687, 39745 S Hwy 101, cabin $39, tent site $13-17, hiker/biker per person $5) Eight tent sites besides the hiker/biker area. Three miles north of Port Orford. This wooded campground is near the ocean and has eight miles of hiking trails. Humbug Mt. State Park, six miles south of Port Orford, is also awesome.

CHOW DOWN
Both Redfish and Paula's Bistro are higher-end options.

Crazy Norwegians
(541-332-8601, 269 6th St, Wed-Sun 11:30am-7:30pm) Famous fish and chips.

Paradise Cafe
(541-221-8104, 518 19th St, 6am-2pm) Classic greasy spoon breakfasts.

Seaweed Natural Grocery & Cafe (541-332-3640, 832 Oregon St, Mon-Sat 11am-5pm) Tiny natural grocery that offers healthy tidbits from its cafe.

Rays Food (www.gorays.com, 541-332-1185, 1555 Oregon St, 7am-10pm) Conventional grocery store.

YOGA
Vital Current Yoga (vitalcurrentyoga@yahoo.com, 541-366-1011, drop-in $10) Heather Lambright teaches on weekdays. I haven't been to a class, but she seems awesome and I would go in a second.

DAY SIX
Port Orford to Brookings
58.7 miles
Elevation Climbed 4,900 ft.

The Oregon coast doesn't skimp on the scenery for your final jaunt. You pass plunging cliffs, gardens of gigantic beach rocks that seem impervious to the frothy barrage of waves, a deep-cover slot canyon and ocean vistas where the sea expands unfathomably.

Though the shoulder is narrow in places, the ocean-side cycling is what you've come here for. After you land in the small fishing burg of Brookings, the border of Cali is just about six miles down the road. You've arrived.

Oregon Coast

Brookings

Pop. 6,000
Elevation 203 ft.

USEFUL WEBSITES
Brookings Chamber of Commerce
www.brookingsharborchamber.com

LODGING
There are a handful of B&Bs in Brookings and budget-friendly, low-end motels on Hwy 101. You might want to check out VRBO. com for rentals.
Ocean Suites
(www.oceansuitesmotel.com, 541-469-4004, 16045 Lower Harbor Rd, $89-119) Off the main drag and right on the water, this is an economical alternative to the Best Western. Equipped with kitchenettes.

CAMPING
Beachfront RV Park
(541-469-5867, 16035 Boat Basin, $11-16) Right (and I mean right) on the ocean, this RV park has some tent camping and shower facilities; but don't expect shade. Less than a mile from restaurants on Lower Harbor Rd.
Harris Beach State Park
(www.oregonstateparks.org, 541-469-2021, reservations 800-452-5687, 1655 Hwy 101, yurt $39, tent site $16-20, hiker/biker tent site per person $5) 63 sites. With easy access to wide beaches dotted with eroded sea stacks, this park is pretty sweet and about two miles north of Brookings. Sites are under a canopy of trees.

CHOW DOWN
These restaurants are near the Beachfront RV Park and Ocean Suites.
Zola's Pizzeria
(541-412-7100, 16362 Lower Harbor Rd,

Mon-Sat 11am-9pm, Sun till 8pm) New York-style pizza from a wood-fired oven. Tasty Oregon microbrews.
The Hungry Clam
(541-469-2526, 16350 Lower Harbor Rd, 11am-8 or 9pm) This little eatery by the water serves acclaimed chowder and fish and chips.
Grocery Outlet
(www.groceryoutlet.com, 541-412-7264, 16261 Hwy 101, Mon-Sat 8am-9pm, Sun 9am-8pm) Conventional grocery store.

BIKE SHOPS
Escape Hatch Sports and Cycle Shop
(541-469-2914, 642 Railroad Ave, hr) These guys will box your bike for shipping or taking on the bus.

YOGA
Visana Yoga
(www.visanayoga.com, 541-254-0485, 603 Hemlock Suite 3C, drop-in $10) A variety of classes Monday through Saturday.

CASCADE CLASSIC

The Sweet Sauce of Central Oregon

Five days and four nights
Begin and end at Harbick's Country Store in Rainbow
Total miles 248

THE SKINNY

PRICE POINT: You can do this with a **small to bulging purse**. There are places to camp each day and good options for restocking groceries. However, any type of splashy splurge can be found in Bend and Sisters. There are also moderately priced lodging options each day.

DIFFICULTY RATING: 7.2 The climbing on Day 1, 2, 3 and 5 is substantial (thousands of feet each day and four mondo passes), though the mileages aren't tremendous.

JAW-DROP FACTOR: 8.9 Iconic Cascadian passes, lakes, snow-capped volcanoes and two Scenic Bikeways (see page 7). Shazam.

STAND OUT CAMPING: There's spectacular camping on Cascade Lakes Hwy (Day 2, page 85).

STAND OUT LODGING: Five Pine Lodge in Sisters has a brewery *and* spa on its campus. The cabins are the bomb (Day 4, page 95).

AVERAGE TEMP IN JULY: Low 50, high 82 degrees

AVERAGE TEMP IN FEBRUARY: Low 30, high 50 degrees

*colder at high elevations, warmer in deserty areas

Fist Bump!

- The **Aufderheide Scenic Bikeway** (Day 1, page 82)
- Drinking **English ale** in Oakridge (Day 1, page 82)
- The **Cascade Lakes Hwy** (Day 2, page 82)
- Picnicking at **Devils Lake** (Day 3, page 86)
- Descending on **Century Dr** into Bend (Day 3, page 86)
- Happy hour at **900 Wall** in Bend (Day 3, page 91)
- **Mountain biking** in Oakridge, Bend and Sisters (See "Trade your Slicks in for Knobbies," page 76)
- Lunch at **Poppies** in Sisters (Day 4, page 95)
- **Dee Wright Observatory** on top of McKenzie Pass (Day 5, page 96)

With lungs like an operatic soprano, this tour screams quintessential Oregon.

The route covers a lion's share of Oregon gems: McKenzie Pass, two Scenic Bikeways (see page 7) (one with a six-volcano vista); the mountain-chic towns of Sisters and Bend, where you can eat well, drink deeply and schmooze with Patagonia-clad locals; the sparkling lake-lavished Cascade Lakes Hwy that begs for picnicking; the English ale-swilling hamlet of Oakridge, touted as the mountain biking

Cascades

Cascades

capital of the Northwest; and the famous 60-mile Robert Aufderheide Memorial Drive, a remote wilderness road and scenic byway that laces through the viscera of the Willamette National Forest.

Unlike some of the other routes in this book, which only explore remote locations dotted with tiny towns, this tour dips in and out of far-flung locations and comes up for breath in the more urbane Bend and Sisters, where you can drink craft brew, check out the local art scenes, go to a yoga class, visit the Farmers Market or sip a soy chai. The combo makes this a perfect route for honeymooners, people on splurge-iversaries or your city slicker cyclist friend who can't be away from an espresso machine for longer than 48 hours.

Noting another layer of awesome, this route penetrates deep into the heart of famous mountain bike country, which comes with three premium mountain bike towns (Oakridge, Bend and Sisters). If you have the time, will and resources, you could make this an equal parts cycling tour and mountain bike trip. Complete bike gluttony!

The splendors of this ride do not come for free. You will sweat for the superior views, secluded pedaling and ecstatic descents as you bag numerous mountain passes. That, of course, makes leaning back in an Adirondack at the end of the day, with a frosty beverage in hand, all the more euphoric.

HISTORY TIDBITS

Starting in the 1850s, pioneers traveled over the Cascades between Boise and Eugene, but only people who could walk or ride horseback made the trip. The trail was too rough for covered wagons. A private company was formed to hack a road through the forest and over the mountains; they completed McKenzie Pass in 1874, but it remained unpaved for decades afterwards. In 1964, a faster alternative highway, South Santiam Hwy, was completed and lured the majority of traffic from the McKenzie Hwy. In 2011, the McKenzie Hwy was designated as a Scenic Bikeway, and it's listed on the National Register of Historic Places.

The major city in this area, Bend, was originally called "Farewell Bend" due to its location at a prominent double-bend in the Deschutes River, one of the few places a loaded wagon could cross. Before crossing the Deschutes, the pioneer trail had followed the river's bank for many long miles. After the crossing, the trail veered away. Thus the "farewell" to the river.

Although many of the pioneers and first settlers in this area were ranchers, lumber put the Central Cascades on the map. Between 1920 and 1950 lumber was king in Bend, and the mills ran day and night. In Bend, a population of 500 in 1910 boomed to almost 9,000 by 1930. Alas, the aggressive clear cutting on private land, without replanting, and denial of access to federally managed forests meant that the lumber industry was done by 1950. Although a small amount of lumber was produced in Bend until 1993, the economy began to shift toward outdoor recreation in the 1960s.

ENVIRONMENT

The dramatic landscape you see over the course of this tour was the result of the bulldozing power of ancient glaciers, carving rivers and the volatility of enormous volcanoes. These forces of nature left jagged mountains covered in trees and snow that are surrounded by lakes and the remnants of lava flows. The area is a patchwork of coniferous woods, shrubs and grassland. Ponderosa pines, cedar, hemlock, spruce and fir all make their home here as well as juniper and sage in the more arid zones.

Big mammals that dwell in the area include black bears, elk, mountain lions, coyote and deer. There is also a rich diversity of small animals, such as weasels, raccoons, rabbits and otters. Bird enthusiasts love it here because of the diversity of species: hawks, eagles, wood peckers, larks, jays, thrushes, etc.

RIDING SEASON

This route has to be done mid-July through September, unless you have a snow-impervious Pugsley bike. Both the McKenzie Pass and the parts of the Cascade Lakes Hwy leading up to the Mt. Bachelor Pass are closed due to snow until mid-summer. As far as summer crowds go, a post-Labor Day, mid-week trip would be less trafficked and allow for easier claims on last minute campsites or hotel rooms. However, we went in mid-August, and the riding was lovely and traffic minimal. Summer holidays will be more hectic in this popular Cascadian area.

WEATHER

The typical Cascade summer will have warm or hot days and cool nights, but, as you are cycling through the mountains, riders should be prepared for anything that Mother Nature could hand out—especially during the fall shoulder season. As you near the summit of a mountain pass, the temperature will drop.

ARRIVING / LEAVING

The tour begins at Harbick's Country Store, which is technically a part of the town of Blue River but actually resides in a little blip of a place called Rainbow. If you don't arrive via your own car, get yourself to Eugene where you can choose to cycle, take public transit or hire a shuttle to the beginning of Aufderheide Scenic Dr.

Bend would be a logical place to begin this ride because it's very accessible by car or bus. I begin the tour at the beginning of the Aufderheide, which is near Eugene, because Bend seems like a lovely place for a mid-tour rest day, where you might get a hotel room and lollygag about.

TO / FROM EUGENE

Airplane

In addition to Eugene, there is also an airport in Bend (www.bend.or.us, 541-389-0258).

Eugene Airport (EUG, www.flyeug.com, 541-682-5544, 28801 Douglas Dr) As the second largest airport in the state, it provides nonstop service to Portland, Seattle, San Francisco, Oakland, Los Angeles, Denver, Salt Lake City, Las Vegas and Phoenix-

Mesa. Allegiant Air, Delta Connection, Horizon Air and United Express all serve this airport.

Car

You could rent a car and drop it off in Eugene. **Hertz** (www.hertz.com, 800-654-3131, 655 West 7th Ave, Eugene, mini-van per day from Portland $124) and **Avis** (www.avis.com, 1-800-331-1212, 3030 Gateway St, Eugene, mini-van per day from Portland $80) are a couple of centrally located companies that have one-way rentals. A **U-Haul** (www.uhaul.com, 800-468-4285, from Portland $124-135) is also an option.

Bus

You can take **Greyhound buses** (www.greyhound.com, 800-231-2222) from far and wide and end up in Eugene (see Bus, page 14). From Portland, it takes 2.5 hours and costs $25. You have to box your bike, and there's a fee.

Train

Amtrak's gorgeous **Coast Starlight** line (www.amtrak.com, 800-872-7245, from Portland $25) connects Seattle to Los Angeles (see Train, page 14). The trip from Portland to Eugene is about two hours and 40 minutes.

Bike

If you're looking to get to Eugene from Portland by bike, check out the Willamette Valley Scenic Bikeway (see page 7). Free maps and cue sheets are downloadable online.

TO / FROM RAINBOW

Car

From Eugene, head east on Hwy 126 for about 50 miles. You can park in the very back at Harbick's Country Store. That's what we did after we bought some drinks and asked nicely. They were really sweet about it.

Bus

From Eugene, you can take **Lane Transit District 91 bus** (www.ltd.org, 541-687-5555, $1.50-3) to McKenzie Bridge, which is about five miles from the beginning of the Aufderheide. Buses have two bike racks on the front. Since it's a rural route, they might allow a couple other bikes inside in the handicap area. If someone comes aboard who needs that space, though, you hit the road.

Shuttle

McKenzie River Mountain Resort (www. rivermountainresort.com, 541-822-6272) in Blue River offers shuttle services for bicyclists. You can talk with them about arranging a shuttle to the beginning of the tour from Eugene. The cost depends on a number of factors but should be around $25 per person.

Bike

I thought about beginning this tour in Eugene but didn't because, though scenic in some parts, Hwy 126 is not a nice place to ride due to traffic, sprawl and narrow shoulders in places. The ride is doable, but is a good 40-50 miles (you can avoid the highway some) of ickiness.

Cascades

USEFUL WEBSITES
Lane County's Visitor's Association
www.travellanecounty.com
Deschutes County Bicycle & Pedestrian Advisory Committee
www.bikecentraloregon.org
Outdoor Guide to Central Oregon
www.explorecentraloregon.com
Central Cascades Geotourism Project
www.thecentralcascades.com; info on sustainable tourism

LODGING
Options abound in Oakridge, Bend and Sisters. In between these locations, choices are sparse. Bend and Sisters both cater to an upscale tourist market, so you can find posh accommodations, but bargain lodging is harder to come by (especially in Sisters), though moderate options are available. Between Memorial Day and Labor Day, it's particularly busy and reservations are recommended, especially on weekends and holidays.

CAMPING
You can camp every night on tour. There is a nice campground right in Sisters. In Bend, it's a little more inconvenient, as the nearest nice campground is 6.5 miles from town. The Cascade Lakes Hwy has premium—meaning naturally splendiferous—campgrounds.

FOOD AND DRINK
The foodie craze has infiltrated the tourist towns of Bend and, on a smaller scale, Sisters. Many of the restaurants and cafes that flourish here step into pace with the Pacific Northwest cuisine that features fresh, local, sustainable and organic food. There are a surprising amount of gluten-free and vegetarian/vegan options in restaurants. Outside of Bend and Sisters, you will find more of the standard all-American menu with burgers, pasta, etc. The area worships the almighty brew, with 11 breweries in Bend and surrounding towns alone.

HYDRATION
In some places, like the Cascade Lakes Hwy or parts of Hwy 58, there is a ton of water on route if you bring a purification method. If not, I suggest being cognizant about carrying enough water plus a bit extra. Potable water stops can be few and far between.

MAPS
The McKenzie River Ranger District and the Middle Fork Ranger District North **motor vehicle use maps** (www.fs.usda.gov, 541-225-6300) cover the first day on the Aufderheide. The maps are free and downloadable under the "maps and publications" tab. The **Deschutes National Forest map** (www.store.usgs.gov, 888-275-8747, $12) covers most of Day 2, all of Days 3 and 4 and most of Day 5. The **Benchmark Oregon Atlas** (www.benchmarkmaps.com, 541-772-6965, $22.95) also shows the route.

GENERAL RIDING TIPS AND HEADS UP
• Be prepared to climb. Be prepared for Cascadian mountain weather.

• Check with the Willamette National Forest Service (McKenzie River Ranger District, 541-822-3381) and the Deschutes National Forest Service (541-383-5300) before your tour to find out about the status of forest fires, construction or possible road closures
• Make sure to have blinkies and reflective garb for the short tunnel on Hwy 58 on Day 2.

CELL COVERAGE
You can get cell service every day at some point, but it's definitely in and out. Bend, Sisters, Oakridge and Harbick's Country Store have solid service.

HOSPITALS
There are small clinics in Blue River, Oakridge and Sisters.
St. Charles Medical Center
(www.scmc.org, 541-382-4321. 2500 NE Neff Rd, Bend) 24/7 emergency care.

EXTRACURRICULAR ACTIVITIES
This tour has tons of fishing opportunities in lakes and streams on route, especially on the Cascade Lakes Hwy (Day 2 and 3 pages 82 & 86). If you have the energy, hiking trails are also plentiful near many of the campgrounds and stops on route. Let's not forget mountain biking; check out the Trade in Your Slicks box (page 76).

Don't Forget your Fishing Rod
By Joel Grover, lover of bike touring and owner of Splendid Cycles (www.splendidcycles.com), a specialty cargo bike shop in Portland

Blame it on my childhood. I grew up on a fish hatchery in Washington's Cascades in the 1970s. In my rural wonderland, as a 12-year-old, fishing for trout and steelhead became an obsession. I spent many hours standing in streams, learning the craft, intently focused on the prize.

It just so happens that my Sears three-speed bicycle was a co-conspirator on many of those fishing trips. I did not think twice about heading out with my fishing rod to explore the Wind River by bike. All too often I found the most joy in my solitude while riding my bike or standing in a river. And it sure was an adrenaline rush when 10-pound "steelies" took me on a one-way ride to the nearest log jam.

Fast forward three decades to a time when I'd pushed riding my bike and fishing to the back burner because of my busy schedule.

That's when I fell in love with bike touring. I became dependent on the annual week or two of getting away on my bike to press the reset button and transform my mind and body by threading my way to a destination.

On quite a few of my bike tours, I've brought a lightweight four-piece fly rod and small fanny pack with just enough

Cascades

tackle to allow for late afternoons of fishing on a beautiful river and focusing my mind.

Bike touring is eminently complimentary with my long lost love of fishing. I cannot think of any bike touring route here in the Northwest where world-class fishing could not be part of the program.

While some may scoff at the additional weight or bulk of the tackle, to me, the extra couple of pounds is well worth it. Standing in a 60-degree river on a hot day during late summer is a wonderful way to spend an afternoon. Moreover, the icy water goes a long way in helping your aching muscles and joints recover from cycling.

So what more could you ask for? A healthy meal? If and when you catch that juicy trout, you've earned a delicious dinner! Not that you're hungry, right?

Joel Grover with his trailer

Trade in Your Slicks for Knobbies

This tour offers the possibility for true cycling gluttony. Oakridge, Bend and Sisters all have full-service mountain bike shops with rentals, plus Bend and Oakridge have shuttle and guiding services. Adding singletrack adventures in these pristine Cascadian mountains will make for a dynamic, unbeatable and deliciously exhausting tour. And you'll end up with a keen understanding of the heart and soul of the landscape, earned through the dirt in your teeth and your sweat-soaked do-rag. (Extra points if you actually wear a do-rag.)

I haven't ever done a hybrid mountain bike tour, but it makes me drool to think about doing it. Please let me know how your adventure unfolds if you do make this combination a reality.

Oakridge is known as the Northwest's mountain biking capital because of its lavish options for riding technical and exquisitely beautiful singletrack. Every year Oakridge hosts major fat tire events like Mountain Bike Oregon, the Cascade Cream Puff and Fat 55 Oakridge. Little Oakridge even has created its own bike skills park in town. **Willamette Mountain Mercantile** (www.oakridgebikeshop.com, 541-782-1800, 48080 Hwy 58) is a full service shop that rents mountain bikes (per day $55-75), and **Oregon Adventures** (www.oregon-adventures.com, 541-968-5397) is a mountain bike guide outfitter in town that can tailor a sweet ride for you.

Bend, also a famous mountain biking mecca, is more known for swoopy, buff trails that are fast and fun. **Cog Wild Tours** (www.cogwild.com, 541-385-7002, 255 SW Century Dr, half day $60, full day $90) is a bicycle tour company out of Bend that guides single and multi-day tours and also provides shuttle services and rentals (per day $25-75).

In Sisters, you can rent mountain bikes at **Eurosports** (www.eurosports. us, 541-549-2471, 182 E Hood Ave, 9am-5:30pm, rentals $20-40), which is just six blocks away from access to the acclaimed Peterson Ridge Trail.

MORE TOUR!

If you want to connect this route to the **Crater Lake and Beyond** tour (page 100), go south from Oakridge (see Crater Lake Butt-kicking Connector, page 109) for an excessively awesome mountain tour. **The True West** (page 103) tour isn't too terribly far away either—maybe a day of hard riding for 80 to 90 miles—but it does necessitate taking Hwy 126, which is scenic but has significant traffic. From Eugene, it's just a day or two of touring till you hit the coast (see map, page 49).

Overnighting near Harbick's Country Store

There are a number of good options near the start of the Aufderheide.

Harbick's Country Inn (www.harbicks-country inn.com, 541-822-3805, 54791 McKenzie Hwy, $70-110) Simple rooms, nice folks.

Delta Campground (www.reserveameria. com, 541-822-3317, Aufderheide Drive, tent site $16-30) 38 sites. May-Sept you can reserve sites with five days notice. Potable water and vault toilets. Located at the very beginning of the Aufderheide. From the campground entrance, you ride in one-mile ride. The short Delta Old Growth Nature Trail provides a quick hike.

COST OPTIONS

Budget camping tour: Day 1, Oakridge RV Park (page 82); Day 2, Lava Flow Campground (page 85); Day 3, Tumalo State Park (page 90); Day 4, Sister Overnight Park (page 95). There are grocery stores in Oakridge, Bend and Sisters where you can restock.

High falootin' credit card camping: Day 1, Oakridge Hotel (page 82); Day 2, Crescent Creek Cottages (Page 82); Day 3, Oxford Hotel (Page 90); Day 4, Five Pine

Cascades

Lodge (Page 95). You can hit restaurants every day, though on Day 3 there is only one before you reach Bend.

DAY ONE
Harbick's Country Store to Oakridge
63.9 miles
Elevation Climbed 4,360 ft

"Most beautiful road ever."

"Rip-roaring, dippidee fun descent."

"Made me wet my shorts. Of course I did ride it on a 95-degree July 4th day. Highly recommended."

Many cyclists will recall their interlude with the Aufderheide Scenic Drive with nostalgia. Over the years, the road has evolved into an Oregon classic. Tucked into conifer and hardwood forests and flanked with nationally designated Wild and Scenic Rivers, this paved back road meanders about 60 miles through remote areas of the Willamette National Forest. The road, a mostly gradual up-and-over ride, has a prize at the top: Constitution Grove, a cluster of trees more than 200 years old. The short interpretive hike under the trees' canopy is worth the stop.

At the end of the day, the Aufderheide channels you into Oakridge, a town branded as the Northwest's mountain biking capital. You could easily linger for a day, rent a mountain bike (see Trade in Your Slicks for Knobbies, page 76), ride the world-class trails right out of town and drink delicious, locally brewed English ale (see Brewers Union, page 82).

RIDING TIPS AND HEADS UP
• There are absolutely no services for the duration of the Aufderheide. Bring all the water (unless you purify) and food you'll need, plus a touch extra for safety's sake.
• The Aufderheide doesn't have very many signs. Follow the pavement! Ignore the gravel roads that veer away.
• Keep your eyes peeled for the Office Covered Bridge as you head into Oakridge. It's the longest covered bridge in Oregon, at 180 feet, and the only one with a secondary pedestrian lane.

EXTRACURRICULAR ACTIVITIES
The short ¼-mile hike to **Terwilliger Hot Springs** (locally known as Cougar Hot Springs, per person $5) from the Aufderheide (mile 9.7) is an indulgent way to visit six natural soaking pools and a swimming hole. Clothing is optional. This is a well-loved spot, so a mid-week, late or early visit might mean fewer crowds. Make sure you can convince your lax muscles into the 20 odd more miles of climbing ahead of you to the top of the Aufderheide pass.

There are fishing and hiking opportunities along the way...if you have the energy.

See Trade in Your Slicks for Knobbies (page 76) for the lowdown on how to throw a sick mountain bike ride into your tour.

Cascades

Day 1

to Blue River
to Eugene

SCALE of MILES

0   5   10

N

126

Willamette

National

Forest

58

WESTFIR

Fivefoot Point Reservoir

to Eugene

19

21

END
Oakridge

58

Aufderheide Memorial Dr.

Klahanie

Terwilliger
Hot Springs

French
Pete

Red
Diamond

19

Aufderheide Memorial Dr.

Roaring
River

3749'
Constitution
Grove

Frisell
Crossing

Wuldo
Lake

Three Sisters Wilderness

START
Rainbow

McKENZIE
BRIDGE

126

242

to Sisters

Day One
Harbick's to Oakridge

0	•	From Harbick's head south on Mill Creek Rd
.1	☞	McKenzie River Rd
.5	☜	W King Rd, over covered bridge
.6	☞	W King Rd
2.3	☞	At stop sign, unsigned Cougar Dam Rd
2.6	☜	Onto unsigned Aufderheide Dr
9.3	•	Gravel section
9.4	•	End gravel section
9.7	•	Terwilliger Hot Springs
13.2	•	French Pete Campground
17.2	•	Red Diamond Campground
23.8	•	Frissell Crossing Campground
24.3	•	Roaring River Campground
40.6	•	Kiahanie Campground
60.3	☜	At stop sign, to 'Oakridge'
63.8	☜	E 1st St
63.9	•	Brewers Union Local 180

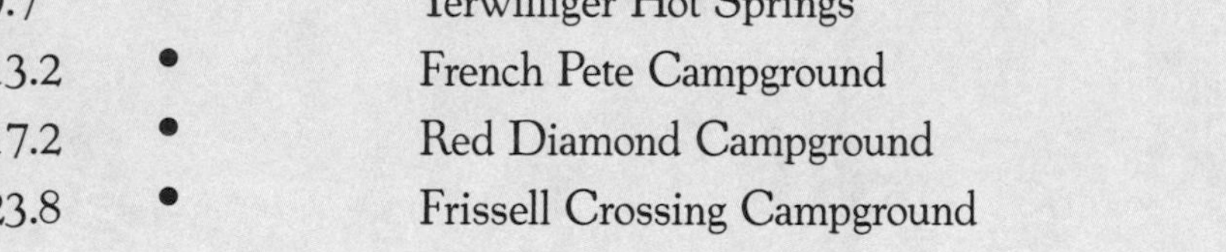

ELEVATION (ft.)

RAINBOW to OAKRIDGE

Rainbow

Oakridge

4000
3000
2000
1000

0   MILES   10   20   30   40   50   60

Cascades

CAMPING AND LODGING ON ROUTE

French Pete Campground
(Mile 13.2, www.publiclands. org, 541-822-3381, tent site $14) 17 sites. Potable water and vault toilets. 3.5 miles from the hot springs.

Red Diamond Campground
(Mile 17.2, www.publiclands.org, 541-822-3381, tent site $14) Three sites. No potable water. Vault toilets. Reserve online at www.recreation.gov. Hiking trails and fishing near grounds.

Frissell Crossing Campground
(Mile 23.8, www.publiclands.org, 541-822-3381, tent site $12) 12 sites. Potable water and vault toilets. First-come, first-serve.

Kiahanie Campground
(Mile 40.6, www.publiclands.org, 541-782-2283, tent site $10) 19 sites. Potable water and vault toilets. In a grove of old-growth forest.

Oakridge
Pop. 3,220
Elevation 1,250 ft.

USEFUL WEBSITES

City of Oakridge
www.ci.oakridge.or.us

Oakridge Chamber of Commerce
www.oakridgechamber.com

EVENTS OF NOTE

Concerts in the Park
Free live music at Greenwaters Park at various times throughout the summer.

Keg and Cask Festival
(www.keg-caskfestival.blogspot.com) Outdoor festival where breweries from 100 miles around share their beers and raise money for charity.

Mountain bike events (See Trade in Your Slicks, page 76)

LODGING
Heads up that motels can book out a year in advance of local mountain bike events (see Trade in Your Slicks for Knobbies, page 76). There are a number of hotels in town. The following are locally owned and close to the brewery (muy importante).

Oakridge Hostel
(www.oakridgehostel.com, 541-782-4000, 48175 E First St, dorm with shared bath $35 or $25 if you arrive by bicycle, room with shared bath $75-105) They give a discount to cycle tourists, have a drying room and hot tub, and serve a healthy breakfast. It's near the brewery. Winner to me.

Oakridge Hotel
(www.theoakridgemotel.com, 541-782-2432, 48197 Highway 58, $45-65) This family-owned, small hotel is a bargain and also offers several larger house rentals nearby.

CAMPING
Oakridge RV Park
(www.oakridgervpark.com, 541-782-2611, 48229 Hwy 58, two people $25) Hot showers, laundry, wifi–it's got all the fancy camping accoutrements.

CHOW DOWN
There are a handful of restaurants in town. Here are the choicest.

Brewers Union Local 180
(www.brewersunion.com, 541-782-2024, 48329 E 1st St, Sun-Wed 12-9pm, Thurs 12-10pm, Fri & Sat 12-11pm) With a strong nod to the English pub, this place crafts its own tasty English-style ale. On the wall you'll find wilderness maps (love), and they have billiards to entice you to kick back after a long day of cycling. Bangers and mash, anyone? How about tempeh and mash?

Trailhead Coffeehouse
(541-782-2223, 47406 Hwy 58, hours are notably unpredictable but more consistent in summer) This place will load you up with a strong breakfast and good coffee. We also got sandwiches to go for lunch. Sweet patio.

Ray's Food Place (www.gorays.com, 541-782-4283, 48067 Hwy 58, 7am-10pm) Conventional grocery store.

BIKE SHOPS
Willamette Mountain Mercantile
(www.oakridgebikeshop.com, 541-782-1800, 48080 Hwy 58) A full-service shop that also does mountain bike rentals (per day $55-75).

DAY TWO
Oakridge to Quinn River Campground (or Crescent Creek Cottages)
63.5 miles
Elevation Climbed 5,700 ft

Today, you climb. For a long time.

For the first half of the day, you climb up Hwy 58. Then you meander into a more remote area in the Deschutes National Forest on the Cascades Lake Hwy. Though Hwy 58 is one of the more trafficked sections of the tour, the road never lets you forget that you are in sumptuous mountain country with lots of evergreen, lake-dappled goodness. Plus, there is a nice shoulder most of the way.

The Cascade Lakes Hwy is one of those roads that you dream about during dreary winter months. Mt. Bachelor towers in the distance, crystal clear mountain lakes are sirens to sweaty cyclists, and the unbothered forest smells fresh and crisp.

I've chosen to highlight three different overnight options. Quinn River Campground is for the campers who like more amenities (like potable water). Lava Flow Campground is for those on a budget who want to still enjoy a sweet, but primitive, campground (free). Both campgrounds are lovely and off the Cascade Lakes Hwy. Finally, the Crescent Creek Cottages are for those who like roofs over their heads (though staying here makes the next day significantly longer because of the location).

Day 2

21

19

START
Oakridge

58

Blue Pool

Willamette

National Forest

SCALE of MILES

0   5   10

N

Diamond Peak Wilderness

△ Diamond Peak

tunnel

Odell Lake Resort

Crescent Creek Cottages

Crescent Lake

CRESCENT LAKE JCT.

Sunset Cove

Princess Creek

5125'

Odell Lake

Waldo Lake Wilderness

Waldo Lake

Pacific Crest Trail

Deschutes National Forest

Davis Lake

Davis Lake

Lava Flow

N. Davis Lake

Rock Creek

Crane Prairie Reservoir

END
Quinn River
campground

Cultus Lake Resort

58
Crescent Cutoff Rd.

to Crescent

46

Cascade Lakes Hwy.

42

to Bend

Day Two

Oakridge to Quinn River

0	•	From Brewers Union head east on E 1st St
One Block	☞	Beech St, becomes Hill St
.7	☜	Unsigned Hwy 58
9.6	•	Blue Pool Campground
20.9	•	Tunnel
27.5	•	Odell Lake Campground and Shelter Cove Resort
28.8	•	Princess Creek Campground
31.7	•	Sunset Cove Campground
32.2	•	Odell Lake Lodge and Resort
34.2	•	Crescent Lake Resort turnoff (3 miles)
34.3	•	Willamette Pass Inn
36.2	•	Crescent Creek Cottages and RV Park

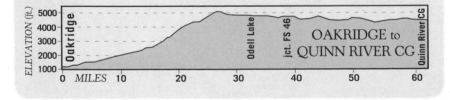

RIDING TIPS

• Be prepared for zero services or potable water until mile 34.4, where there are a couple of restaurants and a small grocery store. While you're at that stop, you'll need to get food for that night and the next riding day if you are planning on staying at a campground on the Cascade Lakes Hwy.

• Start the day mentally prepared for over 30 miles of climbing with little respite from the ascending grade.

EXTRACURRICULAR ACTIVITIES

Lots of the campgrounds off the Cascade Lake Hwy are on lakes or creeks known for fishing. Some places only allow fly-fishing, but many spots also allow lures. For more info, contact the Deschutes National Forest (541-383-5300). These campgrounds tend to have hiking trails nearby as well.

HEADS UP

On Hwy 58, there is a short but narrow tunnel. We got a car to ride slowly behind us while we rode through it. If we didn't have that car follow, I would have walked the debris-laden sidewalk in the tunnel. I'm sure braver souls would have ridden the tunnel with blinkie lights brandished, but that seemed sketchball to me. Either way, blinkie lights and reflective garb are essential.

LODGING AND CAMPING ON ROUTE

In the first 32 miles, you can camp at Odell Lake Campground, Shelter Cove Resort, Princess Creek Campground, Sunset Campground and Odell Lodge and Resort. Both Shelter Cove and Odell Lodge also have lodging.

Willamette Pass Inn (Mile 34.5, www.willamettepassinn.com, 541-433-2211, Hwy 58 Milepost 69, $86-145) All the rooms at this rustic-themed inn have kitchenettes. They also rent "chalets," which are cottages with full kitchens.

E Davis Lake Campground (Mile 47.5, 541-433-3200, Cascade Lakes Hwy, tent site $9-11) 33 sites. The grounds have vault toilets and potable water.

N Davis Creek Campground (Mile 55.4, 541-383-4000, Cascade Lakes Hwy, tent site $14) 17 sites. The grounds have vault toilets and potable water. Situated right on Wickiup Reservoir.

Rock Creek Campground (Mile 61.9, 541-383-5300, Cascade Lakes Hwy, tent site $14) The grounds have vault toilets and potable water. The sites are near the Crane Prairie Reservoir.

END OF DAY CAMPING AND LODGING

Lava Flow Campground (mile 51.3, www.publiclands.org, 541-433-3200, Cascade Lakes Hwy, free) 12 primitive sites. Take a short dirt road to get to the campground. There are vault toilets, but no potable water. Right on Davis Lake. Interesting lava flows decorate the water's edge. There are hiking trails near the campground. You can only fly-fish on Davis Lake, but lures can be used at nearby Odell Creek.

Quinn River Campground (mile 63.5, www.publiclands.org, 541-383-4000, Cascade Lakes Hwy, tent site $14) 41 sites.

Cascades

Right on the Crane Prairie Reservoir, the campground has vault toilets and water pump. Reservations can be made in advance (www.recreation.gov, 877-444-6777). If you brought your fishing rod, rainbow trout, brook trout, mountain whitefish, kokanee salmon, largemouth bass, black crappie and bluegill all roam these waters. There is a hiking trail to Lemish Lake that starts at the campground.

Crescent Creek Cottages and RV Park (mile 36.2, www.crescentcreekcottages.com, 541-433-2324, 19100 Hwy 58, tent site $15, cabin $75-95) These cute cottages come with fully-equipped kitchens. You'll hit a grocery store and restaurant right before this place, at mile 34.4, if you want to grab a bite or stock up on food.

DAY THREE
Quinn River Campground to Bend
47.2 miles
Elevation Climbed 2,560 ft.

With a gurgling brook to one side, the otherwise quiet, forest-lined Cascade Lakes Hwy sticks to a mellow grade, which makes for a sparkly, peaceful jaunt before the beginning the ascent over Mt Bachelor's pass and descent into Bend. On your way to the climb, you'll skirt a number of alpine lakes and a broad, high-country prairie that parades the big-mountain scenery. The area is so iconic and beautiful that I imagine forest sprites and mountain elves use the forest for their annual hula-hoop competition, or however they celebrate the glory of nature.

This day will invite you to get your picnic on and/or go for a revitalizing swim. Right as the highway veers east, you'll hit Devils Lake (mile 19.7) with other-worldishly turquoise waters. Dreamy. Then comes Sparks Lake (mile 20.5), which you might share with a paddle boarder serenely sliding across the emerald-colored surface.

Getting up and over the pass to Bend isn't as brutal as the previous climbing of the first two days. Sometimes the grade gets steep, but the climb isn't too long, and it's magnificent. You achieve great heights and then you cruise down, down, down and down on an epic descent into Bend.

Though some label Bend touristy (lots of people think it's a super fun place to visit), I like this small city. Bend is like a primo outdoors-freak sundae (gluten- and dairy-free, made with unprocessed sugar, of course) decorated with hiking poles, topped with yoga sprinkles and lock-off carabiner crumbles, smothered with a delicious glop of biking crazies and washed down with a

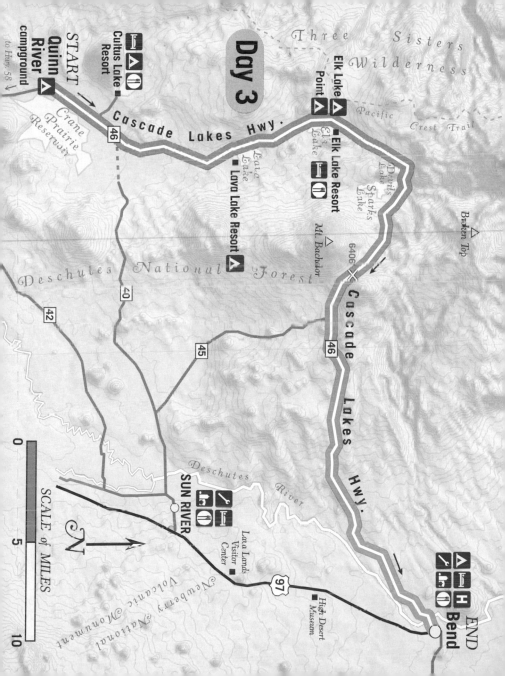

Day 3

Three Sisters Wilderness

Pacific Crest Trail

START
Quinn River
campground
to Hwy. 58

Cultus Lake Resort

Cascade Lakes Hwy.

46

Crane Prairie Reservoir

Elk Lake Point

Elk Lake

Elk Lake Resort

Lava Lake

Lava Lake Resort

Sparks Lake

Devils Lake

6406

Broken Top

Mt. Bachelor

Deschutes National Forest

40

42

45

46

Cascade Lakes Hwy.

Deschutes River

SUN RIVER

Lava Lands Visitor Center

N

SCALE of MILES
0   5   10

Newberry National Volcanic Monument

97

High Desert Museum

END Bend

Day Three
Quinn River to Bend

0	•	From Quinn River Campground head north on Cascade Lakes Hwy
2.1	•	Cultus Lake Resort (two-miles up the road)
9.7	•	Lava Lake Resort and Campground
14.1	•	Point Campground
15	•	Elk Lake Campground
15.1	•	Elk Lake Resort
19.7	•	Devils Lake
20.5	•	Sparks Lake
26.5	•	Top of pass, Mt Bachelor Ski Resort
45.1	🖑	Century Drive through roundabout
45.4	☞	Colorado Ave at roundabout
46.1	🖑	Through roundabout
46.6	🖚	Bond St.
47.2	•	Deschutes Brewery and Public House

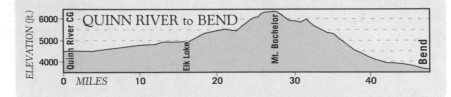

local craft microbrew. Extreme athletes and ultra-healthy people wearing Lululemon and Patagonia flood the streets, which makes the scene homogenous, but very pretty. Even if you're wearing a jersey that smells like the road kill you passed at mile 24, it's well worth indulging in Bend's pleasures for a day or two.

RIDING TIPS

• The Cascade Lakes Hwy is busier on summer weekends, as is Bend. It's not the end of the world, but if you can finagle your tour to hit it mid-week, that would be ideal. We rode this section on a Friday in August and the traffic was extremely low.
• There are a few places to grab food and water on route today. If you want to take a two-mile diversion from the route, you can head to the restaurant and gas station-like store at Cultus Lake Resort (mile 2.1). Lava Lake Resort (mile 9.7), also a small distance from the route, has a very basic store. The only other restaurant on route is the eatery at Elk Lake Resort (mile 15.1).
• The long descent down into Bend has divots that make it bumpy. It's not crazy to take breaks from braking.

EXTRACURRICULAR ACTIVITIES

There's fishing in the various lakes and streams off of the Cascade Lakes Hwy.

Among many lakes you pass, there are pretty hikes around **Sparks Lake** (mile 20.5) and **Devils Lake** (mile 19.7).

Bend has tons of entertaining things going on. Consult its free weekly, The Source (www.tsweekly.com).

Bend is mountain bike heaven (see Trade in Your Slicks, page 76).

Bend

Pop. 76,600
Elevation 3,600 ft.

USEFUL WEBSITES
Bend Chamber of Commerce
www.bendchamber.org; the website has a downloadable city map, among other tourist information.
Bend Visitor Association
www.visitbend.com; a fancy site with tons of tourist information. The lodging listings have coupons.
Bend's bike scene news
www.bikearoundbend.com
Bike Central Oregon
www.bikecentral.org; bike events in Bend and central Oregon.

EVENTS OF NOTE
Road, mountain bike and cross races
(www.visitbend.com) Year round.
Bend Summer Festival
Hosted in July by the Downtown Business Association featuring a festival of food, wine, beer, art and music on the downtown blocks.
Free Summer Concerts
(www.bendconcerts.com) Sunday afternoon outdoor concerts at the amphitheatre.

LODGING
Even though there are other worthy areas to explore in Bend, I chose spots close to Bend's vibrant downtown, where everything is highly walkable.

Cascades

Days Inn (www.daysinn.com, 541-383-3776, 849 NE 3rd St, $89-129) One of the cheaper downtown hotels. They have a hefty continental breakfast included and a hot tub.

Old St. Francis School
(www.mcmenamins.com, 541-382-5174, 700 NW Bond St, $135-185) A quirky McMenamins overnight experience gets even cooler with a decadent saltwater Turkish soaking pool that is available to guests for free (and non-guests for $5). They rent a couple of cottages, too.

Oxford Hotel
(www.oxfordhotelbend.com, 877-440-8436, 10 NW Minnesota Avenue, $239-309) Splurge central! Holy boutique hotel-hot tub-pillow menu-spa-saunagasm! I went here on my bike tour honeymoon and it ROCKED.

CAMPING

There are limited options close to town.

Tumalo State Park
(www.oregonstateparks.org, 800-452-5687, 64120 O B Riley Rd, tent site

$21, hiker/biker rate per person $5) The park is 6.5 miles from downtown Bend and not on route, but it's a super nice camping option, the best really, with a discounted hiker/biker loop open in the summer. Shower facilities.

Skandia RV Park (www.scandiarv.com, 541-382-6206, 61415 Hwy 97 #59, tent site $22) Though the park is only 2.5 miles from downtown, Skandia has just a couple of (expensive) tent spots, which aren't especially nice as they are right by the bathrooms.

CHOW DOWN
Alpenglow Cafe
(www.alpenglowcafe.com, 541-383-7676, 1133 NW Wall St #100, 7am-2pm) An Alpenglow breakfast will put some zoom in your pedal stroke. The breads are baked fresh daily, and dishes include local, sustainable ingredients.

Parilla (541-617-9600, 635 NW 14th St, 11am-10pm) Mountain biker-recommended burritos.

Deschutes Brewery Bend Public House (www.deschutesbrewery.com, 541-382-9242, 1044 NW Bond St, Mon-Thurs 11am-11pm, Fri-Sat till 12am, Sun till 10pm) Widely renowned brew. Black Butte Porter has been one of my favorites for years. Seems like a shame not to stop here. For a less established brewery with excellent suds, go to the nearby tasting room at **Boneyard Brewing** (www.boneyardbeer.com, 541-323-2325, 37 NW Lake Pl #B, Mon-Sat 11am-6pm). You won't find food here, but the tasting room is filled with snowboard stickers and a bad boy attitude, not to mention hop bomb IPAs. Grrr.

900 Wall St (www.900wall.com, 541-323-6295, 900 NW Wall St, 11:30am-10 or 11pm) This place is a bit fancy shmance, but they try to stick with local, sustainable ingredients and have a killer happy hour from 3-6pm. If you get there at the right time, you can snag some righteous outdoor seating.

Devore's Good Food and Wine Store (541-389-6588, 1124 NW Newport Ave, Mon-Sat 8am-6:30pm, Sun 10am-6pm) This is a sweet, locally-owned alternative to the Whole Foods Market (which is well outside of downtown on gnar gnar Hwy 20).

Bend Farmer's Market (www.bendfarmersmarket.com, summer only, top of Drake Park, Wed 3-7pm; St. Charles Medical Center, 2500 NE Neff Rd, Fri 2-6pm) I got a chance to peruse the goodies here. Great place to pick up a snack for the road. Fresh goat cheese. Mmmm.

Safeway (www.safeway.com, 541-312-6480, 642 NE 3rd St, 6am-1am) Conventional grocery store near downtown.

BIKE SHOPS

While there are a ton of bike shops in Bend, the following have been chosen for their cycle tourist-friendly elements:

Sunnyside Sports (www.sunnysidesports.com, 541-382-8010, 930 NW Newport Ave, 9am-7pm)

Pine Mountain Sports (www.pinemountainsports.com, 541-385-

8080, 255 SW Century Dr, Mon-Fri 10am-6pm, Sat-Sun 9am-6pm)

Hutch's Bicycles (www.hutchsbicycles.com, 541-382-9253, 725 NW Columbia St, Mon-Sat 9am-6pm, Sun 9am-5pm)

YOGA
Mandala Yoga Center
(www.mandalayogabend.com, 541-678-5183, 55 NW Minnesota St, drop-in $10) A much-trusted yogi friend suggests classes with Ulla Lundgren, but there is a full schedule of classes from which to choose.

CAMPING AND LODGING ON ROUTE
Lava Lake Resort (Mile 13.3, www.fs.usda.gov , 541-382-9443) 43 camp sites. No reservations. Vault toilets and potable water. Good fishing in Lava Lake. Store nearby with basic supplies.

Elk Lake Campground (Mile 18.6, 541-383-5300, Cascade Lakes Hwy, tent site $14) 26 sites. No reservations. There are vault toilets and potable water.

Elk Lake Resort (Mile 18.7, www.elklakeresort.net, 541-480-7378, Cascade Lakes Hwy, rustic cabin $29-58, cabin $199-329) Their mountain country cabins are hewn from knotty wood, and the "luxury" ones are fully-equipped with kitchens. The rustic cabins are basically a roof over your head—you'll need to bring your sleeping bag, use external bathrooms and eat at the restaurant (or BYO camp food).

Cascades

DAY FOUR
Bend to Sisters
28.6 miles
Elevation Climbed 950 ft.

You've gotten some solid ride days under your belt, so it's about time for a cruiser day. Compared to your other days, this one seems like a toodleloo ride you could pedal while twirling a baton with one hand. The short day just gives you more time to explore Sisters, a community that loves art and specializes in mountain-town cuteness.

The landscape on today's ride diverges from the dense forest and mountain pass motif to which you've become accustomed. You'll head into the more arid, sagebrush speckled ranchland in between Bend and Sisters. The open vistas give you plenty of chances to check out the snow-dolloped peaks in the surrounding mountain ranges.

Besides getting out of Bend, about two miles on Hwy 20 and a quick six miles on Hwy 126, the route has low traffic and scenery good enough for cowboys in a beer commercial.

RIDING TIPS
• Some of the back roads you ride today will have divots that make for a somewhat jolting ride.
• You pass Devore's Good Food and Wine Store (page 91) on the route out of town. It's a good place to get snacks for the road.

Sisters
Pop. 6,200
Elevation 3,100 ft.

USEFUL WEBSITES
Sisters tourist guide
www.sistersoregonguide.com
Sisters Chamber of Commerce
www.sisterscountry.com

EVENTS OF NOTE
Sisters Folk Festival
(www.sistersfolkfestival.org) A late summer, three-day, American roots music celebration.
Sisters Mountain Bike Festival
(www.sistersmountainbikefestival.com) September conclave of mountain bikers partaking in a ridefest. Sometimes on the same weekend as the **Sisters Fresh Hop Festival**.

LODGING
Sister's Motor Lodge
(www.sistersmotorlodge.com, 541-549-2551, 511 W Cascade Ave, $89-299) This place maintains its quirky 1939 character while providing cozy, quilt-loving accommodations. There's a hot tub. They require minimum stays over some holidays.

Cascades

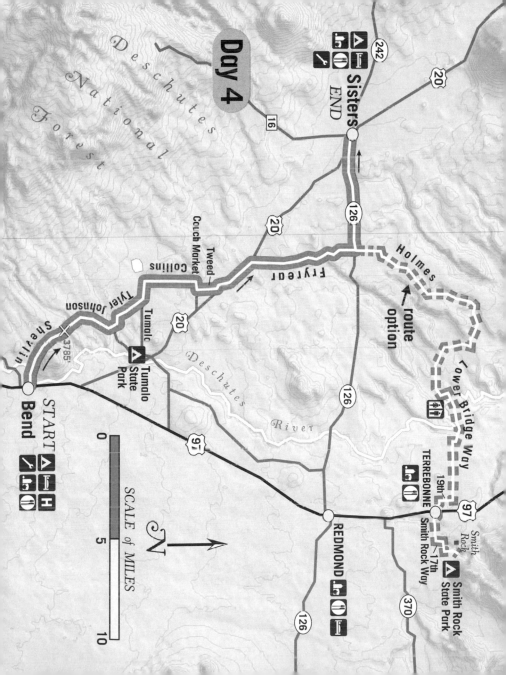

Day 4

Sisters
END

242

20

16

126

20

Holmes

route
option

Deschutes

National

Forest

Collins
Tweed
Couch Marker

Tyler Johnson
3785'
Shevlin

Fryrear

Tumalo

20

START
Bend

H

Tumalo State
Park

Deschutes

River

97

Lower Bridge Way

TERREBONNE
Smith Rock Way

19th

17th

97

370

Smith
Rock

Smith Rock
State Park

126

126

REDMOND

20

SCALE of MILES

N

0

5

10

Day Four

Bend to Sisters

Cascades

0	•	From the Deschutes Brewery head northeast on Bond St
1/2 block	☞	NW Greenwood Ave (becomes Newport Rd then NW Shevlin Park Rd then Johnson Rd)
0.8	•	Sunnyside Sports bike shop
6.7	☞	Tyler Rd
8.7	☞	Tumalo Reservoir Rd
10	☞	Collins Rd
12	☞	Couch Market Rd
12.8	☞	Tweed Rd
14.7	☞	Hwy 20
17	☞	Fryrear Rd
22.5	☞	Hwy 126
27.9	•	Merge with Hwy 20, Sisters
28.5	☞	S Elm St
28.6	•	W Main St, Angeline's Bakery one building down

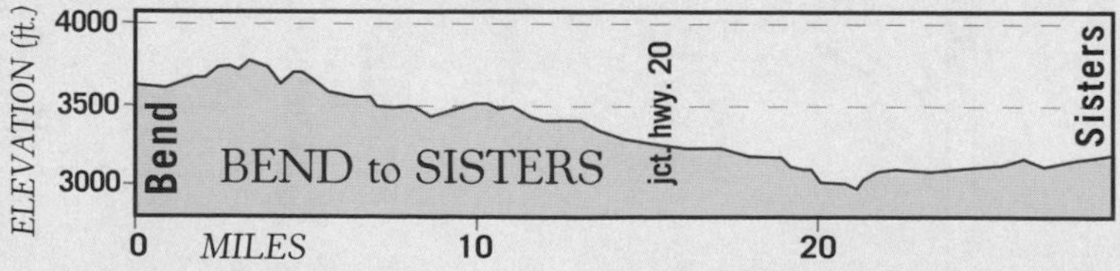

BEND to SISTERS

ELEVATION (ft.) — Bend — jct./hwy. 20 — Sisters

0   MILES   10   20

Five Pine Lodge

(www.fivepinelodge.com, 866-974-5900, 1021 Desperado Trail, $179-$292) Super-luxury experience wrapped up in a log cabin! Three Creeks Brewing on site, plus a movie house and spa. Lots of nature trails out the back door. Two-night minimum.

CAMPING

There is also a KOA campground four miles southeast of Sisters on Hwy 20.

Sisters Overnight Park

(www.ci.sisters.or.us/parks, 541-323-5220, tent site up to six people $12) Though this campground can get crowded, it feels as woodsy as possible being that it's off Hwy 20 and a short walk from downtown Sisters. Sites are first-come, first-serve. There is a restroom facility with showers.

CHOW DOWN

Angeline's Bakery

(www.angelinesbakery.com, 541-549-9122, 121 W Main Ave, 6:30am-6pm) Delicious baked goods, salads and soups include gluten-free and vegan options (that taste good).

Poppies

(541-549-1033, 221 W Main St, Wed-Sun 11am-3pm, 4:30-7pm) The beef is from a local ranch, the eggs are from a neighbor and produce is as local and organic as you can get. Poppies' food is scrumptious, from burgers to gluten-free vegan fare. They are awfully nice folks, too.

Three Creeks Brewery

(www.threecreeksbrewing.com, 541-549-1963, 721 Desperado Ct, Sun-Thurs 11:30am-9pm, Fri till 10pm) The patio is the place to be post-ride, and the fish tacos are pretty good, too.

Jen's Garden

(www.intimatecottagecuisine.com, 541-549-2699, 403 East Hood Ave, 5-8:30pm) If you are looking for a super-special night out, come here for high-end, French-inspired cooking in a cozy, garden-loving, Craftsman-era atmosphere.

Melvin's Fir Street Market (541-549-0711, 160 S Fir St, 8am-8pm, Sun till 7pm) The go-to natural/gourmet food store.

Sisters Farmers Market (541-420-3730, Main St and Ash St, Summers, Friday 3-6pm) Fresh, local food!

Rays Food Place (www.gorays.com, 541-549-2222, 635 North Arrowleaf Trail, 6:30am-10pm) Conventional grocery store.

Bend's Cycle Pub and Ale Trail

Of course you have the option of drinking microbrews while collectively pedaling a mobile pub along the streets of Bend. This is Oregon; what do you expect?

Cycle Pub (www.cyclepub.com, 541-678-5051, 90 minutes or two hours, per person with 14 participants about $21) is usually rented by group, but there is always a chance you could hop a ride (so to speak) with another group that hasn't reached the 14-person maximum. Advance reservations are required. The Cycle Pub will take you on **Bend's Ale Trail**, a route that highlights Bend's world-renowned breweries. (P.S. There is a Bend Ale Trail app for the Android and iPhone. High tech.)

Cascades

BIKE SHOPS

Eurosports (www.eurosports.us, 541-549-2471, 182 E Hood Ave, 9am-5:30pm) A shop with mountain bike rentals among other cycling and outdoor sporting goods.

Blazing Saddles (www.blazinsaddleshub.com, 541-719-1213, 413 W Hood, 9am-5:30) This shop was highly recommended by a lovely friend who is a local cyclist. He loves the service here.

YOGA

Life.Love.Yoga. (www.lifeloveyoga.com, 541-390-5678, 164 North Elm St, drop-in $12)

DAY FIVE
Sisters to Harbick's Country Store in Rainbow
44.7 miles
Elevation Climbed 2,500 ft

The McKenzie Pass. Cyclists pilgrimage to pedal this pass from far and wide. Because of the diverse landscape, geologically dramatic scenery and low traffic, Oregon designated the McKenzie Hwy as a Scenic Bikeway (see page 7). If you are gearing up for McKenzie Pass right now, know that I am jealous.

The newfangled Hwy 126 usurped most of the car and truck traffic from the McKenzie Hwy. The former wagon trail is now left for the lollygaggers, in car and on bike, who wish to explore a quiet forest and gaze over a 65-square-mile lava flow, which dominates the landscape when you get closer to the top.

At the apex of the 5,325 ft pass, you'll hit the Dee Wright Observatory, which is crafted in part by the pumice and lava remnants that completely engulf the area around it. The short stair climb to the top of the observatory rewards you with a 360-degree panorama that flaunts six monstrous Cascadian peaks.

The grade on the climb up the pass won't harsh on you; it's almost angelic...for a 14-mile climb. The descent down the other side, on the other hand, is devilish. It would inspire carsickness were you in a vehicle, but YOU are on a bike, so you will whoosh hedonistically around the hair-pin turns that penetrate thick forest. To boot, you get to descend more than you climbed today, so it seems all the more sinful. Vaguely related side note: I once scared an elk off this road while descending!

At the end of the day, you have to ride 7.5 miles on Hwy 126, which wouldn't be bad scenery-wise except for the significant traffic. As you are on a very slight decline, the mileage goes quickly, and before you know it, you've completed your terribly awesome tour and are drinking as iced tea at Harbick's. Nice job.

It's perfect that the ride ends in a place called Rainbow. Solid Gold.

RIDING TIPS

• There are no services until you hit Hwy 126, basically all day.

• Though the traffic on Hwy 126 leaves something to be desired, the shoulders are wide.

Day Five

Sisters to Rainbow

0	•	From Angeline's Bakery head west on W Main St
.1	🖘	N Oak St
.2	🖙	W Hood Ave
.5	🖘	W Cascade Ave, Hwy 242
15.1	•	McKenzie Pass, Dee Wright Observatory
26.7	•	Alder Springs Campground
35.8	•	Limberlost Campground
36.8	•	Camp Yale
37.2	🖘	Hwy 126, to 'Blue River'
38	•	Paradise Campground
39.4	•	McKenzie River Ranger Station
41.8	•	McKenzie Bridge
44.7	•	Harbick's Country Store

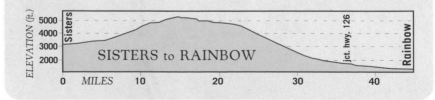

- As always, summer weekends and holidays mean more crowds, both on the McKenzie Hwy and on Hwy 126.

EXTRACURRICULAR ACTIVITIES

At Dee Wright Observatory (mile 15.1) there is a short interpretive hike through the lava rock, which is pretty cool and interesting.

Smith Rock State Park Option
35 miles (one-way)

Including this side trip in your Cascadian adventure will diversify the tour's prevailing mountain forest motif with dramatic desert landscapes. The route to **Smith Rock State Park** heads northward along the Deschutes River into the desert and has rolling terrain with mountain views.

Mostly known as an international climbing destination, hikers and mountain bikers alike are drawn to Smith Rock's beauty. Inside the park, the Crooked River loops its way around the valley at the base of the famous, multi-hued rock formations that seem to shoot vertically from the ground. Some outcroppings seem to have been crafted by a Dada artist. Keep an eye out for Monkey Face.

The route from Sisters to Smith Rock is so fabulous that it has been officially deemed a Scenic Bikeway (see page 7). The info you need to tour this section, from maps to cue sheets, can be found at the State of Oregon's website (www.oregon.gov/oprd/parks/bike). There is camping at Smith Rock and a good pub in nearby Terrebonne, but lodging isn't an option.

Cascades

CRATER LAKE AND BEYOND
Southern Oregon

Five days and four nights
Begin and end in Ashland
245 miles total

THE SKINNY

PRICE POINT: You can do this with a **small to moderately bulging purse.** Summer tourist mark-ups can be significant, but prices outside the Crater Lake National Park are still fairly reasonable. There are a few luxury options.

DIFFICULTY RATING: 8 While the mileage isn't killer, there's lots of climbing, some at high altitudes.

JAW-DROP FACTOR: 9.2 Knock your chamois off.

STAND OUT CAMPING SPOT: Aspen Point Campground, Lake of the Woods (Day 4, page 123)

STAND OUT LODGING: Jo's Motel in Fort Klamath (Day 4, page 124)

AVERAGE TEMP IN JULY: Low 42, high 85 degrees

AVERAGE TEMP IN FEBRUARY: Low 21, high 42 degrees

* Cooler at high elevations

Southern Oregon is flush with cycling opportunities. This tour hits some highlights that truly represent some of the best of the best in the entire state. Just make sure to have your climbing legs ready and your camera battery charged.

Even though Crater Lake is the sweetheart of this tour, the route would still be epic if the Crater Lake rim ride were taken out completely. You get to experience the Shakespeare-crazy, bike-enamored city of Ashland, head up into high-alpine mountain country—where you share forest service roads with deer and squirrels—swim in clear lakes surrounded by extinct volcanoes, fish all you want and rub elbows with locals who are happy to share a story or re-fill your thermos with hot water.

Crater Lake is a phenomenal bonus. Since the lake's first documented description in 1853, when explorer John Hillman named her "Deep Blue Lake," she has been called "mystical," "of the

Great Spirit," "Mystery Lake," "Glorious Work" and "still and mysterious in the bosom of the everlasting hills."

It's fitting that people use words like "mystery" and "magic" to describe Crater Lake. From the edge of the rim, the lake is unavoidably grand and inexplicably wonderful.

When you cycle up to the rim of Crater Lake, you feel saturated by the same awe that Native Americans and American pioneers must have felt upon first view as you gaze on the azure waters cradled by sheer, weather-beaten cliffs. Cycling around the rim introduces you to this national treasure in a very intimate manner and is, by my calculations, 43.7 times better than seeing it from a car. It was a ride of a lifetime for me.

Crater Lake Trivia

• In 1898, cycle touring pioneers Earl Cleveland and G.W. Edwards bicycled 989 miles from Portland to Crater Lake, Ashland, Klamath Falls and back to Portland. No matter what, they had it rougher than you.

• Among other incredible feats, William Steel organized a U.S. Geologic Survey expedition that required a 900-pound survey boat to be carried down the steep walls of Crater Lake to take the first depth measurements of the lake.

• At the turn of the century, Joaquin Mille, Poet Laureate of Oregon, spent several days camping on the rim. He wrote, "The lake took such hold of my heart, unlike other parks...I love it almost like one of my family."

Fist Bump!

• **Standing Stone Brewing** in Ashland (Day 1 and 4, page 111)

• The **Shakespeare Festival** (Day 1 and 4, page 113)

• **Butteville-Prospect Rd and NFD 37** (Day 2, page 117)

• **Becky's pie** (Day 2, page 117)

• Ride around **Crater Lake rim** (Day 3, page 121)

• **Jo's Organic Grocery and Deli** (Day 4, page 105)

• **Fishing and swimming at Lake of the Woods** (Day 4, page 123)

• **Barton Flat Rd** (Day 5, page 127)

• The descent on **Green Springs Hwy** (Day 5, page 127)

HISTORY TIDBITS

A legend from the local Klamath tribe explains the creation of Crater Lake and is widely believed to be based on a first-hand account of the eruption of Mt. Mazama, the mountain that stood where Crater Lake is today. In this legend, Chief Llao of the Below World and Chief Skell of the Above World engage in a great battle. In the end, Chief Llao is defeated and his home, Mt. Mazama, is destroyed.

More than 7,000 years later, Crater Lake National Park was established in 1902 largely due to the efforts of William Gladstone Steel. He was so moved by

Crater Lake

Crater Lake

Crater Lake that he fought tirelessly for 17 years to create a National Park because he saw what the future would hold if the area was not protected. He was one of many fiery advocates for Crater Lake National Park to whom we all owe gratitude. To this day, it is the only National Park in Oregon.

Ashland, the start and finish of the ride, is home to the Oregon Shakespeare Festival, which has been in operation since 1935. The origin of the festival goes back even further, inspired by the Chautauqua movement of the late 1800s, which focused on bringing arts and culture into rural parts of the United States. The festival has grown from a local event to one of national significance; these days festival commissions new theatrical works in addition to performing the Shakespeare canon, and about 350,000 theatre-lovers from around the world attend the festival each year.

ENVIRONMENT

Violent volcanic activity culminated 7,700 years ago with what geologists believe was the largest eruption in the Cascades during the last one million years. It forced Mt. Mazama—now Crater Lake—to collapse in on itself. Those eruptions, along with monolithic glaciers, created the dramatic mountains, valleys and lakes you see over the course of the tour. There are a number of active but dormant volcanic peaks in the region, like Mt. McLoughlin, which shows itself in various places on the route.

You will pass through a plethora of coniferous forests that include pines, firs, hemlocks and other evergreens. Huckleberry bushes are abundant and bear delicious fruit in late summer or early fall. Logging and the suppression of forest fires has altered the natural habit of the forests, but this area is still considered a safe-haven for many native species of plants, trees and animals.

The region is rich with bird species like the spotted owl, jays, crows, eagles, water birds and falcons. The forests are also home to animals such as the black bears, chipmunks, coyotes, elk and more.

RIDING SEASON

If you cut out the spectacular Crater Lake rim ride, this tour could be done late June through early October.

But the window of opportunity to actually ride Rim Dr in a prime cycling time is relatively small. Rim Dr isn't open until mid-July during most seasons due to snow pack, though sometimes it can be open a bit earlier. By mid-October, the weather makes the riding icky and the higher elevation roads can start to close. Check with **Crater Lake National Park** (www.nps.gov/crla, 541-594-3000) for information on road closures. Hoards of tourist flock to the illustrious Crater Lake during the summer, making the weekends, and to a significant degree, the weekdays, quite crowded. Therefore, the faintly shouldered Rim Dr becomes sketchier and less pleasant to cycle. I suggest visiting mid-week after Labor Day, when the weather is still good and crowds diminish.

WEATHER

The typical Cascade summer will have warm, possibly hot, days and cool nights, but, as you are riding through the mountains, you should be prepared for anything that Mother Nature could hand out—especially during shoulder seasons.

As you gain in elevation, the temperature will drop. And you gain lots of elevation on this tour. Ashland is a different story. Summers are hot with milder nights.

ARRIVING / LEAVING
Airplane

The **Rogue Valley International-Medford Airport** (MFR, www.jacksoncounty.org, 541-772-8068) is 16 miles from Ashland. Airlines that serve it include: Horizon Air, United Express, Delta Connection and Allegiant Air. These carriers offer flights daily to and from San Francisco, Portland, Seattle, Los Angeles, Phoenix, Denver, Las Vegas and Salt Lake City. **Medford Rogue Valley Transit District** (www.rvtd.org, 541-779-2877, Ashland $1-3) will get you to Ashland and has buses equipped with bike racks. Take the #1 bus (hourly, 6:30am-6:30pm Mon Fri) to the RVTD transfer station in Medford then the #10 bus to Ashland (about three per hour, 5am-6:30pm Mon-Fri). **Cascade Shuttle** (www.cascadeshuttle.com, 541-488-1998, $28) is one of the shuttle companies serving MFR and Ashland. Just make

Crater Lake

reservations in advance (pay with cash or checks only) and let them know you have a bike.

Car

Take I-5 straight to Ashland. The bigger chain hotels in Ashland will most likely let you park your car in their lot for the duration of your trip. The others near downtown, not so much. Parking is free east of downtown in the residential areas and should be okay for five days. That's what we did. The chamber of commerce suggested talking to the police about arranging a daily rate at the hourly parking garage in downtown.

You can rent a mini-van at any **Enterprise** (www.enterprise.com, 800-261-7331, from Portland, $185) and drop it off at the airport in Medford, 16 miles from Ashland. More convenient, though less comfortable, for two to four people would be to rent a U-Haul (www.uhaul.com, 800-468-4285, from Portland $140) and drop it off in Ashland. From the Medford airport, you can take the Rogue Valley Transit District buses (see Airplane 103) to get to Ashland. Even better, you can ride to Ashland via the **Bear Creek Greenway** (www.bearcreekgreenway.com, 541-774-8184, free downloadable map online) a partially paved multi-use path from Center Point through Medford to Ashland.

Bus

You can take **Greyhound/Trailways buses** (www.greyhound.com, 800-231-2222, from Portland 9.5 hours, $67-84)

from far and wide and end up in Ashland. You have to box your bike, and bike fees may apply.

Train

Amtrak's **Coast Starlight** (www.amtrak.com, 800-872-7245, from Portland $72) connects Seattle to Los Angeles (see Train, page 14). It passes through Klamath Falls where you can easily connect with the tour loop from the east. To hook up with the route, you can ride busy Hwy 140 westward till you meet the route at the intersection of Dead Indian Memorial Rd at mile 45.7 on Day 4 (see page 114). This adds 32 miles one-way to your route. A less trafficked route is through Keno heading to Dead Indian Memorial Rd via Clover Creek Rd. That adds 33.3 miles one-way to your route and hits the tour at mile 7.2 on Day 4 (see page 123).

Crater Lake

USEFUL WEBSITES
Crater Lake Institute
www.craterlakeinstitute.com; a non-profit advocating for Crater Lake's preservation and educating about its history and natural environment.
Crater Lake National Park
www.nps.gov/crla; current conditions, services and other visitor information.
Jackson County
www.co.jackson.or.us

FOOD AND DRINK
Ashland is similar to its I-5 Corridor relatives—Seattle, Portland and Eugene— in that foodies abound. There are a number of interesting and diverse restaurants and bars in Ashland, and for those preferring local, sustainable, gluten-free or vegetarian choices, you will have options. Outside of Ashland, you'll get the standard rural, mountain country fare that usually comes with French fries on the side. Jo's Organic Deli, an exception in Fort Klamath, serves healthy, fresh food. The Crater Lake Lodge restaurant is supposed to

be fancy, and is surely expensive, but we opted for the rehydrated lentil soup and the wine from the Mazama general store, which we opened by pushing the cork in the bottle with an Allen wrench.

Ashland is right next to Rogue Valley wine country, which boasts 40 established wineries. In Ashland, the Winchester Inn has a wine bar (see page 106) that specializes in local wine. The Ashland Vineyard and Winery (see page 115) is the only winery you pass on route— you go by it at the beginning of the first day—where you can buy "Shakespeare" wine. The Southern Oregon Wine Association website (www.sorwa.org) has more information.

LODGING

Ashland has a wide array of lodging options from hostels to high-end B&Bs. On the rest of the route, lodging is sparse. You'll find several "resorts" with camping, cabins and even rentable RVs that cater to Crater Lake tourists, hunters, anglers and nature seekers. These lodging choices are simple, cozy and range from $75-165 per night. The fanciest option is Crater Lake Lodge (see page 121) on the rim of the crater. During the summer, advance reservations are highly suggested.

CAMPING

There is an abundance of campgrounds along the route, ranging from primitive to village-like. They are maintained by Jackson County, the National Forest rangers, the BLM and private resorts. They cost $6-26 per night. A number don't have potable water sources, so bring a purification method if you want to play the tour by ear or go budget, as these sites are usually cheaper. During the summer, advance reservations are highly suggested.

HYDRATION

If you don't bring a purification method, you will need to be careful about stocking up on water. Potable water sources can be few and far between, depending on the day.

MAPS
City of Ashland's Bike Map

(www.rideoregonride.com/maps/ ashland_trails.pdf) is downloadable and free. The **Jackson County Bike Map** (www.jacksoncounty.org, 541-774-8184, 10 South Oakdale, $6 with shipping) shows major routes, traffic volumes, substantial hills and the presence of paved shoulders. It's tear and water resistant, and most of the bike shops in the area carry it. **Rogue River National Forest map** ($4) from the Forest Service covers most of the tour and marks all campgrounds. There is only a bit of the tour near Fort Klamath that's not on the map and is covered on the **Upper Klamath Basin map** ($15) from the Oregon Recreation Maps Series. Both maps can be purchased in Ashland at the **Northwest Nature Store** (www. northwestnatureshop.com, 541-482-3241, 154 Oak Street, 10am-6pm) where they give 20% of their profit to local, community enhancing organizations.

RIDING TIPS

• There will be much climbing. Low gears will make you happy.

• In the mountains, the weather can change unpredictably, so be prepared for all varieties.

• Grocery restock options will generally be Spartan before and after Jo's Organic Grocery in Fort Klamath (page 123).

HEADS UP

You ride through official open range country on sections of this tour, so always keep a heads up for cattle guards. See

Moo-ve Over (page 219). Also, check with the Forest Service (Prospect Ranger District, 541-560-3400) before your tour because there can be forest fires, prescribed and not, in these areas. It's a good idea to check with them about construction or possible road closures as well.

CELL COVERAGE

Coverage is spotty on this route. Every day I got some reception, even on Crater Lake's rim (just barely, though). Mazama Village (see page 118) has a pay phone but no cell reception.

HOSPITALS

Ashland Community Hospital

(www.ashlandhospital.org, 541-201-4000, 280 Maple St, all hours). 24/7 emergency care.

Sky Lakes Medical Center

(www.skylakes.org, 541-274-6176, 2865 Daggett Ave, Klamath Falls, all hours). 24/7 emergency care.

EXTRACURRICULAR ACTIVITIES

Fishing, swimming and hiking on

the creeks, lakes and trails along the way could make this an incredibly interdisciplinary trip.

COST OPTIONS

Budget camping tour: Day 1, Whiskey Springs Campground (page 114); Day 2 and 3, Mazama Campground (page 118); Day 4, Willow Point Campground (page 128); Day 5, Emigrant Lake (page 11). You can graze general stores.

High Falootin' credit card camping: Day 1, Willow Lake Resort Cabins (page 114); Day 2 and 3, Mazama Village Cabins or Crater Lake Lodge (page 121), Day 4, Lake of the Woods Resort Cabins (page 123); Day 5, Columbia Hotel (page 110). You can eat out most days.

MORE TOUR!

If you want to connect this route to the **Cascade Classic** tour (page 69) by going south from Oakridge, that would make a righteously epic mountain tour. There is a killer connector route (see Connecting the Tours, page 109).

Alternatively, head from Ashland to the **Coast** tour (page 46) going from Grants Pass to Merlin then out on Galice Rd, which become Bear Camp Rd/ FR 23, to Agness. From Agness, take Agness Rd (then 595) to Gold Beach. It's an extremely difficult but gorgeous 1-3 day route, with a lot of climbing after Grants Pass. From Agness, the downhill stretches almost all the way to Gold Beach.

Crater Lake

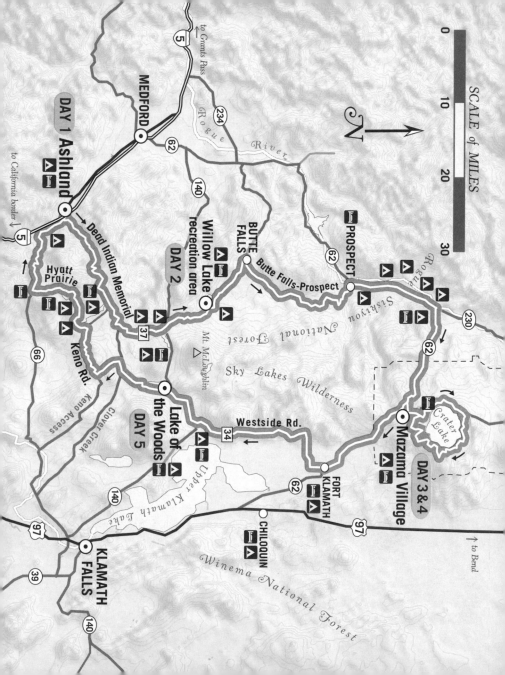

Crater Lake Butt-kicking Connector

By Brian Wilson, trail shredder and touring enthusiast

Back in 2005, after a long history of road and mountain biking, my girlfriend convinced me to try bicycle touring. Reluctant at first, I did finally agree. Bicycle touring had the joys of backpacking and cycling combined, and I liked it.

Eventually, I concocted a route (that I now ride annually) going north to south through the Oregon Cascades, which includes the most challenging, and therefore the most scenic, roads in Oregon. I stay mostly on paved roads and end in Klamath Falls, where Amtrak takes me home. Part of my route connects two of Ellee's tours: the **Cascade Classic** and **Crater Lake and Beyond**. She asked me to elaborate on the connecting route for you, so here it goes:

Leaving Oakridge is always bittersweet. I know what awaits me will both inspire and punish. Being the hardest day of my tour, the route is indirect but is the only paved access to the **N Umpqua Hwy 138** (which leads to Crater Lake).

After turning away from Hills Creek Reservoir onto **Larison Rock Rd**, a (minimum) three-hour climb begins on roads that redefine what a bicycle tourist might consider remote. The gradient is

relentless for miles at a time and the only way to digest the road ahead is to "sit in the angry chair" and continue pedaling. After 10 miles on Larison Rock Rd, **FR 5850**'s asphalt (with a couple of short sections of gravel) is as crunchy as it gets, but the ridgeline is ultra-picturesque.

After 20 miles of non-stop ascending, there's a descent on the recently paved Hwy 22. This spirited plunge leads to Bryce Creek. Its opalescent pools and perfect campsites always test the decision to roll on.

On **Sharps Creek Rd** begins one of the most merciless ribbons of road on my

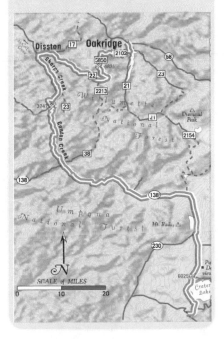

Crater Lake

entire Cascade route. The steepness of this remote climb is so perplexing that one might wonder why this road was ever paved at all. And the challenge sharpens on **Martin Creek Rd** with its body-jarring section of chip-seal.

Once at the summit, the motive for suffering becomes clear: a sweet descent. The cruise down deserted **Canton Creek Rd** passes perfect swimming holes and beautiful camping opportunities. Giddy after 85 miles and 9,500 feet of climbing, it is usually difficult to choose a site. After an unpleasant bear encounter at milepost 10 by Canton Creek, I now choose to camp farther toward the Umpqua River.

On the final two days of my ride, I take **N Umpqua Hwy** to the free hiker-biker campground at **Diamond Lake** (the pizza place right next door is always appreciated), then the next day I ride to the Crater Lake rim. And that concludes the epic connector route.

Ashland

Pop. 21,000
Elevation 1,900 ft.

USEFUL WEBSITES
Oregon Shakespeare Festival
www.osfashland.org
Ashland Chamber of Commerce
www.ashlandchamber.com
Southern Oregon's Visitors Association
www.southernoregon.org

Siskiyou Velo
(www.siskiyouvelo.org)
An active Southern Oregon bike club.

LODGING
I've chosen locally-owned, centrally-located places so you can easily walk or bike to food and shops. I also mention the Best Western on the outskirts of town because, if you stay with them, the hotel will let you leave your car there while you're on tour.

The Ashland Hostel
(www.theashlandhostel.com, 541-482-9217, 150 N Main St, dorm $28, shared bath $40-59, family room with private bath $89) Close to downtown, this place is frequented by cycle tourists. They have an organic coffee and tea service and a communal kitchen.

The Ashland Commons
(www.ashlandcommons.com, 541-482-6753, 437 Williamson Way, dorm $26, private room per person $35-65) Just a couple of blocks away from the United Bicycle Institute, and close to downtown, this hostel provides bike racks outside or an out building for bike storage. There's nearby street parking where you could leave your car.

The Columbia Hotel
(www.columbiahotel.com, 541-482-3726, 262 E Main St, shared bath $95-149, private bath $169-179) The charm of this downtown, period hotel entices tourists to spend $100 and more on shared-bathroom accommodations.

Best Western Windsor Inn

(www.book.bestwestern.com, 541-488-2330, 2520 Ashland St, $120-145) Though this chain hotel is a couple of miles away from city center, it's right on route, allows you to leave your car there during your tour and has a pool and hot tub.

CAMPING

Glenyan Campground (mile 47.7 Day 5, www.glenyanrvpark.com, 877-453-6926, 5310 Hwy 66, tent site $22.50) 25 tent sites. General store on site.

Emigrant Lake Park (mile 47.5 Day 5, www.jacksoncountyparks.com, 541-774-8183, 5505 Hwy 66, tent site $18) 42 tent sites. Reservations recommended. Showers.

CHOW DOWN

Brothers' Restaurant

(www.brothersrestaurant.net, 541-482-9671, 95 N Main St, 7am-2pm) Breakfast joint that uses local produce and sustainable meat and fish sources.

Pangea (www.pangeaashland.com, 541-552-1630, 272 E Main St, 11am-8pm) Soups, salad, sandwiches and wraps. Great for lunch.

Standing Stone Brewing

(www.standingstonebrewing.com, 541-482-2448, 101 Oak St, 11:30am-midnight, Sat from 8am) Super cool pub with bike-friendly practices that have won the brewery an Alice B Toeclips Award from the Bicycle Transportation Alliance and a silver award from the League of American Bicyclists. The food (locally and sustainably sourced when possible) and beer rock.

Ashland Food Coop

(www.ashlandfood.coop, 541-482-2237, 237 N 1st, 7am-9pm) Southern Oregon's only consumer-owned natural food grocery store.

Ashland Farmer's Market

(www.rvgrowersmarket.com, Tuesday 8:30am-1:30pm, May-Oct, on Oak St between Lithia Way and E Main St) Fresh snacks!

Straight from the Local's Mouth
by Bill Heimann, Ashland local and bike touring aficionado

For me, bicycle touring is about traveling into the heart of another culture, knowing the food and becoming familiar with the basics of people's lives. As a result, I have friends all over the world. Journeying in the mind and soul of the country is what touring is for me and what inspires me to search for new roads.

Ashland offers so much for the bicyclist. You can climb big mountains on roads winding through dark forests or ride through rolling hills of white pear blossoms. My wife Annette and I bike toured the US, Europe, the Middle East and Central America searching for our new retirement town. Our searching narrowed the selection to four towns: Chiang Mai; Thailand, Antigua; Guatemala; Ashville; NC; and Ashland. After having invested at least a month in each, Ashland won.

Crater Lake

United Bicycle Institute: Ashland Bonus!

If you want to take a superb bike maintenance class from a bicycle university, the **United Bicycle Institute** (www.bikeschool.com, 541-488-1121, 401 Williamson Way), near downtown Ashland, is ideal. UBI's classes include a one-week basic bicycle maintenance course, wheel building, frame construction and more.

Safeway (www.local.safeway.com, 541-482-4495, 585 Siskiyou Blvd, 6am-1am) Conventional grocery store.

BIKE SHOPS

Cycle Sport (www.roguecycle.com, 541-488-0581, 191 Oak St, Mon-Sat 9:30am-5:30pm, Sun 11am-5pm) Recommended because it's the most tourist-friendly and right on the route.

Other bike shops in town:
Siskiyou Cyclery
(www.siskiyoucyclery.com, 541-482-1997, 1729 Siskiyou Blvd, Mon-Sat 10am-6pm, Sun 11am-4pm)
Bear Creek Bicycle
(bearcreekbicycle.powweb.com, 541-488-4270, 1988 Hwy 99N, Tue-Sat 9:30am-6pm)
Ashland Bicycle Works
(www.ashlandbicycleworks.com, 541-482-3440, 1632 Ashland St, Mon-Sat 9:30am-6pm, Sun 10am-5pm)

YOGA
The Ashland Yoga Center
(www.ashlandyogacenter.com, 541-488-4448, 485 A St, drop-in class $10-12) Yoga and cycling = fabulous combination.

DAY ONE
Ashland to Willow Lake
42.6 miles
Elevation Climbed 4,850 ft.

Starting this day jacked up on coffee or yerba mate is highly suggested. Within the first 16.5 miles, you'll do the hardest climbing of the tour to the top of the pass on Dead Indian Memorial Rd (see page 114). The sustained, sometimes steeply graded, climb cuts through the remote, curvy foothills east of Ashland where the summer sun frizzles the grasses blonder than the clientele at an L.A. hair salon.

As you work your way up the exposed road, the valley and mountain vistas increase in drama, and trees eventually start to dapple the arid landscape. After cresting the pass, you

descend into an expansive high-prairie where the mighty Mt. McLoughlin lords over the land.

The last part of the route is refreshingly wooded. National Forest Rd 37 is nugget of cycling ambrosia on a day already filled with splendor. Barely intruding on the Rogue River National Forest, this road (mostly used by squirrels) cuts narrowly through massive conifers that crowd and tower over the chip seal.

Almost as alluring, the Fish Lake-Butte Falls Rd may out-charm the 37 with its gravity advantage. You careen downhill for much of the way to the day's end at Willow Lake Recreation Area.

RIDING TIPS

• The first potable water sources are at Hyatt Lake and Howard Prairie campground (mile 20.6, off route 3.5 miles) and Lily Glen Equestrian Park (mile 21.6, hand pump right off the road). A creek is accessible at various places on the climb up Dead Indian Memorial Rd and requires purification. If you don't have a way to purify water, take extra, especially if it's a hot day. The burly climb up to Dead Indian Memorial Summit up is really exposed.

• BYOF. Unless you're planning on hunting and gathering, you best bring food. The closest thing you'll get to food on the route is the restaurant at Hyatt Lake Resort, 3.5 miles off route at mile 20.6 (see page 128), which is open for breakfast, lunch and dinner; or the small store and Tadpole Cafe at Fish Lake Resort (see page 114) which is open for breakfast, lunch and dinner during the summer and is 1.5 miles off route from the intersection of Hwy 140 at mile 33.3.

Ashland is but a Stage, Thanks to the Oregon Shakespeare Festival

Attracting a world-wide audience, the Oregon Shakespeare Festival (www.osfashland.org, 541-482-4331) is a year-round professional arts group and a premier live theatre and performance institution, not to mention one of the coolest things about Ashland and a precious Oregon resource.

Since its inception in 1935, with three performances of two plays, the OSF has grown to include a full-time professional staff that coordinate performances of 11 different plays over eight months for an audience that exceeds 350,000 people. Having grown beyond the Shakespearian canon, OSF routinely commissions new works from top modern playwrights.

Going mid-week or getting discount tickets far in advance will make ticket prices more accessible. If you have the opportunity, take off your cleats for a night and catch a show.

EXTRACURRICULAR ACTIVITIES

You can fish and swim at Willow Lake and Fish Lake, 1.5 miles off route at mile 33.3. There are other places to fish as well, especially along NFD 37.

Crater Lake

CAMPING AND LODGING

Howard Prairie Lake Resort (mile 20.6, www.howardprairieresort.com, 541-842-1979, tent site up to six people $18, trailer rental $95-115) Rent your very own RV! Includes hotel amenities and kitchen. 300 tent sites. There are shower facilities, wifi access and a three-meal restaurant.

Lily Glen Equestrian Park Campground (mile 21.6, www.jacksoncountyparks.com, 541-774-8183, tent site up to 8 people $16) 12 sites, no reservations. Water pump but no showers. Vault toilets.

Fish Lake Resort (mile 33.3, www.fishlakeresort.net, 541-949-8500, cabins for 4-8 people $160-240, tent site up to 4 people $19) 44 tent sites. A mile and a half off route. Showers, laundry, cafe and store on site. Canoe, paddle boat and motor boat rentals.

North Fork Campground (mile 32.8, www.publiclands.org, 541-865-2700, tent site $10) Six tent sites. No reservations. Potable water. Hiking trail to Fish Lake. Right on Little Butte Creek. People love fishing here.

Whiskey Springs Campground (40.9, www.fs.usda.gov, 541-618-2000, tent site $10) 34 tent sites. No reservations. Potable water. One mile interpretive hike around Whiskey Springs Pond.

Willow Lake Recreation Area

(www.jacksoncountyparks.com, 541-774-8183, 7800 Fish Lake Rd, tent site $16, yurt $35, cabin $100-125, reservation fee $8) Set on a lake at an elevation of 3020 ft near the base of Mt. McLoughlin, this county park has four cabins, two yurts and over 70 campsites available for

Dead Indian Memorial Road... Wait, Did I Read That Right?

It can be disconcerting to ride the "Dead Indian Memorial Road" on the first and fourth days of this tour. Behind the macabre name lies a rich dose of some of Oregon's tarnished history.

The creepy moniker refers to one of Southern Oregon's oldest trans-Cascadian routes that was once a path used by Takelma and Klamath Native Americans for trade. During the 1850s, the Euro-American settlers and gold-hungry pioneers instigated bloody conflicts and pogroms with the native populations. In 1854, a number of dead (most likely murdered) Native Americans were supposedly discovered along this road. After that, the area was locally known as "Dead Indian Country" and the road, "Dead Indian Road."

As those names are entirely offensive and massively inappropriate, Jackson County changed the road's name to "Dead Indian Memorial Road" in 1993 in an attempt to acknowledge the incredible number of Native Americans who suffered and died in this valley as a consequence of westward expansion.

The name obviously still scores pretty high on the are-you-freaking-kidding? scale, but we can use its jarring effect to remind us of the history, plight and destruction of the people who used to call this land home.

rent. Reservations can be made in advance online 15 days to nine months in advance. BYO bedding for the cabins and yurts. There are restrooms with showers.

Crater Lake

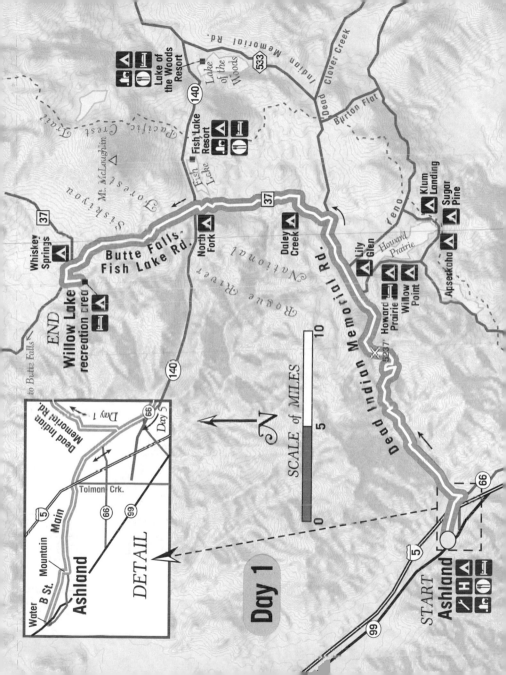

Lake of the Woods Resort

Fish Lake Resort

Lake of the Woods

533

Dead Indian Memorial Rd.

Dead Clover Creek

Byrton Flat

140

Klum Landing

Sugar Pine

Apserkaha

37

Mt. McLoughlin

Siskiyou National Forest

Pacific Crest Trail

Whiskey Springs

37

Butte Falls-Fish Lake Rd.

North Fork

Daley Creek

Lily Glen

Howard Prairie

Willow Point

END
Willow Lake
recreation area

to Butte Falls

Rogue River National

140

3237

SCALE of MILES

10

5

0

N

DETAIL

Day 1

66

Day 5

Dead Indian Memorial Rd.

Tolman Crk.

Main

5

66

99

Water

B St.

Mountain

Ashland

Dead Indian Memorial Rd.

5

66

START
Ashland

99

Day One

Ashland to Willow Lake Recreation Area

0	•	From Blue Bird Park, head east on Water St
.1	☞	B St
.15	•	Ashland Cycle Sport
.9	☞	Mountain Ave
1	☜	E Main St
3.4	☜	Ashland St
3.6	☜	Dead Indian Memorial Rd
16.5	•	Dead Indian Summit 5237 ft
20.6	•	Hyatt Lake and Howard Prairie Campground
21.6	•	Lily Glen Equestrian Park
25.2	☜	To 'Fish Lake,' NFD 37
26.8	•	Daley Creek Campground
32.8	•	North Fork Campground
33.3	☞	Hwy 140
33.4	☜	To 'Willow Lake,' CR 821 N
	☟	To Fish Lake
40.9	•	Whiskey Creek Campground
42.6	•	Willow Lake Recreation Area

ELEVATION (ft.)

5000 — Ashland

4000 —

3000 — ASHLAND to WILLOW LAKE

2000 —

jct. FS 37

jct. hwy. 140

Willow Lake

0   MILES   10   20   30   40

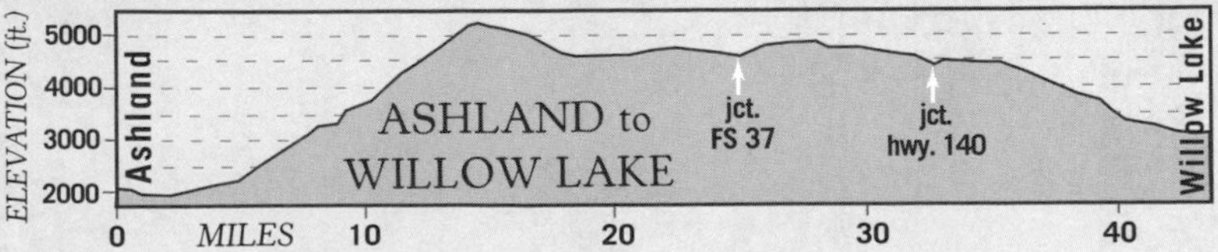

DAY TWO
Willow Lake to Mazama Village
62.7 miles
Elevation Climbed 5,800 ft.

Today, you will put on your climbing pants and accept your upward journey with Yoda-like acceptance because much ascending there will be. The final haul to Mazama Village is sustained, though forgiving, and the grade won't crank you except for inclines during the last five to six miles. If you amble towards your destination at a chillaxed pace, the ascent becomes secondary to the forest and mountains that engulf you in emerald sparkly, pine-smelling, sun-dappled, forest-dominated nature magic.

As you get closer to Mazama Village, the scenery amps up the high-alpine drama, but I have to say that it was the Butte-Prospect Road winding through Rogue River National Forest that charmed me with its *minimalisimo* traffic and pleasant forest ways.

If you start early enough, you can enjoy some tasty treats along the route. One mile off route, you can get calorie-packed, down-home breakfasts and a cinnamon roll for the road at the friendly **Butte Falls Cafe** (mile 6.7, 541-865-7707, 443 Broad St). Make sure to say "hi" to the smart alecky, self-proclaimed "old BSers," Alvin and Darwin, who are there lots of mornings.

Another gem right on route is the pie at Becky's Cafe in Union Creek (mile 45.3, page 117). A foodie loses a taste bud every time a wheat-and-sugar-eating cyclist passes by this cafe without stopping. Most of their menu is similar to any other road stop cafe....until you get to the PIE menu. Holy tasty bombs, their pie is delish. There were ten pies (made fresh every morning) to choose from, and I chose a huckleberry pie, which was filled with berries that had been picked by the restaurant staff. It was a not-too-sweet, ecstatic drum circle in my mouth.

RIDING TIPS
• If you don't take the detour to Butte Falls (mile 6.7), Prospect (mile 30.6) is your next hope for food and potable water. There are a couple of restaurants and a glorified mini-mart. After Union Creek (mile 45.3), which has Becky's Cafe, an ice cream joint and a small general store, there are no food stops until Mazama Village.
• While still scenic, the traffic on Hwy 62 between Prospect (mile 30.6) and the turnoff to Crater Lake (mile 46.6) is the busiest of the day.
• Spend too much time chatting with Alvin and Darwin in Butte Falls? There are plenty of ditch out campgrounds on Hwy 62 to save you.

EXTRACURRICULAR ACTIVITIES
Fishing! Cop a squat on the various water sources along the way. Medco Pond on the Butte Falls-Prospect Rd comes recommended.

Crater Lake

Crater Lake

CAMPING AND LODGING

City Park Butte Falls (mile 6.7, www.southernoregon.com/buttefalls) A mile off route. The camping here is unofficial, not private, and might not be available. There are restrooms and water. It's free, but please patronize the cafe or store to create positive associations with cycle tourism.

Prospect Historic Hotel (mile 30.6, www.prospecthotel.com, 541-506-3664, 391 Mill Creek Dr, $140-205) If your day's journey ends in Prospect, this history-rich inn from the turn of the 20th century will take you back to the days of pioneer Crater Lake tourists such as Teddy Roosevelt. In the age of Best Westerns, I dig it!

River Bridge Campground (mile 35.1, 541-560-3400, tent site $6) Almost a mile off route, including gravel. 11 sites. No reservations. No potable water, but on the Rogue River. Vault toilets. Pack out trash.

Natural Bridge Campground (mile 40.8, 541-560-3400, tent site $6) .3 miles off of route. 17 sites. No reservations. No potable water, but on the Rogue River. Vault toilets. Pack out trash.

Union Creek Resort (mile 45.3, www.unioncreekoregon.com, 866-560-3563, 56484 Hwy 62, lodge room for two-four people with shared bath $60-64, cabin for two-four people $90-130, cabin for six-10 people $145-235) These rustic, well-equipped cabins are right next to Becky's Cafe (see page 117). Enough said.

Union Creek Campground (mile 45.3, 541-560-3400, tent site $11) 77 sites. No reservations. Potable water and vault toilets.

Farewell Bend Campground (mile 46.3, 541-560-3400, tent site $16) 60 sites. No reservations. Potable water and flush toilets.

Mazama Village

(www.craterlakelodges.com, 888-774-2728, tent site $21, every person over two add $3.50, cabin $138, $10/extra person) Seven miles away from Crater Lake's rim at 6,020 ft, this "village" is a National Park entity that corners the Crater Lake tourist market. It's a tourist circus, a mini-town in the middle of nowhere, which includes a campground, restaurant, store, pay showers, laundry facility and cabins for rent. With tens of thousands of visitors per year, advanced reservations are highly recommended, and essential on weekends, though they maintain a number of first-come, first-serve sites at the campground.

The campground is very well run with beautiful tent sites among Ponderosa pines. There is a tent-only loop that excludes RVs; there's another loop that has a free shower facility, but it tends to run out of hot water. Pay showers and laundry close at 7pm. Note that Lost Creek Campground east of Crater Lake (see map page 119) is much smaller, quieter and more primitive than Mazama, but getting there adds a lot of climbing

START
Willow Lake
Recreation Area

Butte Falls-
Fish Lake Rd.

BUTTE
FALLS

821

Day 2

PROSPECT

62

Butte Falls- Prospect Rd.

River
Bridge

Abbott
Creek

Natural
Bridge

Farewell
Bend

to Diamond Lake /

230

Crater Lake Hwy.

62

Mill
Creek

UNION CREEK

32

37

922

34

Rancheria

Lodgepole

Rogue

River

Siskiyou

National

Forest

37

Bessie Crk.

62

N

SCALE of MILES

0

5

10

Winema   National

Forest

6208'

END

Mazama
Village

Rim
Village

Crater
Lake

Westside

34

Upper
Klamath
National
Wildlife
Refuge

FORT
KLAMATH

62

Sevenmile

Winema

National

Sun Mountain Rd.

Upper Klamath Lake

Agency
Lake

97

CHILOQUIN

97

→ to Bend

Winema   National   Forest

Day Two

Willow Lake Recreation Area to Mazama Village

0	•	From Willow Lake Campground, head northwest
6.7	☞	Butte Falls-Prospect Rd
	or 👆	To 'Butte Falls'
30.6	☞	To 'Union Creek'
31.2	☞	At stop sign, to 'Union Creek,' Hwy 62
33.2	•	Mill Creek Campground
35.1	•	River Bridge Campground
37.3	•	Abbot Creek Campground
40.8	•	Natural Bridge Campground
45.3	•	Union Creek Campground and Resort, Becky's Cafe
46.3	•	Farewell Bend Campground
46.6	☞	Hwy 62 E, to 'Crater Lake'
62.4	☜	To 'Mazama Village,' 'Crater Lake'
62.7	☞	Turnoff to Mazama Campground

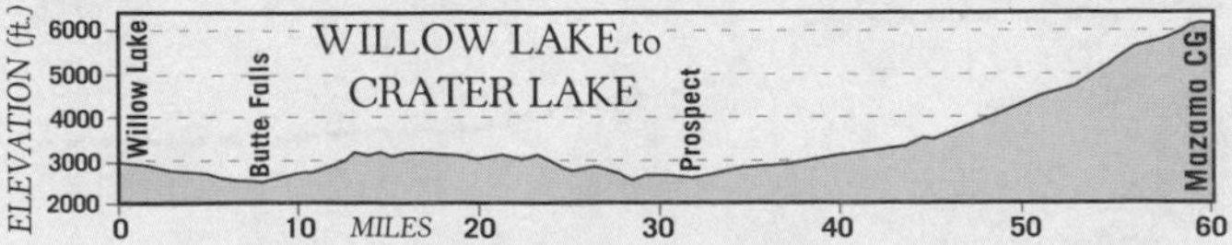

WILLOW LAKE to
CRATER LAKE

ELEVATION (ft.)

6000
5000
4000
3000
2000

Willow Lake
Butte Falls
Prospect
Mazama CG

0   10   *MILES*   20   30   40   50   60

Crater Lake

and almost 14 miles to your day.

The rental cabins are wifi-free, no frills places to hang your hat, but the roof-shower-bed combo might seem like five-star accommodations after cycling up to Mazama Village.

Annie Creek Restaurant is by the campgrounds and cabins. Its hours vary from May to September, but it is usually open for breakfast, lunch and dinner and serves the standard American fare. Also nearby is the store that sells basic camping supplies, some food, wine and beer and other helpful items.

DAY THREE
Rim Drive Day Ride from Mazama Village
39 miles
Elevation Climbed 4,900 ft

Today holds the literal and figurative apex of this tour: Crater Lake.

Eons ago, an ash eruption from the center of Mt. Mazama caused the peak to sink into its own body, ripping bizarre stone cliffs and flinging pumice as it plunged. The resulting crater filled with deep azure water that makes sapphires glower with envy.

While riding the rim—which never dips below 6,500 ft and tops out at 7900 ft—the lake pops in and out of view. For me, each time I saw the lake the water shocked me with its radiant blue layers cradled by precipitous crags and bluffs.

Crater Lake Lodge...One Day I'll Stay There

Originally a private sector operation, **Crater Lake Lodge** (www.craterlakelodges.com, 888-774-2728, open late May to mid October, $164-290) started receiving visitors in 1915. Over the next seven plus decades, the lodge was well loved, but the owners couldn't afford the costly maintenance of a lodge that endured such extreme conditions and remoteness. The National Park Service took over ownership in 1967 but didn't get around to improvements till 1991, when the building was deemed unsafe.

Now this 1920s-style lodge is a proper hotel sitting prettily aside an uncanny natural wonder. If you want to stay here, you can't just snag a reservation the weekend before. It books out up to a year in advance because, while it's spendy, it's the only accommodation that's actually on the rim. While waking up to the view of Crater Lake might be worth a hefty price, there's zero competition to keep quality in check, which is worrisome. But the folks I talked to who stayed there said they loved it.

Second prize: Sneak onto the lodge's deck for a cocktail during happy hour. You could also make a dinner reservation to eat in the lodge restaurant, but allow for enough daylight to pedal down to the plebeian digs at Mazama Village.

Crater Lake

Cycling this cloud-grazing route is like floating around the ether as you cruise along a rim left behind by a bizarre geologic catastrophe. Besides ogling the lake, you can see an ocean of mist-colored mountains boiling voluptuously in the valleys far below, as well as blankets of blue-green forests, meadows perfect for lumbering alpine bears, and Mt. Thielsen's glacier-sharpened peak.

The diversity of the outrageous landscape you witness around Crater Lake makes this ride the stuff of bucket lists. That doesn't mean you should underestimate the road's butt-kicking potential. More than one cyclist has commented on the surprising amount of energy required for this relatively short, 39-mile day.

RIDING TIPS

• The Park entrance fee is $5 per bicycle with a ceiling of $10 for a family-size group.

• Staff will give you a free, detailed map of Crater Lake when you check in at Mazama Village and when entering the Park.

• There are only two places you can stock up on potable water and food after you leave Mazama Village: the Steel Visitor Center (mile 3.7) and Rim Village (6.4). I suggest coming prepared and bringing extra rations. There are tons of turnouts where you'll want to stop, gawk and eat.

• If you don't want to dally another day in Mazama Village, Jo's Motel is an easy

16.4 miles down the road and is equipped with a wicked organic deli and store as well as tent sites.

EXTRACURRICULAR ACTIVITIES

There are a number of hiking trails in the Crater Lake area, including the **Cleetwood Cove Trail** (2.2 miles round trip, 724 ft of elevation gain) which is the only legal access down to the water. You can lock your bike and take a dip. Boat tours ($29 per person, seven tours per day) run from the cove, weather permitting. First-come, first-serve tickets are sold at the Cleetwood Cove Trail parking lot (make sure to buy them before hiking down).

HEADS UP

If for some reason you are doing this ride during peak tourist season, be aware that road shoulders are tiny, the road winds a lot and tourists tend to gape at Crater Lake while driving.

DAY FOUR
Mazama Campground to Lake of the Woods
47.7 miles
Elevation Climbed 1,850 ft.

Today you drop down from the heights of Crater Lake National Park as you cruise along the Volcanic Legacy Scenic Byway (www.volcaniclegacybyway.org). Heading toward Fort Klamath, the landscape suddenly turns into expansive, flat prairie land with mountains grazing the distant horizon.

In teeny Fort Klamath, the organic deli and store at Jo's Motel offers an oasis of fresh food that inspires air-humping. After that, the pancake-flat Sevenmile Rd takes you right up against the foothills of Winema National Forest where the route gets bit more rolling.

The six miles that you ride on Hwy 140 grate on the nerves due to heavy traffic and to the fact that up until this point the tour has spoiled you rotten. The climb during this section seemed harder than more difficult climbs on tour because of the whooshing vehicles.

Once you turn, yet again, onto Dead Indian Memorial Rd (see page 114), the quiet, forest-crowded roads resume. It's not long till you hit Lake of the Woods Resort and Campground, a killer spot to stop for the night that offers fishing, swimming, a store, restaurant and a lake that seems to be fashioned for explosive sunsets. The cabins are so stinking cute you may have to take a cute elixir.

RIDING TIPS

• Potable water and food are never more than 20 miles away, for a change.

• The **Solar Cafe** (mile 40.6, www.solarcafeusa.com, 541-356-2400, 31011 Mountain Lakes Dr, check for summer hours) loves solar power and energy efficient constructions as much as food. You'll find gluten-free and vegetarian options here, as well as an espresso bar.

• An early start can help you avoid the winds on the prairie that can be pushy in the afternoons and early evenings.

EXTRACURRICULAR ACTIVITIES

There is a hike around Lake of the Woods. People are gonzo for fishing in this area and other points along the way, like Rocky Point Resort. Bait is available. Crater Lake B&B (page 124) arranges fly fishing, canoe, rafting and water fowl hunting trips with local guides.

CAMPING AND LODGING ON ROUTE

Wilson Cottages (mile 11.1, www.thewilsoncottages.com, 541-381-2209, 57997 Hwy 62, with kitchens $75-110) With a two-night minimum, this place may not work with your itinerary, but it's a family built (1937) and operated hotel which is reasonable and right on Annie Creek.

Jo's Motel and Campground (mile 16.4, www.josmotel.com, 541-381-2234, 52851 Hwy 62, Fort Klamath, suites with kitchens $110-130, tent site for 2 people $10) I love this place! The owners are

sweet hearts and have revamped this 1947 hotel. The minimal decorations, rich hardwood and clean lines create a simple and welcoming effect, and the organic deli and store is the healthiest and tastiest since Ashland.

Crater Lake Bed and Breakfast (mile 16.7, www.craterlakebandb.com, 541-381-0960, 52395 Weed Rd, Fort Klamath, including breakfast and taxes $140) This three-room B&B can also book fly-fishing, water fowl hunting, rafting and canoeing trips with local guides.

Rocky Point Resort (mile 36.9, www.rockypointoregon.com, 28121 Rocky Point Rd, Klamath Falls, tent site up to two people $22, room $85, cabin $140-160) Facilities include laundry, showers, a fish cleaning station and a small store that also sells bait.

Lake of the Woods
Lake of the Woods Resort
(www.lakeofthewoodsresort.com, 866-201-4194, 950 Harriman Route, cabins $119-299) At an elevation of 4,950 ft, the wooden cabins are comfortable, well-

equipped and adorable, with just enough country flair to make them charming. The website says there is a two-day minimum for renting the cabins, but we arrived there without reservations in October and it wasn't a problem to stay just one night. There is a restaurant on-site that does not mess around when it comes to breakfast. There is also a small general store.

Aspen Point Campground
(www.recreation.gov, 541-949-8032, 15300 Dead Indian Memorial Road, tent site $17) 39 sites. Reservations must be made at least four days in advance. Flush toilets. Less than a mile north of the resort. On the lake near a beach.

Sunset Campground
(www.recreation.gov, 541-949-8032, 15300 Dead Indian Memorial Road, tent site $17) Reservations must be made at least four days in advance. Flush toilets. 1.5 miles south of the resort. On the lake near a beach.

DAY FIVE
Lake of the Woods to Ashland
52.9 miles
Elevation Climbed 2,850 ft.

This is yet another spectacular day. You begin on Dead Indian Memorial Rd (see page 114), a dreamy cycling road through national forest. But eight miles later, Barton Flat Road comes straight from cycle touring heaven.

Crater Lake

Day 3

Pacific Crest Trail

N

7683'

START & END
Mazama Village

62

SCALE of MILES

62

Visitor Information Center

Rim Village & Lodge

Crater Lake

Wizard Island

to Diamond Lake

Cleetwood Cove trail

Cloudcap overlook

R i m   D r i v e

7908'

7412'

Lost Creek

Pinnacles Rd.

the Pinnacles

Mt. Scott

N a t i o n a l

C r a t e r   L a k e

P a r k

Day Three
Day Ride Around the Rim

0	☞	Leaving Mazama Campground
3.7	•	Steel Visitor Center
6.4	🖐	To 'Rim Drive West'
	☞	To 'Rim Village' and Crater Lake Lodge
12.3	☞	To 'East Rim'
16.8	•	Cleetwood Cove Trail
23.4	👈	To 'Phantom Ship Overlook,' Hwy 62
35.4	☞	To 'Mazama Village'
39	•	Turnoff to Mazama Campground on left

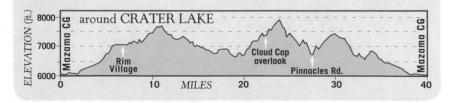

Crater Lake

For several days, we had been asking locals whether Barton Flat was paved or not. Two of our maps said no; one said yes. No one had even heard of the road....even locals living eight miles away. We indeed found that the road was paved, though it was just a one-lane wide, no frills black line sneaking around the forest floor. It seemed to have been laid for logging trucks then forgotten. We saw no one.

Keno Access Rd is a little more developed, as it was wider, but is still pretty deserted and wonderfully tucked into a contour line on the side of a wooded mountain. Occasionally, the road allows voluminous vistas of the valley and surrounding foothills.

The route skirts both Howard Prairie Lake and Hyatt Lake, which do a deft job in their roles as picturesque high-country lakes. Camper Cove (mile 30.1) on Hyatt Lake is your first chance for services. When we visited the restaurant there, the sweet waitress gave continual refills of scalding tea to our drenched, cold, oddly-clad cyclist selves, and she didn't hesitate at my request for foot-sized plastic bags.

The descent into Ashland on the lightly used Green Springs Hwy compensates you heartily for all your climbing. As you head back down the arid slopes above Ashland, the trees give way to a broad panorama of distant sylvan mountains. This swooping, mountain-clinging road makes your bike—which is bloated with panniers and other such hitchhikers—an elegant, whooshing glider...an excellent note on which to end the tour.

RIDING TIPS

• Much of the ride today is super-remote, so make sure you have all the supplies, food and water you'll need.

• The two places to buy food are Camper's Cove Restaurant (mile 30.1) and Green Springs Inn Restaurant (mile 34.1). You can find water at various campgrounds along the way as well.

EXTRACURRICULAR ACTIVITIES

You can fish along the way and drink beer in Ashland.

CAMPING AND LODGING ON ROUTE

Klum Landing Campground (mile 22.2, www.jacksoncountyparks.com, 541-774-8183, Dam Rd, tent site up to eight people $18) 30 sites. No reservations. Restrooms and showers. On the shore of Howard Prairie Lake, which has trout and bass fishing.

Asperkaha Campground (mile 23.6, www.jacksoncountyparks.com, 541-774-8183, Dam Rd, tent site up to eight people $12-16) First-come, first serve unless a group has booked the entire grounds. 12 sleeping cabins for rent. Showers and restrooms.

Willow Point County Campground (mile 24.8, www.jacksoncountyparks.com, 541-774-8183, Dam Rd, tent site up to eight people $16, reservation fee per site $8)

Crater Lake

Crater Lake

41 sites. Potable water. Vault toilets and fish cleaning station. On the shore of Howard Prairie Lake.

Hyatt Lake Campground (mile 31.5, www.blm.gov, per site $12-15) 54 sites. No reservations. Showers, restrooms, fish cleaning station. On Hyatt Lake.

If sites are full, the smaller Wild Cat Campground is around the corner.

Green Springs Inn (mile 34.1, www.greenspringsinn.com, 541-890-6435, 11470 Hwy 66 Ashland, lodge $79-109, cabin $195-245) They aim to be a "sustainable getaway" by using solar energy and local, sustainably-sourced lumber for their buildings.

Hyatt Lake Resort (www.hyattlakeresorts.com, 541-482-3331, 7900 & 7979 Hyatt Prairie Rd, cabins $129-169) Some of these styled-out cabins are located next to the restaurant at Camper Cove and some are just up the way. ALL have hot tubs.

Emigrant Lake Recreation Area (mile 47.5 , see Ashland lodging page 111)

Glenyen RV Park and Campground (mile 47.7, see Ashland lodging page 111)

Day Four

Mazama Village to Lake of the Woods Resort

0	•	From Mazama Campground, head to 'Hwy 62'
.3	↘	To 'Klamath Falls'
11.1	•	Wilson Cottages
16.4	•	Jo's Motel and Organic Deli • Fort Klamath
16.7	☞	Volcanic Legacy Scenic Byway, to 'Lake of the Woods'
	•	Crater Lake B&B
18.4	☞	Seven Mile Rd, to 'Lake of the Woods'
36.9	•	Rocky Point Resort
39.8	☞	Hwy 140
40.6	•	Solar Cafe
45.7	↘	Dead Indian Memorial Rd
47.2	☞	To Lake of the Woods Resort, Aspen Point Campground
47.7	•	Lake of the Woods Resort

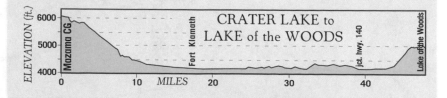

Crater Lake

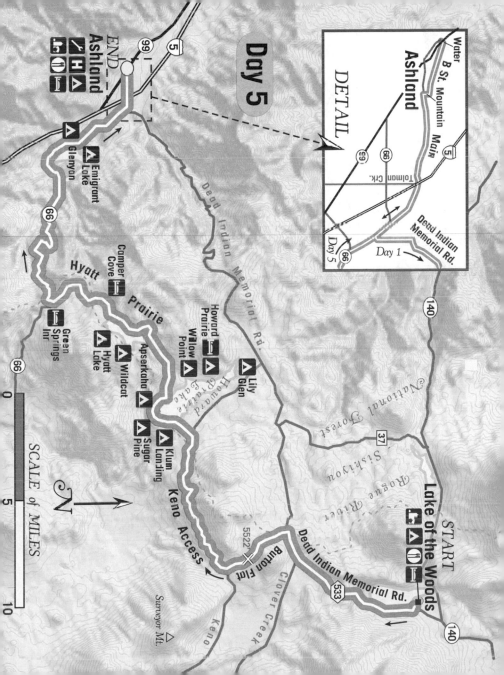

Day 5

DETAIL

Ashland

Water
B St.
Mountain
Main

Tolman Crk.

99
66
5

Dead Indian
Memorial Rd.

Day 1

Day 5

66

END
Ashland

99
5

Emigrant
Lake

Glenyon

66

Hyatt

Prairie

Camper
Cove

Green
Springs
Inn

Hyatt
Lake

Wildcat

Apserkaha

66

Sugar
Pine

Klum
Landing

Keno Access

Howard
Prairie

Willow
Point

Lily
Glen

Howard Prairie Lake

Dead Indian Memorial Rd.

National Forest

140

37

Siskiyou

Rogue River

Surveyor Mt.

5522'

Burton Flat

Clover Creek

Keno

Dead Indian Memorial Rd.

533

START
Lake of the Woods

140

SCALE of MILES

N

0   5   10

Day Five

Lake of the Woods Resort to Ashland

0	•	Leave Lake of the Woods and head south on Dead Indian Memorial Rd
1.4	•	Aspen Point Campground
8.5	↩	Barton Flat Rd
12.6	☞	Unsigned, paved Keno Access Rd
20.7	↩	At Howard Prairie/Hyatt Lake informational sign
22.2	•	Klum Landing Campground
22.9	•	Sugar Pine Campground
23.6	•	Asperkaha Campground
24.8	•	Willow Point Campground
25.5	☞	Hyatt Lake Rd, to 'Hyatt Lake'
30.1	•	Camper Cove and Hyatt Lake Resort
31.5	☞	To 'Green Springs Hwy'
	or ↩	Hyatt Lake Recreation Area
34.1	☞	Green Springs Hwy
	•	Green Springs Inn
47.5	•	Emigrant Lake Recreation Area
47.7	•	Glenyan RV Park and Campground
52.8	☞	Mountain Ave
52.9	↩	B St
53.7	↩	Water St (for one block)
53.8	•	Bluebird Park (E Main and Water St)

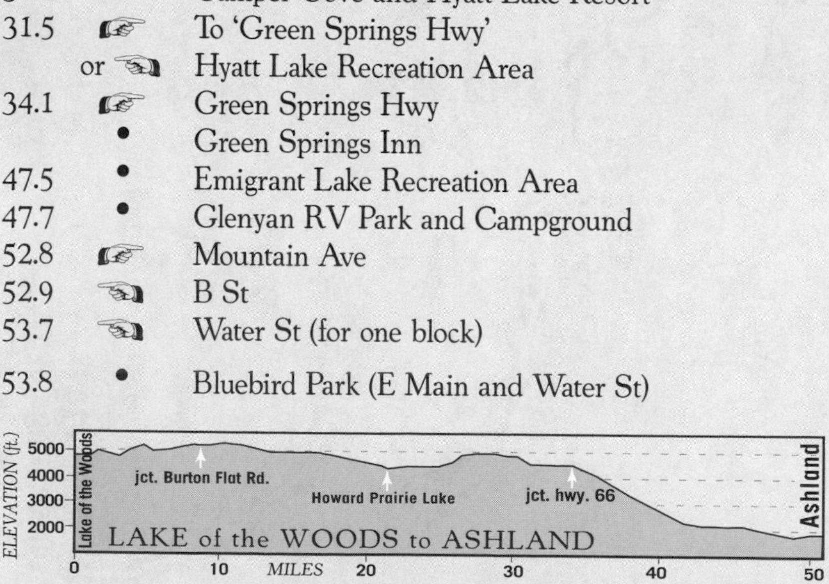

Crater Lake

ELEVATION (ft.) 5000 4000 3000 2000

Lake of the Woods

jct. Burton Flat Rd.

Howard Prairie Lake

jct. hwy. 66

Ashland

LAKE of the WOODS to ASHLAND

0   10   *MILES*   20   30   40   50

ᕫTHE TRUE WESTᕬ

Paleo Lands to the Strawberry Mountains

Seven days and six nights
Begin and end in Mitchell
271 miles total

THE SKINNY

PRICE POINT: You can do this with a small or medium purse. Camping at BLM campgrounds is free. Hotels are very reasonable. There is no tourist-motivated food mark up in the grocery stores. The hotels and B&Bs are comfortable but nothing approaching luxury options.

DIFFICUTLY RATING: 7.7 I planned some high-mileage days and some big climb days, but there are low-mileage days thrown in the mix. Services are far between in some areas, so being a more experienced rider (knowing the needs of your body and your bike) is suggested.

JAW-DROP FACTOR: 9 Insane, pinch-yourself gorgeous scenery.

STAND OUT CAMPING: Trout Farm Campground on the ride around the Strawberries (Day 3, page 154).

STAND OUT LODGING: River Bend Hotel (Day 2, page 145) earned points in this area for its decorative charm, large coffee maker, functional AC and comfortable bed.

AVERAGE TEMP IN FEBRUARY: Low 25, high 48 degrees
AVERAGE TEMP IN JULY: Low 50, high 88 degrees
* Cooler at high elevations

Fist Bump!

• **The Painted Hills** (Day 1, see page 142)
• Bike Shuttles that let you **raft the John Day River** (Day 2, see page 139)
• Microbrews at the **Outpost Pub** in John Day (Day 3 and 4, see page 153)
• Riding the **Forest Service roads around the Strawberry Mountains** (Day 4, see page 154)
• **Ritter Hot Springs** (Day 5, see page 158)
• John Day **Fossil Beds National Monument** (Day 3, page 149)
• **Thomas Condon Paleontology Center** (Day 3 and 7, page 150)
• **James Cant Ranch Museum** (Day 3 and 7, page 150)

Although Oregon tends to be famous for its Cascadian wilderness and idyllic coastline, the riding in Eastern Oregon is nothing short of spectacular. It would behoove you to pay this far-flung country some heed.

The True West

The sheer natural diversity and scintillating scenery on this particular tour will twist your spandies backward.

The voluptuously rounded and smooth Painted Hills (page 142) stand out like a princess amongst craggy desert surroundings and flaunt an ancient history in the cinnamon and rust striations. It's a worthy side trip. Later, empty roads twist through dramatic formations of John Day Fossil Beds National Monument where world-renowned rock outcroppings display millions of years of geologic history. Along the way, the Thomas Condon Paleontology Visitor Center (Day 3, page 150) sheds light on ancient epochs revealed by the surrounding stone and earth.

On the day ride around the Strawberry Mountains (Day 4, page 154), you take respite from the desert. The ride feels like cheating because Forest Service roads dart straight into the viscera of a snow-peaked, crisp, alpine wilderness; it doesn't take hiking for days to experience this backcountry. The ride to Long Creek (Day 5, page 157) brings you through both the wooded Malheur National Forest and high-country grazing plains where Tom Petty's "Into the Great Wide Open" seems to linger in the air from a far-away radio. The Ritter Hot Springs option is a decadent highlight.

On some days, the route ambles beside the roaring John Day River, flanked with desert buttes, and at other times it runs beside a forested stream.

On this tour, I fell into bed lusciously exhausted one night, switched off my cowboy-boot lamp, and went to sleep still savoring the day and the land I just barely washed out of my hair and clothes. Each day had its own little treats beyond just ogling brazen geologic formations and radical landscapes. I befriended motorcycle riders (who were genuinely interested in a bicycle's disc brakes), witnessed bovine love—groaningly and stampingly unrequited due to a road-forced separation—and appreciated a small-town cafe waitress who brought me toast because I was about to eat the napkin.

As much as some folks in this region want to promote tourism, there are no packaged experiences here yet. The winding and desolate roads provide world-class cycling for those who choose to journey into the heart of the true western landscape. But you'll have to snag your adventure. No one will hand it to you on a pretty china plate, and there is a rare glory in that.

HISTORY TIDBITS

John Day (1770-1820)—for whom the county seat, the main river and basin is named—was as manly, pompous and outdoorsy as they come. As a hunter, trapper and frontiersman, he gained fame as a member of the Astor Overland Expedition, the second major group of

HUGE DESERT LOVE

Do you know what it feels like to carry an extra gallon of water on tour? Although my friend Stephanie Edman weighs 120 pounds and carries a monstrous load on her touring bike, I've seen her bungee on an extra gallon of water for the good of the group on a long, waterless day. Even better, she makes geeky anatomy jokes about fascial planes, is a road runner up hills and sees the humor in aiming at a banana peel while peeing. She rides loaded double centuries for fun, cycle tours in the neurotic and unfriendly Pacific Northwest spring, and loves every shivering second of camping in the rain as long as there's a hot spring nearby. She's crazy...and as noble a bike tourist as I've ever met.

That's why I knew she understood Huge Love.

As Stephanie and I pedaled south through the Paleo Lands on a sparkling spring day, a gigantic gust of Huge Love swept through me. The blue heaven filled my brain and the bizarre desert landscape seemed to burst open inside of me. The rush of the John Day gargled in my ears,

and sage wafted through my nose. I wanted to know if she experienced Huge Love, too.

Later, she told me:

"Bicycle touring allows you to fully experience a place. You're able to see everything in more detail with every sense stimulated. When you breathe in, the beauty soaks into your bones then seeps out of your pores, so you feel more beautiful just for having been there. Touring inspires love and appreciation for the world in a way that leaves an indelible mark on your soul. I truly believe bike touring to be the very best way to see the world."

This Huge Love Stephanie and I are talking about isn't like a Jennifer Aniston-romantic-comedy love. Huge Love is a vastness way bigger than yourself, or even the desert. Huge Love turns your breath into a bright thing in your lungs, a liquid sunshine that reaches every last alveoli and saturates your heart. The expansiveness of the feeling inspires gratitude and generosity of spirit. The freedom in the emotion infuses helium to each pedal stroke. Huge Love consciousness makes you a better person because it stretches the potential of your understanding of all which is good in the world.

Huge Love, like a crazy lady on a bike dressed in ruffles tossing orchids from her handlebar basket onto the street, acts on whimsy. The feeling may hit you in a rainstorm or on a perfect day, arrive for a second or last for miles. Either way, Huge Love awaits you at the edge of the horizon.

The True West

Eastern Oregon from a Cyclist's Perspective

by Dan Little, Portlander and Forest Service Manager who lived in John Day for a decade.

It was 1983 and the first day of my first job with the Forest Service fire crew in Grant County. A sparky fire management officer barked at everyone to bring their "rigs" around to the back of the warehouse. To his complete confusion, I wheeled out an early-version mountain bike and asked him where to "park" it. Later that afternoon, lying in the park next to my bike studying the Oregon drivers' manual, a local police officer sauntered over for what I (naively) thought was a welcome but what ended up being an inquisition. "No, I do not have long hair—a beard, yes…"

Since then, my understanding of Grant County has deepened. Over the last couple centuries, much has been taken from this county, from the gold of the late 1800s to the timber of the 1970s. Mostly a skeleton of ranches is all that remains of more prosperous times. Yet, living there means everyone is your neighbor, from the mayor to the hospital nurse to the local ranch hand. Evening rush hour consists of a good portion of the town showing up at Chester's, the local grocery store, where you pick up supplies and catch up on the latest news and gossip.

The John Day Basin, nicknamed the "Valley of Sunshine," is a cyclist's paradise. Noise and traffic obstacles are largely absent, other than the occasional cattle drive (and associated droppings). While riding here, I've come the closest I ever have to meditating while cycling. Needless to say, some of my most soothing cycling memories and closest friendships came from the decade I spent in the John Day area.

explorers to rummage about the western frontier of North America after the Lewis and Clark Expedition.

John Jacob Astor, at the time the richest man in America and by some measures the fourth richest American of all time, financed the expedition, which had a razor-sharp purpose: to expand Astor's dominance of the fur trade on the Pacific Coast.

John Day's name is associated with this area because of the many colorful misadventures he experienced during the expedition, including an incident during which local Native Americans relieved him and his traveling partners of their clothing and supplies, forcing them to travel over 100 miles between the John Day and Umatilla Rivers without so much as a pair of shoes and eat only what they found along the way.

John Day eventually left the area that bears his name and headed east. The experience of his odyssey was his eventual undoing: mental instability caused by the harsh conditions lead to his early demise in Idaho in 1820.

ENVIRONMENT

The John Day Basin, where the majority of this ride takes place, reaches from the Elkhorn Mountains to the Greenhorn Mountains where the John Day River originates. Then it runs from the high desert where the Middle Fork of the river starts, to the Ochoco Mountains in the south, the source the South Fork of the John Day River.

Within the John Day Basin, the Paleo Lands expand from Antelope on the west to Dayville on the east. From north to south, they reach from Condon to Mitchell. The area's lakebeds and volcanic remnants open windows into the earth's ancient history by exposing extraordinary fossils and evidence of prehistoric mammals and dinosaurs.

Many parts of the John Day River system have attained National Wild and Scenic River and Oregon Scenic Waterway status. The lower section of the John Day River, from Tumwater Falls upstream to Service Creek, is frequently rafted.

The Strawberry Mountains give you a taste of a completely different landscape, with its forests and snow-capped mountains. Glacial ice carved these peaks and their seven alpine lakes out of earth and volcanic leftovers. The 1.7-million acre Malheur National Forest, which you ride through on Days 4 and 5, boasts pine and fir trees, as well as juniper and sage.

RIDING SEASON

The best times to ride the John Day Basin are in the spring and fall (June and September). I've ridden here in the summer, and it's alright as long as you play it smart. July and August are H-O-T. Winters are actually on the mild side for the lower elevation areas of the ride. People in the west of the state covet this area's sunshine. Locals tell me that the weather can be unpredictable any time of the year.

WEATHER

The Cascade Range and the Ochoco Mountains block the wet weather to the west, so the area has significantly more sun than the western part of the state. The temperatures in the John Day Basin are milder than the area on Day 3 (page 149), the ride around the Strawberries, which receives a fair amount of snow in the winter.

ARRIVING / LEAVING
Car

We took Hwy 26E to Mitchell all the way from Portland. The nice folks at the Oregon Hotel (page 142) in Mitchell let us park across the street for the duration of our tour. Christy Walder (541-932-4275), owner of the Bike Inn (page 152), can sort out a shuttle to bring you and your bikes back to your car if you plan a non-loop tour.

Bus
To / From Bend

A number of bus companies go to Bend including:

Central Oregon Breeze

(www.cobreeze.com, 541-389-7469, $5 bike charge) They have two buses per day to Bend leaving the Portland Amtrak Station at 1:30pm and 6pm, arriving at 6pm and 10:30pm. Bike boxes required. From Portland it's $50 one-way, $90 roundtrip.

Valley Retreiver/Porter Stage Lines

(www.kokkola-bus.com, 541-757-1797) The early bus to Bend from Corvallis goes through Salem. You can take your bike for free without boxing it. The later bus doesn't go through Salem, and you have to box your bike and pay $30 per bike. Who knows why.

Greyhound Bus (www.greyhound.com, 1-800-231-2222) You're required to use a bike box and the company will charge you between $15-50 to take your bike.

To / From Mitchell
Grant County People Mover

(www.grantcountypeoplemover.com, 541-575-2370, $11.75) runs from Bend to Mitchell at 4pm on Mon, Wed and Fri, arriving at 6:10pm. A couple bikes can fit in the larger bus *if* there are no wheelchair passengers. Reserve as far as you can in advance, and let them know you have bikes, so they can arrange for the proper vehicle. You still aren't guaranteed a spot if a wheelchair passenger decides to ride the bus. They suggest checking 24 hours in advance to get the best idea if you can get on board.

American Shuttle of Central Oregon (541-306-1845, $165, $10/person over two) is a private company that will take you from Mitchell to Bend. Advanced reservations are encouraged. They can fit four people with four bikes comfortably.

USEFUL WEBSITES
Wheeler County

www.wheelercounty-oregon.com

Grant County

www.gcoregonlive.com

LODGING

Lodging options are limited in scope, but basic, clean, quirky mom-and-pop hotels and a number of B&Bs sprinkle the tour route, with some chain hotels being in the city of John Day.

CAMPING

You could camp every night of this tour if you wanted. Word to the thrifty: BLM campsites are all free. Plus, you are technically allowed to camp on BLM land, which is much of the space along the John Day River.

FOOD AND DRINK

Culinary arts are not a high priority of this region. You'll mostly find the standard fare: bacon and eggs breakfast, fried food, traditional steak-and-potato-type choices. We were thrilled to when we found baked potatoes. Vegetarians can get by alright; vegans will find it harder. Gluten-frees, say a hail Mary or come prepared.

HYDRATION

As long as you plan well and bring extra water, you should be fine. But I suggest bringing a water filter or (more weight savvy) tablet purification in case of emergency. You'll be by water sources in lots of the sections without potable water.

RIDING TIPS AND HEADS UP

• Be prepared for potable water sources that are few and far between.
• This is cattle country. Be on the look out for cattle grates, especially if the roads are wet.
• Try not to roll your bike off the roads. Prickly goathead thorns will puncture your tube faster than you can say goathead.
• Don't forget the sunblock.

CELL COVERAGE

In most of the little towns on route, you can get cell service, as well as some places in between (but don't rely on it).

HOSPITALS
Blue Mountain Hospital
(www.bluemountainhospital.org, 541-575-1311, 170 Ford Road, John Day) 24/7 emergency care.
Pioneer Memorial Hospital
(www.scmc.org, 541- 447-6254, 1201 NE Elm St, Prineville) has a trauma unit. West of the route.

EXTRACURRICULAR ACTIVITIES

You can fish in the John Day Fossil Beds Monument and on public lands along the John Day River. Mah-Hah Outfitters (www.johndayriverfishing.com, 1-888-624-9424) is a local fishing outfit.

There's a bicycle-friendly, non-guided rafting outfit in Service Creek (Day 2, page 146) that rents you equipment, meets you at the put-in, and shuttles your bikes to the end of the rafting trip.

The route passes hiking trailheads such as in the Painted Hills (Day 1, page 142), John Day Fossil Beds National Monument

The True West

(Day 3 and 7, pages 149 & 162), and the Strawberry Mountain Wilderness (Day 4, page 154). Also, the **Paleo Lands Institute** (www.paleolands.org,541-763-4480, 333 W 4th St) out of Fossil leads guided hiking and nature education tours in the area.

MORE TOUR!

Connect to the **Cascade Classic** tour (page 77) or the **Grab your Bike by the Elkhorns** tour (page 197)

COST OPTIONS

Budget camping tour: Day 1, Mitchell City Park (page 142); Day 2, River Bend Motel (page 145); Day 3 and 4, Grant County Fairgrounds (page 153); Day 5, Hitching Post RV Park (page 158); Day 6, Lone Pine Campground (page 161).

High falootin' credit card camping: Day 1, Oregon Hotel (page 142); Day 2, Spray Riverfront Park (page 146); Day 3 and 4 Best Western John Day Inn, (page 153);

Day 5, Long Creek Lodge (page 158); Day 6, Monument Motel (page 161).

DAY ONE
Painted Hills Overlook out-and-back from Mitchell
22 miles
Elevation Climbed 2,780 ft.

Whether you are taking a car or public transportation to the start of the ride in Mitchell, the riding day will start late. If you want to throw your bags down and head out for a short day ride, the Painted Hills will not disappoint. It's mostly downhill on the way there. The last mile has a short climb to the overlook. It's worth it. Surrounded by desert buttes and a quaint emerge as a surreal geologic phenomenon with volcanic history appearing at its most artistic. The place has a ceremonious and almost sacred feel to it.

RIDING TIPS

• There are restrooms and picnic tables by the Painted Hills overlook.
• Bring your own food. It can get hot and there's not much cover, so bring plenty of water, too.

EXTRACURRICULAR ACTIVITIES

If you have time, lock or stash your bike at the overlook and take a walk. The **Painted Hills Overlook Trail** is a mile out-and-back or, for more sweeping views, the **trail to Carroll Rim** is three-miles out-and-back. You won't regret perusing these hills.

Mitchell
Pop. 155
Elevation 2,780 ft.

The tiny town of Mitchell used to have a pet bear in town that you could feed. The beast has retired to a local ranch, but folks still talk about him. Mitchell also displays a story-high rocking chair, but you aren't allowed to climb up into it. The town has character, and you'll see it reflected in itsy bitsy eateries and motels.

USEFUL WEBSITES
City of Mitchell
www.mitchelloregon.us

EVENTS OF NOTE
Painted Hills Festival—Labor Day weekend with lawnmower races, music

and more.
Tiger Town Music Festival—Music and food street festival showcasing the town's new theatre every June.

LODGING
Little Pine Cafe and Lodge
(www.littlepinecafe.com, 541-462-3532, 100 E Main St, $45-65) Three simple rooms over a little cafe with a shared bath and living room.
Oregon Hotel (541-462-3027, 104 Main St, $41-91) People here are super nice, cyclist-friendly and will let you park your car out front for the duration of your tour. It's one of those quirky, small hotels.
Painted Hills Vacation Rentals (www.paintedhillsvacation.com, 541-462-3921, SE Rosenbaum St, $80-140, cleaning fee $40-65) Run by a mother/daughter pair, this might be the nicest place in town, and definitely the most expensive. It has a two-day minimum. Located on a hill about a ¼ mile from town.
Sky Hook Motel (541-462-3569, 13101 Hwy 26, $55-65) Owned by the sweetie owners for decades.

CAMPING
Mitchell City Park (541-462-3121, free) No reservations) Has restrooms, shade, a hose and a new BBQ in the gazebo. Nice park.

CHOW DOWN
There is a limited grocery store in town

The True West

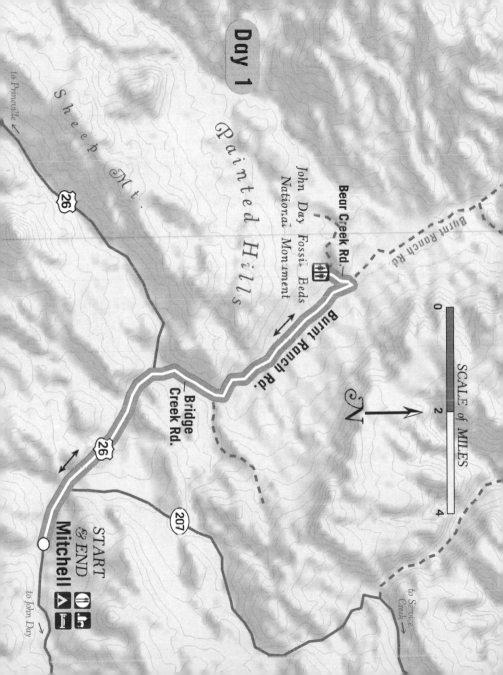

Day 1

Sheep Mt.

Painted Hills

to Prineville

26

26

John Day Fossil Beds National Monument

Bear Creek Rd.

Burnt Ranch Rd.

Burnt Ranch Rd.

Bridge Creek Rd.

207

START & END
Mitchell

to John Day

to Service Creek

N

SCALE of MILES

0   2   4

Day One
Painted Hills out-and-back from Mitchell

0	•	Start at Mitchell information center on 'Mitchell business loop' and head NW
.1		At stop sign, Hwy 26
3.8		To 'Painted Hills Unit' on Burnt Ranch Rd (watch for cattle grates)
9.4		To 'Painted Hills Unit' on Bear Creek Rd
9.7		To Painted Hills Overlook and trailheads
	or	To picnic area
10.8	•	Painted Hills Overlook (Return as you came)

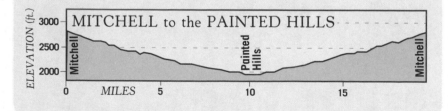

MITCHELL to the PAINTED HILLS

that is open 7am-7pm every day. The only place that does dinner in town is the **Little Pine Cafe** (www.littlepinecafe.com, 541-462-3532, 100 E Main St) and it's closed Sunday and Mondays. The two other place in town are the **Sidewalk Cafe** (541-462-3800, 204 W Main St, closes at 3pm), which might stay open for a big group if you call ahead, and the **Bridge Creek Cafe** (541-462-3434, 218 Hwy 26 W, 8am-2:30pm, closed Wed and Sat). All sport local flavor. You'll see the country kitchen influence and fried food on the menus.

DAY TWO
Mitchell to Spray
37 Miles
Total Elevation Climbed 4,360 ft.

"Touring. Legs. Legs, Touring. Work it out amongst yourselves."

This low-mileage ride is a nice introduction to your touring adventure. It cuts to the chase and launches you into the heart of what this country is all about: huge sky, Western farming enclaves straight out of a hotel painting, sage-infused wind, desolate canyons jutting up and crumbling at the same time, and the rushing John Day River hued with desert sediment.

A hill immediately initiates you into today's ride, with some moderately big ups and downs to follow until Service Creek (mile 24.3), where the road turns east to follow the John Day upstream on a very gentle climb into Spray. Along the way are

a number of basic campsites by the river with vault toilets but no water. You could always haul water from the mini-mart at Service Creek in order to camp at these primitive and free campsites.

When we pulled up to Spray to stay in the River Bend Motel, the rest of the rooms were booked by motorcyclists. They were super friendly and we jibed at each other all night, so it turned out to be a lovely experience. This town is itty-bitty with not a lot going on.

RIDING TIPS

• The general store and cafe at Service Creek (mile 24.3, www.servicecreekresort.com, 541-468-3331, 38686 Hwy 19, 7am-8pm, Sun 5pm close) provide the first potable water since the ride start. Plus, the ice cream you can buy there will lortily you until Spray.

EXTRACURRICULAR ACTIVITIES
Service Creek Stage Stop

(www.servicecreekresort.com, 541-468-3331, 38686 Hwy 19) will rent you rafting equipment *sans* guide if you want to incorporate some lollygagging on the John

Day into your adventure. They will meet you at the put-in (put-ins vary depending on the time of year) and bring your bike to you at the end!

Spray
Pop. 140
Elevation 1,772 ft.

EVENTS OF NOTE
Spray Rodeo and East Oregon Half Marathon (www.sprayrodeo.org) Memorial Day Weekend.

LODGING
River Bend Motel and River Bend Retreat (www.riverbend-motel.com, 541-468-2053, 708 Willow St, room $70, retreat house $100) *Sweet* lodging with cowboy-boot lamps, large coffee makers, water dispensers and comfortable beds. Showers are wonky. We loved it.

CAMPING
Spray Riverfront Park (Old Parish Creek Road, tent site $12) Follow signs off of Hwy 207. It's 0.8 miles from the turnoff from Main St.

LODGING AND CAMPING ON ROUTE
Service Creek Lodge (mile 24.3, www.servicecreekresort.com, 541-468-3331, 38686 Hwy 19, $85-95, per person over two $10) Used to be known as 'Tilly's Boarding House' in the stagecoach days of the 1920s. Includes breakfast.

River's Edge Bed and Breakfast (541-468-2470, 37948 Hwy 19, shared bath $75, private bath $85) Hearty full breakfast. Ginger Cromwell cooks gluten-free, vegetarian or meat bombs. One mile west of Service Creek (mile 24.3).

Big Sarvice Corral (541-468-3265, tent site for 2 people $10, sleep cabins $40) There are shady pine trees and a picnic shelter with refrigeration. 3.1 miles west of Service Creek on Hwy 19 (mile 24.3). There are numerous primitive camping spots—like **Donelly Park** (mile 24) and **Muleshoe Recreation Area** (mile 26.3)— along the river for about the last 14 miles before Spray, but they don't provide potable water.

Day 2

START Mitchell

26

3588'

3560'

Service Creek - Mitchell Hwy.

207

3163'

Brdy

John Day River

Shelton Wayside

SERVICE CREEK

Donelly Service

19

to Fossil

Muleshoe

John Day Hwy.

207

19

Spray END

KIMBERLY

19

207

to Heppner

SCALE of MILES

0   10   20

N

26

Day Two
Mitchell to Spray

0	•	Start at the Mitchell information center and head NW
.1	🖐	At stop sign, Hwy 26
.3	☞	To 'Spray,' Hwy 207
23.9	•	Donelly Service Creek River Access Park (WC)
24.3	☞	To 'Spray,' Hwy 207N
	or 🖐	.3 miles to Service Creek
26.3	•	Muleshoe Recreation Area (WC)
36.6	•	Spray • Lone Elk Market

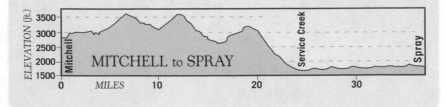

The True West

CHOW DOWN

On the main drag, you can eat at the **River Bend Bar and Grill** (802 Willow St) which is supposedly open till 8pm, but it was closed early when we got there. Next door is the **Lone Elk Market and Deli** (541-468-2443, 800 Willow St., deli 6am-7pm, store till 8pm, Sunday 6am-6pm), which is fully equipped with a wall-sized hunting scene photo. They prefer no cleats inside. The store has a touch more than bare necessities. The deli in the back is open at 6am for alpine-start breakfast.

DAY THREE
Spray to John Day
69 miles
Total Elevation Climbed 3,059 ft

Fascinating museums that *boom* show up the middle of nowhere and mesmerizing desert-scapes spice up this long, desolate day. Start the ride early if you want time to check out: the bizarre geologic formations in the John Day Fossil Beds National Monument, the small, well-done Cant Family Ranch Museum that gives you a glimpse into the local farm culture of pioneer days and the Thomas Condon Paleontology Visitor Center, which emerges in all its spiffy modernity in the middle of a barren canyon. You could spend quite a while there learning about dino-history. Once in Dayville, you could pay homage to (or overnight in) the local church that chooses to let cyclists hostel there for donations (see Eastern Oregon's Quirky Bicycling Hospitality, page 153).

After a bit of a climb at the beginning of the day, Hwy 19 climbs gently south to Dayville, but normally the wind is to your back, so it feels like a milder ride than the numbers indicate. The ride on Hwy 26 through Mt Vernon to John Day is less spectacular and more trafficked, but it's still a relatively gentle climb, and the wind tends to not be against you.

John Day is the largest town on the route and in Grant County. It's a sweet community in the heart of ranching country that is flanked with wilderness and is the gathering place for animal tracking conventions and white water enthusiasts. In town, there are tiny specks of amenities that city slickers are accustomed to: a little natural food store, places to grab a latte, a choice of where to drink a beer at night...but not much.

RIDING TIPS

• If you don't have enough time (or energy) today to spend at the sites, remember the tour passes this way again on the last day.
• Water filling can happen in Kimberly and at the museums along the way before you hit Dayville, but there's no food between Kimberly and Dayville.
• There are beautiful picnic spots off Hwy 19.

The True West

EXTRACURRICULAR ACTIVITIES

There are a number of interpretive hiking trails accessible from the route today in the John Day Fossil Beds. At the John Day Fossil Beds National Monument at mile 21.6, you can cycle up a hill to hit a picnic area, restrooms, drinking water and a trailhead. At mile 26.1, there are trails accessible (without a big climb) at the Blue Basin Area, which is equipped with a killer picnic site and restrooms, but no water.

Cant Family Ranch Museum (mile 29.2, 541-987-2333, Hwy 19, summer 9am-5pm, winter 10am-4pm) Set on the original Cant family homestead and sheep farm, these nicely executed indoor and outdoor exhibitions display the history of early pioneer settlement.

Thomas Condon Paleontology Visitor Center (mile 29.4, 541-987-2333, Hwy 19, summer 9am-5:30pm, winter 9am-4pm) "No region in the world shows a more complete sequence of Tertiary land populations, both plant and animal, than the John Day Basin."—Ralph W. Chaney, paleobotanist and UC Berkley Professor (1890-1971). Woot woot. The modern museum—that houses working paleontologists who you can watch cleaning fossils behind glass—has wonderful natural history and dinosaur exhibits and also showings of a 20-minute documentary.

Kam Wah Chung State Heritage Site (541-575-2800, NW 1st Ave, John Day, May 1- Oct 31, 9am-5pm) This museum commemorates the legacy of the Chinese workforce that played an important, and relatively unsung, part in the history of the John Day Basin. Guided tours on the hour till 4pm.

John Day
Pop. 1850
Elevation 3,200 ft

Useful Websites
City of John Day
www.cityofjohnday.com
Grant County
www.gcoregonlive.com

EVENTS OF NOTE
Grant County Fair
(www.grantcountyfairgrounds.com) Festivities every August
Sol West Renewable Energy Fair
(www.solwest.org) Treehuggers descend in July

LODGING
There other options than these in town, including chain hotels.
Dreamers Lodge Motel (www.dreamerslodge.com, 541-575-0526, 144 N Canyon Blvd, $55-85) They have a larger suite.
Little Pine Inn (541-575-2100, 250 E Main St, $45-75) A little worn down and fraying, but cheap.

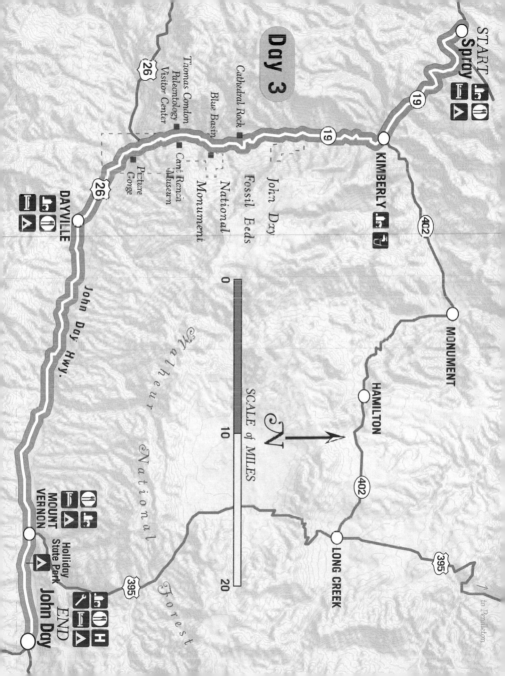

Day 3

START
Spray

19

KIMBERLY

26

Cathedral Rock

Blue Basin

Thomas Condon
Paleontology
Visitor Center

John Day
Fossil Beds
National
Monument

Cant Ranch
Museum

Picture
Gorge

26

DAYVILLE

402

MONUMENT

John Day Hwy.

HAMILTON

402

SCALE of MILES

0   10   20

N

LONG CREEK

395

MOUNT
VERNON

Holliday
State Park

END
John Day

395

to Pendleton

Day Three
Spray to John Day

0	•	From the Lone Elk Market head east
6.7	•	Shady Grove Recreation Site
12.8	•	Kimberly
21.6	•	John Day Fossil Beds National Monument
	or ☞	To WC, Trailheads, H2O
26.1	•	Blue Basin Recreation Area
29.2	•	Cant Family Ranch Museum
29.4	•	Thomas Condon Paleontology Visitor Center
31.4	☞	To 'Dayville,' Hwy 26E
38.1	•	Dayville
38.4	•	To get to Dayville Presbyterian Church, turn right on South Fork Rd
61.2	•	Mt. Vernon
62.5	•	Clyde Holiday State Park
69.4	•	John Day • the Outpost Pub & Grill

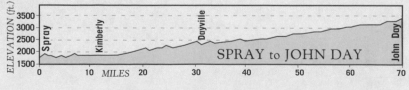

SPRAY to JOHN DAY

Sonshine Bed & Breakfast

(www.sonshinebedandbreakfast.com, 541-575-1827, 201 NW Canton St, $93-104) Quaint B&B right in town.

Best Western John Day Inn

(www.bestwestern.com, 541-575-1700, 315 W Main St, $117) It's the schwankiest place in town, though it's not that schwanky.

CAMPING
Grant County Fairgrounds

(www.grantcountyfairgrounds.com, 541-575-1900, tent site $10) Cop a squat with a Bud next to the RVs. Restrooms with showers. Close to town.

CHOW DOWN

The **Snaffle Bit** (541-575-2426, 830 John Day-Burns Hwy, Tues and Sat 4pm-close, Wed-Fri 11:30am-close), which is at mile 73 returning from the ride around the Strawberries, is supposed to have the best (and priciest) food in town. We enjoyed the nice folk and good breakfast at the **Squeeze-In Restaurant and Deck** (www.squeeze-in.com, 541-575-1045, 423 W. Main St., Mon-Sat 7am-8pm, Sun 7am-7pm). **Outpost Pub and Grill** (www.gooutpost.com, 541-575-0250, 201 W Main St, Mon-Sat 6am-9pm, Sun 6am-8pm) has more health conscious dinner choices, but I would go to the **Grubsteak** (541-575-1970, 149 E Main St, 9am-9pm) any day instead. The service is so much better there, the food is good and it's a genuine John Day experience. But I'd definitely go back to the Outpost for a

Eastern Oregon's Quirky Bicycling Hospitality

There are some very charming bike-friendly places along the tour. You could stay the night or just check them out.

Bike Inn (Day 5, mile 8.6, 541-932-4275, 615 North Mtn Blvd, Mt Vernon, $10-40 donation or work exchange) Christy Walder, owner at large, is a fabulous cycling fanatic. She has guest house (or camping) ever-ready for cyclists. It's equipped with a VHS player and kitchen. A 24 hrs-in-advance phone call is helpful or try dropping-in. The inn is 0.5 miles from Mt Vernon north on Hwy 395.

Dayville Presbyterian Church (Day 3, mile 38.4, just up South Fork Rd to the right, donation) The stained glass in the church portrays a cute little white church with a bicycle riding up to it. The doors are always open to cyclists who can sleep on the floor, cook or do laundry. The visitor journal has fun entries to peruse. On the cork board by the kitchen, there is a list of people to call to check in. So if the first isn't home, try the second, and so on. They ask for whatever donation you can give. Walking into this place warms your heart.

microbrew. In the summer, the **Saturday Farmer's Market** (johndayfarmersmarket@gmail.com, 541-932-2725, SW Brent St

across from The Outpost, June-Oct, 9am-12pm) is worth a meander.
Naturally Yours (541-575-1241, 135 W Main St) is a little natural food store on the main drag, but it has mostly supplements and dry goods. **Chester's Thriftway** (541-575-1899, 631 W Main, 7am-9pm) is a conventional grocery store.

DAY FOUR
Ride Around the Strawberries
74 miles
Elevation Climbed 4,460 ft.

Drop your panniers and take a break from the high desert today. Start by heading up and up into spectacular forests of alpine country on an unobtrusive grade. Humongous snow-capped mountains chaperone you for most of the day, making the air seem crisper and giving your ride more bravado.

County Rds 16 and 15 made me feel like a swindler. They cut through wilderness that you wouldn't normally be able to see without a backpack and long hike in. The long, gorgeous descent on the way back to John Day can be tempered with a head wind. On a sparkling spring day, this ride inspires pagan-like gratitude for the wonders that Mother Nature throws down.

While circumnavigating the Strawberry Mountains, water is available only at certain points unless you have a filter, so be prepared.

RIDING TIPS
• There is visitor information in the hardware store in Prairie City. They give out passable cycling maps, including one of this ride.
• There are spectacular campsites along the way, my favorite being Trout Farm Campground (mile 28.3), which is the first potable water you'll hit out of John Day.
• Bring all the food you will need for the entire ride. There are lovely picnic spots along the way.
• Taking a cinnamon roll from the Squeeze-In for a snack and ending the day with a brewsky at the Outpost worked well for me.

HEADS UP
There are cattle grates on this route. Be extra careful descending.

Day Four
Dayride around the Strawberries from John Day

0	•	From the Outpost Pub & Grill head east on Hwy 26
13.0	☞	Bridge St • Prairie City
13.5	☝	Past Depot Museum and Campground
28.3	•	Trout Farm Campground
30.1	•	Crescent Creek Campground
32.8	•	Highest point of ride - 5,898ft
36.4	☞	CR 16, to 'Hwy 395'
42.1	•	Big Creek Campground
43.7	•	Murray Campground
49.9	☞	CR 15
55.9	•	Wickiup Campground
63.6	☞	At T onto Hwy 395
71.7	•	Canyon City
73	•	Snaffle Bit Restaurant
73.7	☞	At stop light • John Day
73.8	•	Outpost Pub & Grill

JOHN DAY around the Strawberry Mountains

The True West

EXTRACURRICULAR ACTIVITIES

Grant County Historical Museum (mile 71.7, www.gchistoricalmuseum.com, 541-575-0362, 101 South Canyon City Blvd, May 1-Sept 30, Mon-Sat 9am-4:30pm, $4 admission) This museum addresses many of the historical elements that made Grant County what it is today: Native Americans, settlers, gold miners, timber industry, Chinese Immigrants, ranchers, etc. It has an original log cabin on display as well as a supplanted jail from Greenhorn, Oregon.

DAY FIVE

John Day to Long Creek
(or Ritter Hot Springs)
37 miles
Elevation Climbed 4,880 ft.

In the bathroom of the general store in Spray, Oregon, you will see a picture of eagles flying and the quote:

Climb high, Climb far
Your goal the sky
Your aim the star.

Might want to keep that one in mind today as there is lots of climbing—albeit spectacular climbing—through Malheur National Forest. When you leave the forest and hit a plateau, high-elevation prairies unroll for miles and miles until they reach the seam of a monolithic sky. The almost-ghost town, Fox, is a dot on the way, and then you reach Long Creek (pronounced Long Crick), where you

might meet the mayor at the only store in town. Long Creek has big plans to create showers and camping infrastructure for cyclists (says the mayor). But as of now, they just have a timeworn hotel and an RV park.

You climb a lot today (the first 25 miles are mostly climbing and there's a killer hill out of Fox) and reap only a bit of descent benefit. The real payoff is tomorrow on your way east to Kimberly. Long Creek has one mini-mart, one cafe with a limited menu, one church and one hotel. But after seeing no services all day, the town is like an oasis. Though Long Creek is small, it's scrappy. The nice folks there are enthusiastic about their town.

Schmoozing with the mayor and school superintendant of Long Creek

RIDING TIPS
• In between Mount Vernon and Long Creek there is no source of potable water and lots of climbing, so fill up and bring extra.

Long Creek
Pop. 220
Elevation 3,750 ft

USEFUL WEBSITES
City of Long Creek
www.cityoflongcreek.com

EVENTS OF NOTE
Long Creek 4th of July Celebration

LODGING
Long Creek Lodge (541-421-9212, 171 W Main, $59) This is the only place in town, so you have to love it. It has eight rooms, character and sweet people.

CAMPING
Hitching Post RV Park (541-421-9212, 507 N. Hwy 395, tent site $10) Bathrooms and showers. Go to the Long Creek Lodge to register for your tent site.

CHOW DOWN
Rumor has it that a new bonafide restaurant is opening in town! Until then, head to the **Mountain Inn Cafe and Grocery** (541-421-3141, 110 Main St, Mon-Sat 8am-6pm, Sun 9-4pm, hours depending on crowds), which has a little cafe and basic groceries. Otherwise, BYO from Mt. Vernon or John Day.

—Cycling Hedonist Alert—
If you have the energy to go 20 more miles today, and are a hedonist like me, you could stay at **Ritter Hot Springs** (www.ritterhotsprings.com, 541-421-3846, pool $3, mineral bath $3, both $5). It's a relic from the stagecoach days when Ritter was an overnight spot between Pendleton and John Day for settlers and cowboys. Because of the rusted-out-farm-equipment vibe (which is charming to some), this place is under the tourist radar and cheap. Yay.

The grounds have a 120 year-old basic **hotel**—that used to be rocking during its heyday—and **camping** (cabin $81, hotel room $30-36, camping for two $11). Or make Ritter Hot Springs a day ride from Long Creek. They have a huge warm (85 degree) pool heated by hot springs and four individual soaking tubs with steamy hot spring water. How awesome is that? The devout hot springs pool adheres to the Seventh Day Adventist Sabbath, so it closes from sundown on Friday to sundown Saturday. BYO food.

The first half of the ride to Ritter Hot Springs from Long Creek is rolling hills and the last seven miles loses elevation. Just remember that the return to the route will work you good. Totally worth it to this hedonist.

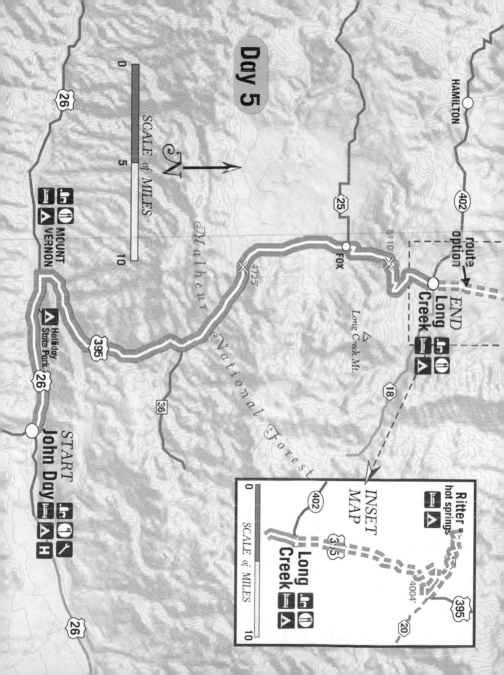

Day 5

SCALE of MILES

0 — 5 — 10

N

26

MOUNT VERNON

395

Holliday State Park

26

36

START
John Day

26

Malheur

National Forest

4725

FOX

5110'

25

△ Long Creek Mt.

END
Long Creek

18

402

HAMILTON

route option

INSET MAP

Ritter hot springs

402

395

Long Creek

4004'

395

20

SCALE of MILES

0 — 10

Day Five
John Day to Long Creek (or Ritter Hot Springs)

0	•	From The Outpost Pub head east on Hwy 26
6.8	•	Clyde Holliday State Park
8.1	☞	To 'Long Creek' on Hwy 395 N • Mount Vernon
8.6	•	The Bike Inn
30.0	•	Fox (no services)
34.3	•	Carter Park Rest Area
37.0	•	Long Creek
	•	Mountain Inn Cafe
or ☝		Continue up Hwy 395N to the turn off to Ritter Hot Springs

The True West

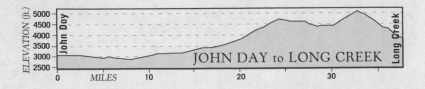

DAY SIX
Long Creek to Kimberly
33 miles
Elevation Climbed 1,820 ft.

You worked hard to make it to Long Creek. Now you face some climbing for almost four miles out of town then some flats and more climbing until around mile nine. The straight-up descent kicks in around mile 12, a killer downhill where you experience the endorphin-rush of your hard work climbing, the energy boost from the sublime and dramatic landscape, and the smooth, swoopy road. Think religious experience at velocity.

The terrain today is fickle. Does it want to be forested hills, desert crags, a lush river valley, an exhibition of outlandish geological formations or wide-open ranch country? It ends up taking all these elements and swirling them together for a generous cocktail of natural beauty.

Around mile 21, the route starts to flatten as you leave Monument (mile 21.2) to follow the John Day River to Kimberly. This is my favorite section along the John Day. The desolation and the outrageous scenery, staring the John Day River, make your soul feel sun-bleached and crusted over with earthy-smelling river sediment. That's a good thing.

The route is Long Creek to Kimberly, but today's ride ends at a campsite called Lone Pine Campground that is 1.7 miles northeast of Kimberly on Hwy 402 right on the John Day. If you want to stay in a hotel, there's one in Monument (mile 21.2). Kimberly is scarcely more than an intersection and a mini-mart by the John Day River.

RIDING TIPS
• This day is short enough to allow for some major hangout time by the river.
• If you wanted come from Ritter Hot Springs today, the ride would be a doable 50 miles.
• There is water and food in Monument and at the store in Kimberly.

LODGING ON ROUTE
Monument Motel and RV Park (mile 21.2, mmrv402@centurytel.net, 541-934-2242, 780 Hwy 402, with kitchenette $65, room $55, tent site $10) is on the route today. No wifi. Smoking allowed right outside of rooms.

Kimberly
Pop. 36
Elevation 4,336 ft.

CAMPING
Big Bend Campground (Mile 32, 541-416-6700, BLM, Prineville District, free) This primitive campsite is not as cool as Lone Pine and about a mile farther north of Kimberly on Hwy 402.

Lone Pine Campground (541-416-6700, BLM, Prineville District, free) This primitive campground right before Kimberly is first-come-first-serve and its five sites are usually available, except maybe on holidays. It's in a gorgeous location by the river. No water. Vault toilets. Kimberly's mini-mart is 1.7 miles down Hwy 402.

CHOW DOWN

Stock up on food supplies in Monument at the **Boyer Store** (mile 21.2, 541-934-2290, 778 Old Highway Rd, Mon-Sat 8am-6pm, Sun 10am-4pm). It has longer hours and will have more options. The **Kimberly mini-mart** (Jct Hwy 19 and Hwy 402, Mon, Thurs, Fri 8:30am-4:30pm, Tues, Wed, Sat till 2:30pm, closed Sun) has your basic mini-mart fare and has a drink machine outside—with water—if you are in desperate straits outside of its finicky hours. They don't take credit cards or checks.

DAY SEVEN
Kimberly to Mitchell
51 miles
Elevation Climbed 2,670 ft

You've already gone down through the Fossil Beds once. Twist your arm to *again* ride past the uncanny geologic formations on swiveling, untrafficked pavement through the glorious Eastern Oregon desert. When conjuring this route, I had the choice of bringing you on Hwy 19 through the Fossil Beds twice or leaving it out entirely. I opted for the Hwy 19 double-take because it didn't feel right to cut out a fabulous road sprinkled with pioneer history, paleo-education and geologic allure. Plus, the wind is usually at your back going south—making the gentle climbing unnoticeable at times—so it can be a lovely jaunt. Hwy 26 to Mitchell has a magical slot-canyon feel (see 'Heads Up'

below) and then eventually gives way to the gargantuan Western sky again.

Speaking of climbing, it lasts for most of the ride, but then you cruise, cruise, cruise into Mitchell and end the tour with a bang.

RIDING TIPS
• If you didn't get to see the Museum or Paleontology Center on the third day (page 150) and there's a streak of history buff in you, make time to see them today.
• Stock up on water at the Cant Museum or Paleontology Visitor Center because there are no on-route hydration opportunities until Mitchell.

HEADS UP
From the right turn on Hwy 26 (mile 20.1), the route—while splendid—has no shoulder for bits and pieces. And while there tends to be less traffic, the locals can exceed the speed limit at times. Be very careful.

Day Six
Long Creek to Kimberly

0	•	From the Mountain Inn Cafe head east to 'Kimberly'
21.2	•	Take a right on John Day St to hit the Boyer Store
	•	Monument
32	•	Big Bend Park
33.2	•	Lone Pine Park

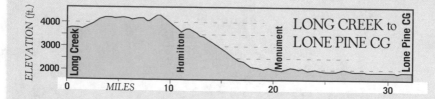

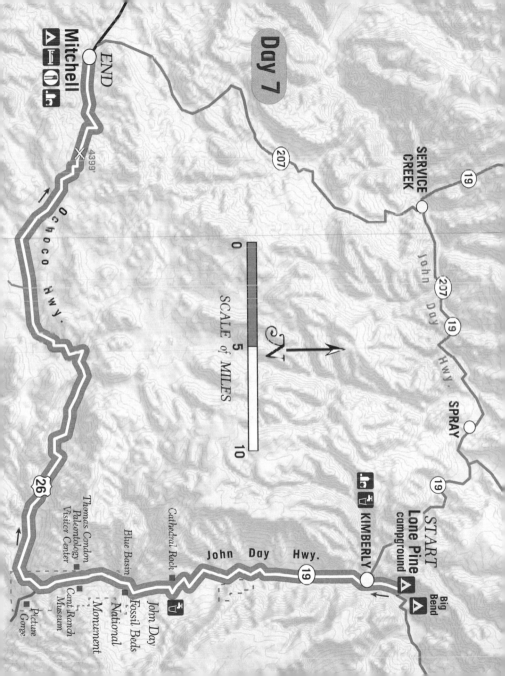

Day 7

SERVICE CREEK

Mitchell
END
4399'
Ochoco Hwy.

John Day Hwy.

SPRAY

START
Lone Pine
campground
Big Bend

KIMBERLY

John Day Hwy.

Thomas Condon
Paleontology
Visitor Center

Blue Basin

Cathedral Rock

John Day
Fossil Beds
National
Monument

Cant Ranch
Museum

Picture
Gorge

0

SCALE of MILES

5

10

N

Day Seven
Kimberly to Mitchell

0	•	From Lone Pine Park head east to Kimberly
1.7	👉	Hwy 19S • Kimberly
10.4	•	Turnoff to 'John Day Fossil Beds National Monument'
15	•	Blue Basin Recreation Area
18	•	Cant Family Ranch Museum
18.2	•	Thomas Condon Paleontology Visitor Center
20.1	👉	To 'Mitchell,' Hwy 26W (Caution! No shoulder)
30.3	•	The Shoe Tree
50.9	👉	Onto Mitchell Business Loop
51.2	•	Mitchell Information Center • Mitchell

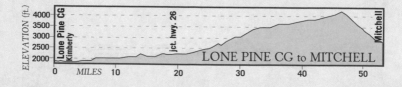

LONE PINE CG to MITCHELL

⌒HELLS CANYON, HELLS YES⌒

Four days and three nights
Begin and end in Baker City
261.7 miles total

THE SKINNY

PRICE POINT: You can do this tour with a **small to medium purse**; camping and groceries are available each day. Joseph is the only stop that has higher tourist priced (but also higher quality) lodging and food. The other stops have reasonably priced accommodations and budget food options.

DIFFICULTY RATING: 8.9 Days 2 and 4 make this score high. Halfway to Joseph on Day 2 is over 70 miles, and half of that distance is spent climbing two huge passes. On Day 4, the ride from Elgin to Baker City definitely has some climbing, but it's the fact that the day is 84 miles long presents the challenge.

JAW-DROP FACTOR: 8.7 Forest Road 39 on Day 2 (page 176) and the Medical Springs Hwy on Day 4 (page 185) will blow your mind. Adding in the out-and-back option from Copperfield (page 180) hikes the score to 9.

STAND OUT CAMPING: Camping off FR 39 (Day 2, page 176) is remote and scenic.
STAND OUT LODGING: Pine Valley Lodge (Day 1, page 175) won me over with comfy rooms, interesting antique decorations and

a general cyclist-friendly attitude.
AVERAGE TEMP IN JULY: Low 48, high 90 degrees
AVERAGE TEMP IN FEBRUARY: Low 18, high 40 degrees
*colder at high elevations

Fist Bump!
- Hitting the big town (well, comparatively) of **Baker City** (Day 1, page 174)
- Descending into **Halfway** (Day 1, page 174)
- **Forest Road 39** (Day 2, page 176) through Wallowa-Whitman National Forest and Eagle Cap Wilderness
- The art, food and brew in **Joseph** (Day 2, page 172)
- Bucolic back roads to **Enterprise** (Day 3, page 182)
- Picnic at **Catherine Creek State Park** (Day 4, page 186)
- **Medical Springs Hwy** (Day 4, page 185)
- The **people of small town Eastern Oregon** (All days)

Way out in the farthest reaches of Oregon's northeastern corner, Hells Canyon remains overlooked by most tourists. I just discovered it myself seven years ago. When

Hells Canyon

I did, I wondered why no one had ever told me about the overwhelming beauty of this canyon, which is even deeper than the Grand Canyon. The hugeness of the craggy walls and gushing river—along with a remoteness that makes solitude lonely—will melt away nit-picky thoughts and the daily worries in the fringes of your mind. There is no room for such trifles while trying to comprehend such a vast phenomenon of geology and nature.

The tour's route follows much of the Hell's Canyon Scenic Byway, which leads you through the rural, Eastern Oregon cattle country, Wallowa-Whitman National Forest, Eagle Cap Wilderness, high-desert landscapes and tiny towns. The loop of the tour circumnavigates the Wallowa Mountains, which do not skimp on dramatic, snowy-peak displays.

The natural beauty of this area is a heavy-weight champion, but another contender for me was chatting with locals about invasive Californians, small-town

Cooking up a Cycling Tour in Wallowa County

by Troy Nave, cycling enthusiast from Enterprise

I approach cycling adventure like I approach cooking: begin with an inspiration, combine a little structure with the freedom to adlib, keep it fun and make the experience memorable. Cycling in Wallowa County is like preparing a meal with an international food market and top-notch kitchen at your disposal. All the finest ingredients for the discerning palate can be found here. Here's a menu, complete with ingredients, for a unique Wallowa County cycling experience. Season to taste.

Appetizers: **Diverse and Breathtaking Landscapes**
Ingredients: Mile-high basalt cliffs that plunge into Hells Canyon's Snake River; deep blue waters of the glacially-carved

Hells Canyon

Wallowa Lake; granite peaks and forested slopes of the Wallowa Mountains; and vast and vibrant Zumwalt Prairie. You may see elk, cougar, raptors, deer and wolves along the way.

Drinks: **Craft Brews, Wine and Booze**
Ingredients: Two local brewpubs create malty goodness in the Pacific Northwest craft brew tradition: bold and liberally hopped. And there are locally produced wines and a distillery that's open for tasting.

Main Course: **Abundant Cycling Options for All Levels**
Ingredients: Winding mountain roads that pair challenging ascents with stunning scenery; easy valley cruising through lush pastureland; single-track trails through the Wallowa Mountains; a 3,500-foot-vertical ascent via gondola, followed by some disc-melting downhill.

Side Dishes: **Slow Food and Accommodations**
Ingredients: Local grass-fed beef, bison meat and fresh produce; a local chocolatier; twice-a-week farmers market. Numerous high-quality B&Bs, motels and campgrounds.

Dessert: **Culture**
Ingredients: A thriving art scene includes several galleries, pottery studios and bronze foundries. History and info about the Nez Perce Indians and their continuing history in Wallowa County at spots along the way.

politics and favorite camping spots. Due to local hospitality, I shot a gun for the first time. It was loud, and I missed the Gatorade bottle.

Even though my most recent tour in Hells Canyon was during a rainy/snowy/soggy spell in October, I am unwavering and partial in my love for this area. I always learn something from the wilderness, empty and butt-kicking roads, austere desert and people who call this wild place home.

HISTORY TIDBITS

I'll use this section to tell a very important, though not joyous, story of this region.

Prior to the arrival of settlers, the Hells Canyon region was home to the Nez Perce Indians. Until 1860, when gold was discovered on their land, the tribe was notably friendly to newcomers. But the settlers' greed for the tribe's land led to a deteriorating state of relations, and war finally broke out in 1877.

In 1855 the Nez Perce had signed a treaty with the United States that granted them a very large reservation that spread across parts of Idaho, Oregon and Washington. After gold was discovered, the government, under pressure from local officials in Oregon and gold prospectors, cut a deal with one faction of the tribe to sell 90% of the reservation, including the area where gold had been discovered, back to the U.S. for about 8 cents an acre. Other groups within the tribe did not agree to this sale; they wanted to keep

Hells Canyon

their ancestral lands. Tensions increased, and violent acts were carried out by both the government and the tribes.

In 1877, the issue came to a head and fighting ensued between a group of Nez Perce led by Chief Joseph and the U.S. government. Knowing his tribe could not endure a long struggle, Chief Joseph led his 200 warriors and 800 non-combatants on a 1,400-mile retreat through Idaho and Montana on the way to the Canadian border while being pursued by more than 1,500 American soldiers. They fought the whole way. This running battle is considered one of the most brilliant fighting retreats in American history.

In the end, the Nez Perce were caught just 40 miles from the border. After a final losing battle, Chief Joseph surrendered. Although the government promised the Nez Perce they could return to their homes, the Chief and his tribe were shipped to a reservation in Oklahoma. Chief Joseph campaigned vigorously for fairness and justice for his people, and they were finally permitted to return to their reservation in 1885. Chief Joseph returned to the Pacific Northwest, but was never allowed to return home with his people, a punishment which was rationalized as protecting "safety." He died on another reservation in Washington in 1904. The town of Joseph, Oregon is named in his honor.

ENVIRONMENT

On the route, you'll observe steep canyon walls, large sandbars next to the Snake River, humongous mountain peaks in the distance, rolling high-desert and thick forest. Hells Canyon itself is the result of huge plates of land smashing into each other millions of years ago and the Snake River powerfully carving the rock. Both Wallowa Lake and the Wallowa Mountains were created by nine mondo glaciers during the last two million years.

As for creatures you might see along the way, keep an eye out for: pika, cougars, badgers, beavers, otters, bobcats, bears, elk, deer, mountain goats and bighorn sheep. The rare wolverine and grey wolf have been spotted on occasion in these parts during the last decade. In the sky, you might see Peregrine falcons, bald eagles, golden eagles, hawks, finches, partridges, woodpeckers or owls.

Logging and cattle grazing have seriously encroached on the forest vegetation, but significant amounts of old-growth forest have survived. Tree species in the Wallowa-Whitman Forest range from high-elevation subalpine fir and lodgepole pine to low-elevation ponderosa pine. Other coniferous tree species include western larch, spruce and Douglas fir. Deciduous tree species you might see include aspen and cottonwood. Wildflowers—including Indian paintbrush, sego lily, larkspur and bluebell—grace the area.

Hells Canyon

RIDING SEASON

Since Forest Road 39 isn't open until sometime in June, late June through September would be the best time to tour, with the premium periods being late June, late August and September when the rides to and from Baker City aren't as scalding. I went in October, and the weather got nasty, but I'm sure beautiful weather occurs during some early Octobers. Crowds aren't usually a problem, though I would book in advance around holidays, rodeos and festivals. As the summer season starts to close, expect businesses to have shorter hours.

WEATHER

Lots of this route explores higher-elevation areas, and weather in the mountains can be volatile—though for the most part, summer days are lovely, and possibly hot. Be prepared for all weather. Nights get chilly. In the lower areas like Baker City and the surrounding exposed desert, summer days can fry your tuckus.

ARRIVING AND LEAVING

See the Elkhorns tour (page 195).

USEFUL WEBSITES

Hells Canyon Scenic Byway
www.hellscanyonbyway.com
Wallowa County Chamber of Commerce
www.wallowacountychamber.com
Eastern Oregon Visitors Association
www.visiteasternoregon.com
Hells Canyon Chamber of Commerce
www.hellscanyonchamber.com

LODGING

On every night of this tour, lodging is available, but in general, lodging is sparse in this remote area. On summer weekends, I would suggest booking in advance because the limited lodging can fill up, especially around events, rodeos and holidays.

CAMPING

You can camp every day of the tour. Forest Rd 39 on Day 2 especially has tons of camping opportunities, from impromptu camping on Forest Service land to developed campgrounds. Also, in Baker City and little towns throughout the tour (including Halfway and Elgin), RV parks accommodate tent camping.

FOOD AND DRINK

The best food of the tour will be found in Joseph; among other options, it has a brewery and pub fully stocked with micro-brews, a chocolatier and the upscale restaurant Calderas (page 180). Baker City has the most restaurants, including two breweries (hallelujah, Oregon!). Enterprise (Day 3, page 182) has the famous Terminal Gravity Brewing. I guess if you like breweries, this is a good tour for you. Other than that, you'll find simple, inexpensive American food in small town restaurants. In the fall, expect restaurant opening hours to be shorter.

HYDRATION

All days but Day 2 (when you are in the woods and beside water for much of the day) you navigate through high-desert. That means exposed riding with high temperatures in the summer. Day 3 has a fair share of refill places...Day 1 and 4, not as much. If you aren't using a water filter, bring some emergency purification tablets. And, as always, bring more water than you need.

MAPS

The **Benchmark Oregon Atlas** (www.benchmarkmaps.com, 541-772-6965, atlas $22.95) shows this route. For a more detailed map, get the Wallowa-Whitman National Forest Map (541-426-5546, PO Box 905, Joseph, OR 97846, $9), which can be purchased over the phone or via the mail (wow). Or buy it online from Discover Your Northwest (www.discovernw.org).

HEADS UP

There is a chance that you might encounter cattle being herded on the Forest Road 39 (Day 2, page 176). See Moo-ve Over (page 219).

CELL COVERAGE

There is cell reception in towns. In between towns, it is much spottier.

HOSPITALS

Halfway, Joseph and Elgin have small medical clinics.

Saint Alphonsus Medical Center

(www.stelizabethhealth.com, 541-523-6461, 3325 Pocahontas Rd, Baker City) 24/7 emergency care.

Wallowa County Health Care District

(www.wchcd.org, 541-426-3111, 601 Medical Parkway, Enterprise) 24/7 emergency care.

EXTRACURRICULAR ACTIVITIES

On the first day, you cruise by the **Oregon Trail Interpretive Center** (mile 7.3, page 175) which has some pretty cool history exhibits. Other stops you might consider are the Elgin Opera House (page 182) or

Hells Canyon

the Union County Museum (page 186). Of course, there are hiking and fishing opportunities in the beautiful rivers and natural areas along the way.

MORE TOUR!

The **Elkhorn Scenic Byway** tour (page 191) also begins in Baker City, and it would be a beautiful and easy 44 miles to connect Sumpter (Day 1 of the Elkhorn tour) to Prairie City, Day 3 of the **True West** tour (page 149), using Hwy 7 then Hwy 26. Now *that* would be one spectacular sampling of Eastern Oregon.

COST OPTIONS

Budget camping tour: Make it to FR 39 on Day 1 instead of riding through on Day 2, and there are free, primitive places to camp on Forest Service land within the first 10 miles of that road; Day 2, Wallowa Lake State Park (page 180); Day 3 Hu-Na-Ha RV Park (page 185); Day 4 Oregon Trails West RV Park (page 199). There are grocery stores in each of the small towns along the way.

High falootin' credit card camping: Day 1, Pine Valley Lodge (page 175); Day 2, Bronze Antler B&B (page 180); Day 3, Stampede Inn (page 182). There are restaurants in all the towns at the end of each day, the tastiest being Mutiny Brewing and Calderas in Joseph (page 180).

TOWN COVERAGE OF BAKER CITY

See the Grab Your Bike by the Elkhorns tour (page 198).

DAY ONE
Baker City to Halfway
53.3 miles
Elevation Climbed 3,270 ft.

Not long after leaving civilization in Baker City, you pedal on a lonely strip of road cutting farther and farther into the vast rolling plains of the Oregon high-desert. Bald and jagged mountain ranges jut into the horizon as you navigate the curvaceous butter- and wheat-colored rollers that drape the valley floor surrounding the squiggly Powder River.

Until you arrive in Richland, the route is gently rollie pollie. The big up-and-over is between Richland and Halfway. It's a long, sustained climb with some steeper sections, and as you climb, the mountain and

Hells Canyon

valley vistas expand to provide a euphoric distraction from the burn of the ascent.

Cruising down to Halfway is like a desert-themed amusement park ride and an excellent way to end the day. Halfway is a tiny town that's part cute, part rugged, part hillbilly, but 100% friendly. I thoroughly enjoyed my stay.

RIDING TIPS
• The farm equipment graveyard on the way out of town is awesome (mile 3.3).
• There are no services till Richland (mile 40.9), so keep your water and food coffers stocked. Richland has several little eateries where you can fuel up before climbing the pass.
• If rain dumps on you (like it did on Pete and me), dry your clothes at the Laundromat at Eagle Valley RV Park (mile 41.2).

EXTRACURRICULAR ACTIVIES
If you get an early enough start, you can check out the **Oregon Trail Interpretive Center** (mile 7.3, 541-523-1843, 22267 Hwy 86, 9am-6pm, $8) that has multi-media history and geology exhibits, plus four miles of interpretive trails.

Halfway
Pop. 337
Elevation 2,660 ft.

USEFUL WEBSITES
Halfway's website
www.halfwayoregon.com

Road updates on FR 39
www.fs.usda.gov/wallowa-whitman, click "Current Conditions" tab.

EVENTS OF NOTE
Halfway Rodeo
(www.halfwayfairandrodeo.com, Labor Day weekend) Yee-haw good time.

LODGING AND CAMPING
Halfway Motel and RV Park (541-742-5722, 170 South Main St, room $55-75, tent site $10) This lodge is good for the budget. You can pitch tent in the RV Park, which has bathroom and shower facilities.

Pine Valley Lodge (www.pvlodge.com, 541-742-2027, 163 Main St, $110-150) Loved our stay here! We stayed in the "shack," which is a refurbished mining shack and the oldest building in Halfway. The kitsch is more interesting and antiqueish than cheesy. The included breakfast has healthy and high-calorie options. It's a cyclist-friendly establishment.

CHOW DOWN

There are two grocery stores in town right across from each other, and between the two of them, open hours are between 7am-8pm. They are slightly larger than mini-marts with the same (poor) quality produce.

Both **Wild Bill's** (541-742-5833, 105 S Main St, 7am-8pm, bar till close) and **Stockman's Restaurant and Lounge** (541-742-2301, 146 North Main St, breakfast, lunch and dinner, hours vary) have your standard hamburger/pasta/pizza type food that is very budget friendly. Both **Levi's Cafe** (241 Main St), which is said to have the best grub in town, and **Stephanie's Bakery** (541-742-7437, Main & Record St, Tues-Sat 7:30am-2:30pm) were just about to open when we were in town.

DAY TWO
Halfway to Joseph
71.4 miles
Elevation Climbed 7,340 ft.

Funny story: I ended up shooting at empty plastic bottles with a rifle at the Hells Canyon Overlook instead of cycling FR 39 (first time ever to shoot a gun!). It's a long story, but in short, when my friend Pete and I were riding this tour, we hit Day 2 at the same time as the first snow of the year. To avoid slippery, snowy roads, we had to hitch a ride over the passes with a local named Jeff who owned a truck

that "wanted to be a semi," i.e. I had to practically rock climb to the cab.

That impromptu day was fun, and I broadened my country music horizons, but alas, it was very sad as well. FR 39 defines epic in the world of cycle touring. This thin ribbon of pavement weaves through the wild and remote reaches of the Hells Canyon Recreation area and Eagle Cap Wilderness. You witness both the monolithic chasm of Hells Canyon still being carved by the Snake River and the Wallowa Mountain range with its jagged cluster of peaks crowding over 10,000 ft into the sky. Adding to the epicness is the fact that half of today's 71.4 miles is spent climbing two giant passes. And I missed riding it.

This lonely corner of Oregon will rock you with its pristine beauty. Pete and I have unfinished business there. We will return. Oh, yes.

RIDING TIPS

• There are no services today. Bring everything you need, food- and water-wise, and some extra. You are beside Pine Creek and cross the Imnaha River during the first half of the ride, so there are water sources, plus potable water at Ollokot Campground (around mile 33.1).

• Around mile 29.4, there's a turnoff to a scenic canyon overlook that is pretty spectacular. You ride a little section of gravel road to get there.

• Please don't underestimate the volatility and severity of mountain weather.

Hells Canyon

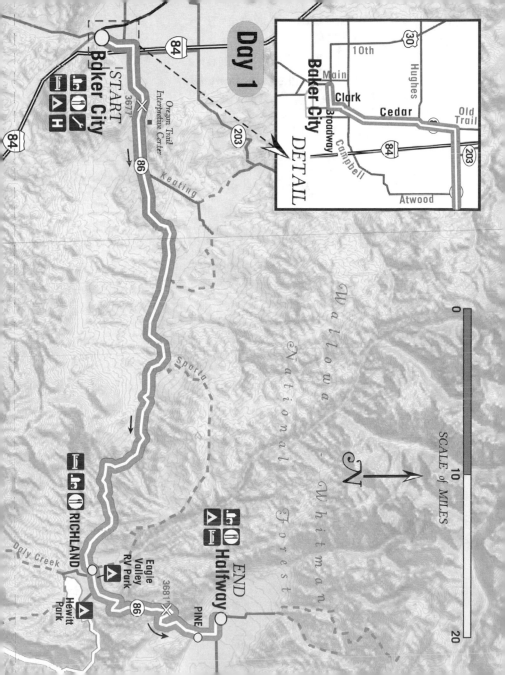

Day 1

DETAIL

Baker City

10th
Main
Clark
Cedar
Broadway
Campbell
Hughes
Old Trail
Atwood

30
84
203

START
Baker City

Oregon Trail
Interpretive Center

3677

Keating

84
84
86
203

Sparta

RICHLAND

Daly Creek

Hewitt
Park

Eagle
Valley
RV Park

86

3681

PINE

END
Halfway

Wallowa - National - Whitman - Forest

N

SCALE of MILES
0
10
20

Day One
Baker City to Halfway

0	•	From Bella Main St Market, head south on Main St
.1	☞ / ☜	Church St / Resort St
.2	☞	Madison St
.5	☜	Clark St (turns into Hwy 86)
3.3	•	Farm equipment graveyard
7.3	•	Oregon Trail Interpretive Center to the left up a hill
26.6	•	Bishop Springs Rest Area
40.9	•	Richland
41.2	•	Eagle Valley RV Park
52.3	☜	To 'Halfway'
53.3	•	Halfway

Hells Canyon

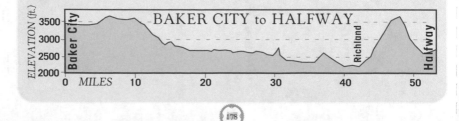

• Winter weather wreaks havoc on FR 39. Check for construction or wash-outs with the Wallow-Whitman Forest Service (www.fs.usda.gov/wallowa-whitman under "Current Conditions" tab, 541-426-5546).

EXTRACURRICULAR ACTIVITIES

You can attempt to do leisure activities like fishing or hiking today, but most likely it will take you the duration of the day and most of your energy to get to Joseph... unless you are so fit you could bounce a quarter off your butt. Or you could take two days to get to Joseph and be more leisurely.

HEADS UP

We came across cattle in the road on FR 39 (see Moo-ve Over, page 219).

CAMPING ON ROUTE

Lake Fork Campground (around mile 15.8, www.fs.usda.gov, 541-523-6391, Hwy 39, tent site $6) No reservations. Vault toilets. May or may not have potable water.

Ollokot Campground (around mile 33.1, www.fs.usda.gov, 541-523-6391, Hwy 39, tent site $8) 12 sites. No reservations. Vault toilets and potable water

Blackhorse Campground (around mile 33.4, www.fs.usda.gov, 541-523-6391, Hwy 39, tent site $8) 16 sites. No Reservations. Vault toilets and no potable water.

Lick Creek Campground (around mile 47.7, www.fs.usda.gov, 541-523-6391, Hwy 39, tent site $6) 12 sites. No reservations. Vault toilets and no potable water.

Hells Canyon

Joseph
Pop. 1,050
Elevation 4,150 ft.

USEFUL WEBSITES
Joseph's official website
www.josephoregon.com

EVENTS OF NOTE
See Joseph's Far-Flung Art Scene (page 181)
Chief Joseph Days
(www.chiefjosephdays.com) Rodeo, parade, carnival and Native American dance in late July.
Bronze, Blues & Brews
(www.bronzebluesbrews.com) Blues festival and beer garden in early August.

LODGING
The following places are all in the town center (where all lodging is taxed 9%). There are a number of good quality bed and breakfasts in downtown, like the cozy **Chandlers Inn** (www.josephbedandbreakfast.com, 541-432-9765, 700 S Main St, $85-160), which has a hot tub and shared bath options, and the cyclist-friendly **Bronze Antler B&B** (www.bronzeantler.com, 541-432-0230, 309 S Main St, $134-250), which has a garage for bikes, a bocce ball court and a two-night minimum on weekends. For slightly lower rates, check out the **Indian Lodge Motel** (www.indianlodgemotel.com, 541-432-2651, 201 S Main St, $90-100).

CAMPING
Wallowa Lake State Park (541-432-4185, 72214 Marina Ln, tent site $20) 119 sites. Wallowa Lake is gorgeous, but can be raucous like an amusement park in the summer. It's seven miles from Joseph, making a ride from Halfway more epic. Being a fully-equipped campground, it has shower and laundry facilities.

CHOW DOWN
Arrowhead Chocolates (541-432-2871, 100 N Main St, Tues-Sun 9am-6pm) We stopped here for some luscious Stumptown Coffee. Can't say we didn't savor a chocolate or two as well.
Mutiny Brewing Company (541-432-5274, 600 N Main St, 11am-9pm) A local pointed me in Mutiny's direction. Oregon's brew culture rocks.
Embers Brewhouse (www.embersbrewhouse.com, 541-432-2739, 204 N Main St, Mon-Sat 11am-close, Sun 12pm-close) With 17 micro brews on tap and gourmet pizzas on the menu (available to go), I'm guessing this place will be a cycle tourist pleaser.

HELLS CANYON DAM OPTION
29.2 miles (Forest Road 39 turnoff on Hwy 86 to the Hells Canyon Dam)
On Day 2, instead of heading north up N Pine Rd/Hwy 39 at mile 10, keep heading straight until you hit **Copperfield**. Cross the big bridge over the Snake River to go up **Hells Canyon**

Rd, which terminates at the Hells Canyon Dam.

If you are a lover of dramatic natural beauty and low-traffic byways, this road, which clings to the side of the canyon, is for you. The verdant and rocky walls of the canyon plummet to the churning Snake River to create a surreal and pleasing pedal. The inclusion of this side trip is worth adding another day to your tour. About six miles north of Copperfield, you can camp at **Hells Canyon Campground**, which is maintained by Idaho Power (www.idahopower.com, tent site $10) and has showers and no reservations. Or there are a couple of B&Bs near Copperfield, such as the **Hillside Bed and Breakfast** or the **Hells Canyon Bed and Breakfast** which is on the Oregon side of the river.

Calderas

(www.calderasofjoseph.com, 541 432-0585, 300 N Lake St) With eclectic, and I'd say fantastic, fused glass and metal art adorning the place, this upscale dinner restaurant is something to savor visually and with your taste buds. The food has local, organic flair, and the menu flaunts gluten-free options. The happy hour is a good way to try these eats on a budget.

Mt. Joseph Family Foods

(www.josephfamilyfoods.com, 541-432-0740, 208 N Main St, summer 7am-10pm) Joseph's grocery store.

Joseph Farmers Market (541-398-0707, cnr of Main St and Wallowa Ave, Saturdays in June-Oct 9am-1pm) Fresh food and local specialties.

BIKE SHOPS

Joseph Hardware

(www.joseph.doitbest.com, 541-432-2271, 15 S Main St, Mon-Sat 7:30am-6pm, Sun 8:30am-4pm) You couldn't find more helpful or friendly folks at this hardware store, which harbors a tiny bike shop in a far room.

Joseph's Far-flung Art Scene

Walking down the main street in downtown Joseph, you can tell this little mountain town has a unique artsy streak. Seven huge western-themed bronze sculptures bedeck the sidewalks. In Joseph you can tour **Valley Bronze Foundry** (307 W. Alder St, 541-432-7551) if you arrange it ahead of time. It's the same deal with **Parks Bronze Foundry** (541-426-4595, 331 Golf Course Rd) in Enterprise.

Wallowa Valley Festival of Arts

(www.wallowavalleyarts.org) happens in the beginning of June and features local, regional and national artists who work with all types of media. Local artists, including painters, textile artists and metalworkers, have a website (www.josephoregonartists.com) that has information about individual artists' work as well as the four galleries in town.

Hells Canyon

DAY THREE
Joseph to Elgin
52.3 miles
Elevation Climbed 2,040 ft.

For Pete and me, the upshot of Hwy 82 (where you spend the majority of this day) was witnessing the round-up of dogies, rural high-desert landscapes unfurling for miles and snowy-peaked mountain ranges in the distance. Still, I have to say the road is not my favorite. Hwy 82 is not bad compared to other high-speed thoroughfares, just a huge change from the wilderness bomb you experienced yesterday. There's more traffic, and vehicles move quickly.

In contrast, the very first 7.7 mile section that navigates quiet back roads to Enterprise—before you hit Hwy 82—gives you a sweet little mountain vista fix and is an excellent start to the morning.

Near the end of your day, you begin a five-mile climb just past Minam (mile 38.6) then cruise down to the classic small Eastern Oregon town of Elgin, where Sig's restaurant is decorated with the cattle brands of all the local rancher families.

RIDING TIPS
• Since today is a pretty moderate ride, have a leisurely breakfast in Joseph, or lollygag enough to arrive at the famous **Terminal Gravity Brewing and Public House** (www.terminalgravitybrewing.com, 541-426-3000, 803 SE School St, 11am-9pm) in Enterprise in time for lunch.
• Hwy 82 can have fast-moving, semi -truck traffic.

EXTRACURRICULAR ACTIVITIES
Besides finding a place to fish along the way, the **Elgin Opera House** (www.elginoperahouse.com, 541-663-6324, 104 N 8th St) sporadically features plays, concerts or movies. You might be in luck.

CAMPING AND LODGING ON ROUTE
Enterprise and **Wallowa** both have lodging and camping options. **Minam** has (and basically is) one motel and Minam State Recreation Area, which has 12 primitive, first-come, first-serve sites.

Elgin
Pop. 1,650
Elevation 2,716 ft.

USEFUL WEBSITES
Elgin Chamber of Commerce
www.elginoregonchamber.com

EVENTS OF NOTE
Elgin Stampede Rodeo
Rodeo fun in July.

Day 2

END
Joseph
Chief Joseph
Monument
Wallowa Lake
State Park

START
Halfway

Wallowa-Whitman National Forest

Eagle Cap Wilderness

Eagle Cap

Wallowa-Whitman National Forest

Copperfield

Cornucopia

Lake Fork

Lick Creek

6,101'

5921'

5392'

Blackhorse
Ollocot
Hells Canyon
Overlook

Hells Canyon
Copperfield
Oxbow Dam

route option

Imnaha Hwy.
to Imnaha
350
39

Imnaha River

Snake River

Hells Canyon Dam

to Cambridge
71
86
39

IDAHO

Payette National Forest

to Cambridge

N

SCALE of MILES
0   10   20

Day Two
Halfway to Joseph

0	•	From Main St head east on Hwy 414 (Record St)
10	☞	To 'Joseph,' N Pine Rd
29.4	•	Turnoff to Hells Canyon Overlook
45.4	•	Wayside Springs Forest Camp
63.3	☞	Hwy 350, to 'Joseph'
71.4	•	Joseph, E Wallowa Ave and Main St

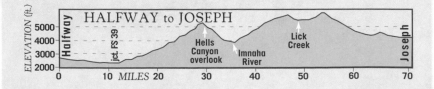

LODGING AND CAMPING
Stumpede Inn (www.stampedeinn.com, 541-437-2441, 51 S 7th St, $50-70) As this inn is directly on the route, it doesn't get much easier...or more budget-friendly. Plus, it's the only place in town.

Hu-Na-Ha RV Park (541-437-2253, 255 Cedar St, $15) Tent area. This RV park in town has showers and laundry facilities.

CHOW DOWN
There are limited options in town.

The Corral Restaurant and Saloon (831 Alder St) Just on the verge of opening at the time of research, this restaurant is considered to be unique, with a focus on fresh, homemade food.

Sig's (541-437-2109, 31 N 8th Ave, Mon-Sat 6am-9pm) We stopped in for hot cocoa on a chilly, rainy ride, and the people there were fabulous. Loved the local cattle brands blazed into the walls for decoration. This is the local tavern where you can eat simple, cheap food.

Foodtown (541-437-2012, 1480 Division St, Mon-Thurs 7:30am-8pm, Fri-Sun 8am-9pm) Conventional grocery store.

DAY FOUR
Elgin to Baker City
84.7 miles
Elevation Climbed 4,040 ft.

Medical Springs Hwy is the shining star of today's route. Even though the quiet back roads along the wide open valley floor to Union are bucolic and picturesque, the Medical Springs Hwy steals the show as it edges along and through the Wallowa-Whitman forest then over a pass between Frazier Mountain and Bald Hill to Baker City.

After you crest the pass, the wooded foothills give way to a completely disparate desertscape on a rolling descent to Powder River. As the trees disappear, the gigantic sky dominates and dwarfs even the snow-capped Wallowa Mountains that grace the eastern horizon. All the while, the dipping and swelling sea of sage-speckled grassland engulfs this one desolate road that you pedal along, each squeak of the gears a bright noise in vast quiet. You wonder if you are on the far edge of an abandoned universe.

Hells Canyon

Re-entering the world, even into little Baker City, from Medical Springs Hwy seems like a cacophonous adjustment. That's okay. A bit of the stillness in Eastern Oregon will stay with you.

RIDING TIPS

• In Summerville (mile 10.2), there is a tiny store. After Union (mile 40), there is nothing until the outskirts of Baker City except for Catherine Creek State Park (mile 48.2), where you can find potable water and beautiful picnic spots.

• The majority of this ride is exposed, so if it's hot, you'll want plenty of water.

• You might be interested in going to La Grande. I was. Though a couple of businesses on Adams Ave, like Mt. Emily Ale House, are cool, biking into the city on the heavily-trafficked roads is craptastic.

• Union (mile 40) is close to the halfway mark of the ride and has a market, nice city park with restrooms and several restaurants.

EXTRACURRICULAR ACTIVITIES

This is a long day, but if you are interested in swinging by the **Union County Museum** (mile 40, www.unioncountymuseum.org, 541-562-6003, 333 S Main St, admission

$4) in Union, you could see the "Cowboys Then and Now" exhibit (yes!) and other historical displays.

Cove, Oregon, about a five-mile detour from mile 32.4, has a **warm (not hot) springs pool** you can swim in. The pool is part concrete and part natural and would feel perfect on a 65- to 80-degree day. There are signs for the springs as you enter town. Fees vary but usually run about $5 per person. Cove also has a cafe and a mini-mart.

CAMPING AND LODGING ON ROUTE

The Historic Union Hotel (mile 40, www.thehistoricunionhotel.com, 541-562-6135, 326 N Main St, $39-119) I would have loved to have stayed in one of their 16 quirky rooms. On the to-do list.

Catherine Creek State Park (mile 48.2, www.oregonstateparks.org, 800-551-6949, Medical Springs Hwy, tent site $9) 20 sites. Vault toilets and potable water. To make a reservation, go to www.reserveamerica.com.

Hells Canyon

Day Three
Joseph to Elgin

Hells Canyon

0	•	From Main St head east on E Wallowa Ave to 'Hurricane Creek,' 'Airport'
7.2	🖛	To 'Elgin,' 'La Grand' • Enterprise
7.7	🖛	E North St, turns into Wallows Lake Hwy
17.7	•	Lostine
25.3	•	Wallowa
25.9	•	Wallowa City Park
32.7	•	Fountain Wayside
35.7	•	Wallowa River Wayside
38.6	•	Minam
43.4	•	Top of climb
52	🖛 / 👉	Hwy 82, to 'La Grande' / Hwy 204, to 'Palmer Jct'
52.3	•	Elgin • 12th Ave and Division St

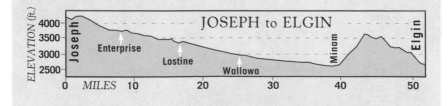

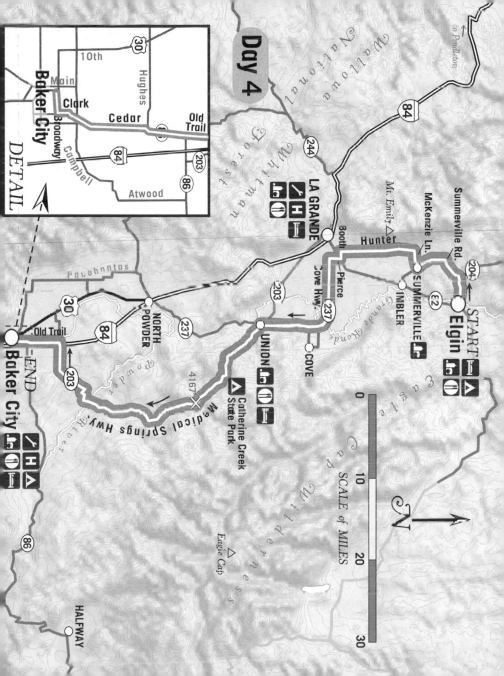

Day 4

DETAIL

Baker City

10th
Main
Clark
Cedar
Hughes
Old Trail
Broadway
Campbell
84
203
86
Atwood
30

N

Baker City
END
Old Trail
84
30
203
86
HALFWAY

Powder
North Powder
237
Pocahontas

Medical Springs Hwy.
4167
Catherine Creek State Park
Eagle Cap Wilderness
Eagle Cap

UNION
COVE
237
203
Cove Hwy.
Pierce
Booth
Hunter
Mt. Emily
LA GRANDE
244
84
to Pendleton

McKenzie Ln.
Summerville Rd.
SUMMERVILLE
IMBLER
204
82
Elgin
START

Grande Ronde
Eagle Cap

Wallowa

Wallowa
National
Whitman
Forest

SCALE of MILES
0   10   20   30
N

Day Four
Elgin to Baker City

0	•	From 12th Ave, head east on Division St
3.1	↩	To' Summerville'
10.2	☞	Unsigned 4th St, to '4H Club,' becomes McKenzie Ln
	•	Summerville
12.3	↘	Hunter Rd
20.9	↩	Booth Ln
22.5	☞	Pierce Rd (gravel)
22.8	•	Cross Hwy 82
24.5	↩	Unsigned Hwy 237
32.4	☞	Phys Rd
	or ↩	To Cove
33.5	☞	Hwy 237, to 'Union'
39.6	↩	Hwy 203, to 'Baker City'
40	•	Union
40.2	↩	Hwy 203, to 'Medical Springs'
48.2	•	Catherine Creek State Park
54.1	•	Summit 4,178
78.5	☜ / ↩	Cross Hwy 84/Old Trail Rd
82.6	☜	Through stop sign, becomes N Cedar Rd
84.1	☜	At stop light onto Clark St
84.3	☞	Broadway St
84.4	↩ / ☞	East St/Broadway St
84.7	•	Bella Main St Market • Baker City

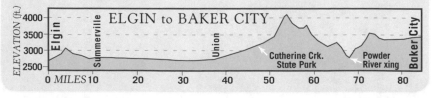

Hells Canyon

GRAB YOUR BIKE BY THE ELKHORNS
The Elkhorn Scenic Byway

**Three days and two nights
Begin and end in Baker City
107.6 miles total**

THE SKINNY

PRICE POINT: You could do this tour with a small to medium purse; you'll work hard to find high prices for lodging or food. The hotels on this tour are some of the most economical in the state.

DIFFICULTY RATING: 5.8 All days have short mileage. The two large passes on Day 2 ups the rating.

JAW-DROP FACTOR: 8.5 From snowy mountains to arid valleys, this tour has been officially deemed a scenic byway. And the scenic byway gods aren't lying.

STAND OUT CAMPING:
Anthony Lake Campground (Day 2, page 210) has tent-only sites cozied into the forest.

STAND OUT LODGING:
Sumpter Stockade (Day 1, page 202) is quirky as hell and will give you bang for your buck.

AVERAGE TEMP IN FEBRUARY: Low 19, high 37 degrees

AVERAGE TEMP IN AUGUST: Low 49, high 86 degrees

I love Eastern Oregon. In this neck of the woods, people don't hesitate to slow their trucks down to engage a cyclist in a bit of curious conversation. It's not uncommon to receive an extra helping of potato salad because you look hungry. A campground host might chase you down the mountain with a pile of laundry in case you were the one who left it behind. It wouldn't be unheard of for a local to pull up a chair next to you at the bar and spill twenty years of regional gossip and family intrigue.

That's why this place wins my heart. Eastern Oregonians showered my pal Barbara and me with friendly vibes and hospitality that you rarely find in urban areas. They didn't even seem to mind our freaky Lycra that smelled like an old sock in a garbage can.

Though the mountainscapes, lakes, valley vistas and empty roads on this tour are enough to gain anyone's admiration, history buffs will also love the off-the-beaten-track museums, ghost towns and historical sites that litter this tour (see page 197). The area is rich with pioneer and Gold Rush era history.

Moreover, this tour is accessible to a wide range of cyclists. I brought Barbara with me, and she had never been on a

Elkhorn

bike tour before. As an adventurer, casual cyclist and someone in moderately good shape, Barbara did fabulously. Point being, this tour has short-mileage days and could be a great initiation tour for a newbie. See what she has to say about her experience (other column).

The challenging day, Day 2, has lots of climbing over two gorgeous passes, one being 7,400 ft. If you wanted to break up the 41 miles of Day 2 into two shorter days, there is appropriately located lodging and camping. Alternatively, mashers could do the whole tour as a day ride. So there's nothing to stop you. Grab a pal, get out there and grab your bike by the Elkhorns.

Fist Bump!

• Hardy breakfast at the locals' pick, **Inland Cafe** in Baker City (Day 1, page 200)
• Cooling off in **Phillips Lake** (Day 1, page 200)
• **Sumpter's eccentric, small town museums** (page 197)
• The ghost town of **Granite** (Day 2, page 194)
• **Blue Springs Summit** (3,800 ft) and **Elkhorn Summit** (7,400 ft) (Day 2, page 209)
• The honey ambrosial sweetness of the **descent into Baker Valley** (Day 3, page 211)

My First Stab at Cycle Touring
by Barbara Borst, world traveler

"Where are we going?" I asked.
"Eastern Oregon," Ellee replied simply.
"Yeah, but where?"
"Middle of nowhere."
"Okay, awesome. But where?"
"Baker City."
I Googled it quickly and came back with, "Wow. That really is the middle of nowhere."
"Told you," Ellee replied, unfazed, though she added, "but Baker City is actually pretty big."
And so began the adventure of my first ever bike tour, guided by my dear friend and bike guru Eleanor Thalheimer. When we arrived in Baker City, I chided Ellee for describing it as "pretty big." From what I could tell, it was made up of an adorable main street, complete with a Wild West facade and a number of offshoot side streets.

Being a pretty laid back and adventurous gal, I hadn't been intimidated to sign up for a bike tour with Ellee. However, on the morning of departure, when I grappled with a fully-loaded bicycle I could hardly hold up, I started to worry that maybe I had underestimated the challenge.

It seemed if I didn't hold the handlebars down tightly, the bike would pop a wheelie and flip over

Elkhorn

backwards. The slightest wavering of the handlebars while riding might make the whole bike topple over. What if I fell into the path of a car?

My momentary panic quickly subsided after I took a test ride without any bailing. Once I was actually pedaling, the weight didn't faze me. Sweet. I patted myself on the back for my impressive bike touring skills (the ability to remain upright), and we rolled out of town on Oregon's Elkhorn Scenic Byway.

Whoever deemed this a "scenic byway" was dead on. Plus, there was little traffic and great pavement for miles and miles and miles. I admittedly have a bit of a chip on my shoulder when it comes to cycling in the States after having pedaled around in many other bike-friendly countries. But Ellee quieted those demons when she introduced me to the beauty of bike touring off the beaten path.

The Elkhorn Scenic Byway revealed Americana at its best: deserted old gold mining towns, dusty saloons, cowboy hats and backcountry roads that were seemingly reserved just for us. I was bowled over by everyone's kindness and openness.

Sometimes it takes getting out of the city to remember how awesome people are. American country-folk reminded me that it's okay to make small talk, smile at and trust strangers.

We were on the receiving end of more genuine helpfulness, kindness and chivalry in just three days than I can remember in a lifetime of city living in this country.

We wouldn't have had that experience from the bucket seat of a car; nor would we have had the aerobic high of reaching the top of a 7,000 ft mountain as the sun set over the valley and the holy-sh$t rush of cruising down at top speed on a fully loaded bike.

Sign me up for the next tour. I'm hooked!

P.S. You might consider taking "hike across the Alps" off your bucket list and adding "bike tour across Middle of Nowhere, America." Trust me, it will be just as fabulous (and way cheaper). Or do both. But don't miss out on bike touring in the Middle of Nowhere.

Elkhorn

HISTORY TIDBITS

See the History Crawl box (page 197) for the low down on the historical sites and museums you can check out on route.

Evidence of thousands of years of Native American inhabitants has been found in prehistoric hunting and plant gathering grounds, rock shelters, remnants of riverside villages and rock art in Baker County. Some of the tribes known to have lived in the area include: the Cayuse, Umatilla, Walla Walla, Nez Perce and Paiute tribes. The ravages of westward expansion led to the near elimination of these peoples.

In 1862, five South Carolinians were making their slow way to California, fueled by dreams of gold. One day they camped at Cracker Creek (in current day Sumpter) and decided to pan for gold. And gold they found. After building a primitive cabin, one that can still be seen today, they named the place Fort Sumter after the famous fort of the Civil War. (The present spelling of Sumpter evolved over time.) By 1903, the city had grown to 3,500 registered voters, not counting Chinese, women or children. The fire of 1917 destroyed the whole town. Simultaneously, hard rock mining was slowing down and Oregon was starting to implement prohibition. That was the end of booming Sumpter.

Also established in 1862, Granite was a booming gold mining town until federal law made gold mining illegal in 1942. Soon after, the town was abandoned to the point that even telephone lines fell into disrepair. Modern telephone service was only reestablished in 2000. Granite, now labeled a "ghost town," with a population of 19, is the second-smallest incorporated town in Oregon after Greenhorn, which has a population of zero.

ENVIRONMENT

The Elkhorn Mountains are a result of different geological events that happened at different times. Ancient seas deposited the currently visible sedimentary rocks. Later, molten rock from volcanic activity displaced the sedimentary rocks and solidified into granite. Subsequent lava flows covered parts of this area with volcanic basalt. The final touch was handed down by glaciers which sculpted the mountains.

While visiting the Elkhorn Scenic Byway area, you might see Rocky Mountain elk, mule deer, hawks, eagles or woodpeckers, to name just a few species.

The Elkhorn Mountains are home to the majority of the rare Rocky Mountain goat (only about 800 live in the state), which were virtually demolished by settlers (aka numbskulls) who overhunted the species in the 1800s. The goats were previously a staple for Native American food and hides, as well as a spiritual symbol. In the Rocky Mountain Goat Management Plan, goats are relocated from the Elkhorns to similar mountainous areas of the state with the hope that new herds will flourish.

The vegetation can vary greatly in this area, from ponderosa pines to fir and larch forests and sagebrush. On Day 2, you might see stands of young Lodgepole pines, which were named because Native Americans used the tree to frame teepees and lodges. Recently, there was a massive mountain pine beetle epidemic that wiped out nearly 90% of the Lodgepole pines. The area is still recovering.

RIDING SEASON

Hwy 73 up to Anthony Lake on Day 2 can be closed through June and even mid-July. Therefore, this tour is doable July till October. Campgrounds start slowing and shutting down between September and November. Sumpter holds a humongous flea market the weekends of Memorial Day, Fourth of July and Labor Day; it's best to avoid the area during those times. A lovely time to do the tour is after Labor Day, in September, because you avoid crowds at campgrounds and lakes while still enjoying good weather.

WEATHER

The Elkhorn Mountains behave like most high-elevation mountain ranges; while summers can be warm, weather can move in quickly and nights are chilly, so come prepared. You navigate bits of Baker Valley on Day 1 and 3; it's exposed and can feel scalding on a hot summer day.

ARRIVING/LEAVING
Airplane
Portland International Airport (PDX, www.portofportland.com, 503-460-4040, 7000 NE Airport Way) is your best bet for an airport hub, though the small Redmond and Bend airports are slightly closer.

Car
Baker City is right off I-84, about a 4.5-hour drive east from Portland. There are no car rental agencies with drop-off locations in Baker City, so unless you want to rent a car for the duration of your tour, you'll have to look into renting a **U-Haul** (www.uhaul.com, 800-789-3638, from Portland starting at $195), which has a drop-off location in Baker City.

Bus
Greyhound Bus (www.greyhound.com, 800-231-2222, 515 Campbell St) travels to Baker City. From Portland, it's a 6.5-hour trip for $70-78. Bike carrying fees may apply. Bike boxing required.

USEFUL WEBSITES
Eastern Oregon Visitor's Association
www.visiteasternoregon.com
Baker County Chamber of Commerce
www.visitbaker.com

Elkhorn

LODGING

Besides Baker City, which has plenty of economical lodging options and one fancier historic hotel (The Geiser Grand, page 199), the towns of Sumpter, Granite and North Powder have lodging options. Nothing is fancy and most have small-town, gold mining-era charm. Plus, you won't spend a lot (around $45-65 per night).

CAMPING

There is plenty of camping on this tour, which makes it easy to split the tour into even smaller bite-sized chunks. Near Baker City there are only RV parks from which to choose.

FOOD AND DRINK

You'll find mostly your standard processed, American food on this route. But it is served with kindness and hospitality. In Baker City, there are two breweries (page 199) that are fun to check out. For super nice cheese, meat, lavender soda and other boutique grocery nibbles, Bella Main Street Market (page 200) in Baker City is your place.

HYDRATION

Potable water is not as hard to come by on this tour as it is on other Eastern Oregon tours. There are places to fill up in the middle of each day, and the longest mileage day is only 41 miles. Plus, there are opportunities to purify water on Days 1 and 2.

MAPS

The **Wallowa-Whitman National Forest map** covers the entire route and shows campgrounds, water sources and trailheads. You can call or write the National Forest office or fill out their online map order form (www.fs.usda.gov/main/wallowa-whitman, 541-523-4476, Baker City Office, 3285 11th Street, Baker City, OR 97814, $9), and they'll mail it to you with no shipping or handling fees. Or you can order it online from Discover Your Northwest (www.discovernw.org, $10.50 plus shipping). The **Benchmark Oregon Atlas** (www.benchmarkmaps.com, 541-772-6965, $22.95) also has good coverage.

CELL COVERAGE

Cell phone coverage outside of Baker City, Sumpter and Haines can get spotty, but occasionally you'll get a signal. There is no coverage around the Elkhorn Summit or Anthony Lake (Day 2, Page 209).

Elkhorn

HOSPITALS
Saint Alphonsus Medical Center
(www.stelizabethhealth.com, 541-523-6461, 3325 Pocahontas Rd, Baker City) 24/7 emergency care.

EXTRACURRICULAR ACTIVITIES
Besides exploring the historical sites and museums, which chronicle the pioneer days and the Gold Rush of Oregon's yesteryear (see page 197), you can fish the rivers and lakes that you ride past. Also, you'll find enough hiking trails along the way to create a hearty, interdisciplinary adventure.

MORE TOUR!
The **Hells Canyon, Hells Yes** tour (page 167) shares Baker City as its starting and ending point. It's easy cheesy to tack on that tour if you have the time (and legs). From Sumpter (Day 1, page 202) it would be a beautiful and easy 44 miles to connect south to Prairie City, which is Day 4 of the **True West** tour (page 154), using Hwy 7 then Hwy 26. An absolutely splendid option.

COST OPTIONS
Budget camping tour: Day 1, Oregon Trails West RV Park (page 199); Day 2, McCully Fork Campground (page 209); Day 3, Anthony Lake Campground (page 210). There's a Safeway (page 200) in Baker City where you can stock up for the trip.

High falootin' credit card camping: Day 1, Geiser Grand Hotel (page 199); Day 2, Sumpter Stockade (page 202); Day 3, Anthony Lake Campground (page 210),

you have to camp unless you stay in Granite (Day 2, page 210) or North Powder (Day 3, page 211).

Make it a History Crawl: Exploring Oregon's Ghost Towns and Gold Fever
The history of early American pioneers and the frantic Gold Rush that took place at during the late 19th and early 20th centuries saturates the Elkhorn Byway region. There are a number of stops on the tour where you can learn more about the area's past:

Baker City (start of the tour)
Historic Baker City, Inc
(www.historicbakercity.com) This website details a DIY historic walking tour of Baker City.
Baker Heritage Museum
(www.bakerheritagemuseum.com, 541-523-9308, 2480 Grove St, 9am-4pm, free admission) Open spring through fall, there are exhibits about the history of industry and agriculture as well as Chinese-American and pioneer culture and wildlife.
Oregon Trail Interpretive Center
(541-523-1843, 22267 Hwy 86, 9am-6pm, $8) If you want to add a bit more mileage onto that first 28-mile day, you can cruise seven miles (one way) up to this interpretive center that has multi-media exhibits and four miles of interpretive trails. See page 173.

Elkhorn

Sumpter (Day 1, mile 28.7)
Sumpter Valley Railroad
(www.svry.com, 541-894-2268, 12259 Huckleberry Loop Rd, $15) This vintage choo choo runs 23 miles from Sumpter to McEwen.
Sumpter Valley Dredge State Park
(www.oregonstateparks.org, 541-894-2486, Hwy 7, free admission) Sumpter's gold digging dredge stopped its work in 1954 and is now a historical site where you can learn about Sumpter's past and even pan for gold (but if you find any, you have to pay for it).
Cracker Creek Museum of Mining
(mile 28.5, Hwy 7, free) This relic-filled beauty caught my eye when cycling into Sumpter. Crazy antique mining equipment is displayed on a front lawn for your self-guided pleasure.
Sumpter Municipal Museum
(www.sumptermuseum.org, 240 Mill St, hours vary, free admission) This is an adorable little museum about local gold mining, logging and ranching. It's housed in a building built in 1899 that it shares with the town's tiny library.

Granite (Day 2, mile 16.3)
Lazy V Adventures
(www.lazyvadventures.com, 541-755-5300) This primarily horse-packing outfit guides historic walking tours of the ghost town Granite. Let them know of your interest in advance.

Haines (Day 3, two-mile detour at mile 21.6)
Eastern Oregon Museum
(www.hainesoregon.com/eomuseum, 542-856-3233, 610 3rd St, May-Sept Wed-Sun 9:30am-4:30pm or by appt, free admission) This little museum has artifacts from cowboy memorabilia to period clothing and a one-room schoolhouse display. Also, in Haines is **Chandler's Cabin** (1861), which is said to be the first known cabin to have been built in Baker County.

Baker City
Pop. 9,450
Elevation 3,400 ft

USEFUL WEBSITES
Historic Baker City, Inc
www.historicbakercity.com

EVENTS OF NOTE
Baker County Fair—August
Baker City Bronc and Bull Riding—July

LODGING
The following hotels are in walking distance of restaurants and shops on Baker City's

Elkhorn

cute downtown Main St.

Bridge Street Inn

(www.bridgestreetinn.net, 541-523-6571, 134 Bridge St, $49-57) This is one of a number of very economical hotel choices in Baker City. When we stayed here, we thought the employees were a kick in the pants and nice as could be. Plus, the price is a great value.

Geiser Grand Hotel

(www.geisergrand.com, 888-434-7374, 1996 Main St, $79-249) Though you pay a bit more, the place is pretty cool—from the restored woodwork and stained glass ceiling to the mini-museum downstairs. Opened in 1889, the Geiser Grand has been through millions of dollars of restoration and, as a result, you feel transported back in time.

CAMPING

There are a number of RV parks near the city that accommodate tent camping and have shower and laundry facilities.

Oregon Trails West RV Park

(www.mtviewrv.com, 541-523-3236, 42534

North Cedar St, tent site $22.69) is right on the route out of town and is about two miles away from downtown's Main St. **Mt View RV** (www.mtviewrv.com, 541-523-4824, 2845 Hughes Ln, tent site for 2 people $22.15) is pretty near the route, has a hot tub and swimming pool and is also about two miles from downtown's Main St.

CHOW DOWN

Barley Brown's Brew Pub

(www.barleybrowns.com, 541-523-4266, 2190 Main St, Mon-Sat 4-10pm) A Baker City go-to that serves small batch, hand-crafted brew.

Bull Ridge Brew Pub (541-523-5833, 1954 Broadway St, Mon-Wed 11am-9pm, Thurs till 10pm, Fri-Sat till 11pm, Sun 12-8pm) At the time of my research, this spanking new brewery wasn't officially selling their own beer yet, but will be when you get there. Let me know what you think.

Bella Main Street Market

(www.bellabakercity.com, 541-523-7490, 2023 Main St, 7am-7pm) This store is

Elkhorn

owned by a cyclist ("Baker Loves Bikes" stickers for sale here), has a cycling mural on the wall in the back and sells scrumptious, high-end food like local goat cheese and kombucha. They have a coffee bar, too.

Inland Cafe (541-523-9041, 2715 10th St, Mon-Sat 7am-8pm, till 7pm on Sun) Locals flood this greasy spoon located away from Main St. You'll experience true Baker City here and will not leave hungry.

Baker Food Coop

(www.bakerfoodcoop.org, 541-523-6281, 2008 Broadway St, Mon-Fri 10am-6pm, Sat 10am-4pm) Baker City's little natural food coop has mostly refrigerator and dry goods, including a bulk foods section. There's a tiny produce selection, too.

Farmers Market (www.bakercityfarmersmarket.org, Grove St and Campbell St, June-Oct, Wed 4-7pm) Fresh, local fruits and veggies.

Safeway (www.local.safeway.com, 541-523-7276, 1205 Campbell St, 6am-1am) Conventional grocery store.

BIKE SHOPS

Flagstaff Sports (541-523-3477, 2101 Main St, Mon-Fri 10am-5:30pm, Sat till 4pm) Probably your best bet for bicycle supplies.

Progression Gravity Lab Bicycle Repair (541-406-0608) Just opening at the time of research, this is a mobile bicycle repair business.

DAY ONE
Baker City to Sumpter
28.7 miles
Elevation Climbed 1,590 ft.

After leaving the outskirts of Baker City, small-town traffic gives way to exposed high-desert plains fringed by a gentle roil of foothills. After the first 10 seemingly flat miles, a minor grade sets in as the surrounding prairie land gradually becomes more forested. Around mile 17, glassy Phillips Lake appears on your left as the Elkhorn Mountains start to make their grand entrance on the horizon to the right. Only a few bonafide climbs punctuate the gently climbing 29-mile route.

You end up in the former gold rush boom town of Sumpter. Nowadays Sumpter caters mostly to hunters, outdoor enthusiasts, snowmobilers and people who attend the gargantuan 10,000-person flea markets that happen three times per year. Yet, the town still nails the rough-hewn-wood, log-cabiny, lazy-wild-west-saloon, antique-mining-settlement aesthetic.

Because of the short mileage on this day, you could feasibly travel to Baker City the same day you begin the tour. Alternatively, you could spend time out of the saddle during the cycling day to explore handsome Phillips Lake—where you can

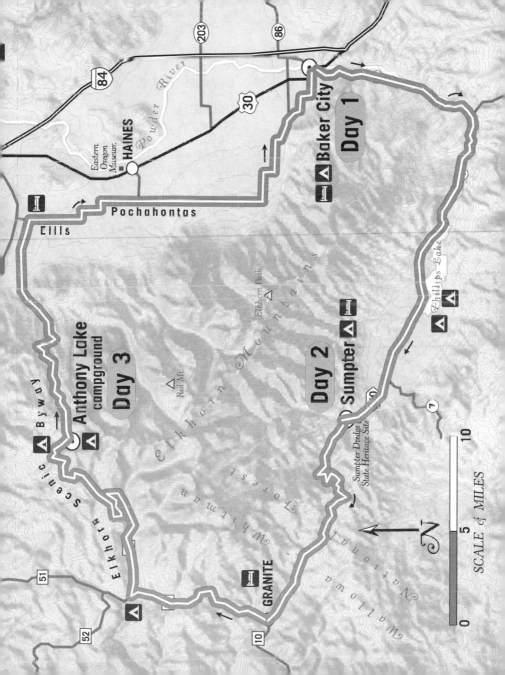

hook a bass or maybe some Coho salmon—and check out historic Sumpter's mining museum, gold dredge or other gold rush era relics scattered about the tiny town (see page 197).

RIDING TIPS

• Avoid Sumpter during its flea markets (see Riding Season, page 200).
• Phillips Lake comes into view around mile 15. There are a number of picnic spots and a campground where you can relax or take a dip.
• Though this day is short, McEwen Country Store (mile 22.6), which is about 6 miles from Sumpter, might be open to sell you a cold drink.

EXTRACURRICULAR ACTIVITIES

Phillips Lake has hiking trails, and all methods of fishing are permitted.

Sumpter has a number of little museums and historical sites if you get there early enough to explore (see page 197).

CAMPING ON ROUTE

Union Creek Campground (mile 18.8, www.reserveamerica.com, 541-894-2393, 17564 Hwy 7, tent site $12) 60 sites. Open May-Sept. It has vault and flush toilets, potable water, lake access and is heavily used. You can reserve sites ahead of time. FYI, on the south shore of Phillips Lake, there are two other campgrounds, Millers Lane and Southwest Shore.

Sumpter
Pop. 191
Elevation 4,400 ft.

USEFUL WEBSITES
Sumpter visitor information
www.historicsumpter.com
More Sumpter visitor information
www.sumpter.org

EVENTS OF NOTE
Sumpter Flea Market
Thousands of folks flood Sumpter for this thrice-annual, three-day event on Memorial Day, 4th of July and Labor Day.
Breakfast Club
(www.sumpterbreakfastclub.org, 3rd Sunday every month, 7-10am, donation only) If you're lucky enough to be in Sumpter the 3rd Sunday of the month, you can indulge in eggs to order and a community breakfast that benefits Sumpter civic projects.

LODGING
The Depot Inn
(www.thedepotinn-sumpter.com, 541-894-2522, 179 S Mill St, $60-75) Simple, reasonably priced rooms right in town.
Scoop-N-Steamer Cabins
(www.scoop-n-steamer.com, 541-894-2236, 363 S Mill St, cabin $65-110) The four adorable, rustic mini-cabins rent for a reasonable price.
Sumpter Stockade
(www.sumpterstockade.net, 541-894-2360, 129 E Austin St, room $65-75, bunk per person $20, camping per person $10) I loved staying in the two-person bunk room here! The other rooms, both spacious and

Elkhorn

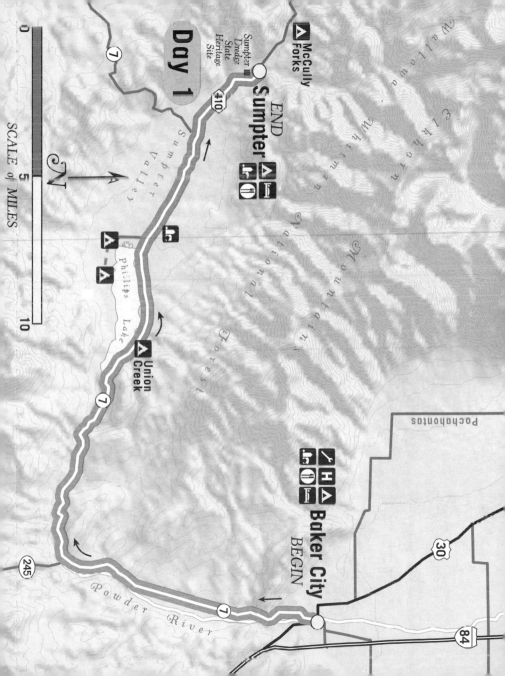

Day One
Baker City to Sumpter

0	•	From Bella Main Street Market head south on Main St
.2	👆	To 'Sumpter' on Hwy 7
.6	•	Take pedestrian walkway on the right instead of underpass
15.7	•	Powder River Recreation Area
18.8	•	Union Creek Campground
20.7	•	Mowich Loop Picnic Area
22.4	•	McEwen Country Store
25.8	☞	To 'Sumpter,' Elkhorn Scenic Byway
27.9	•	Sumpter Pines RV Park
28.7	•	Sumpter Stockade

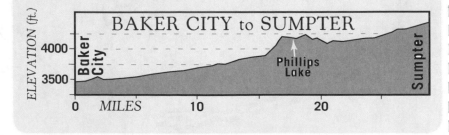

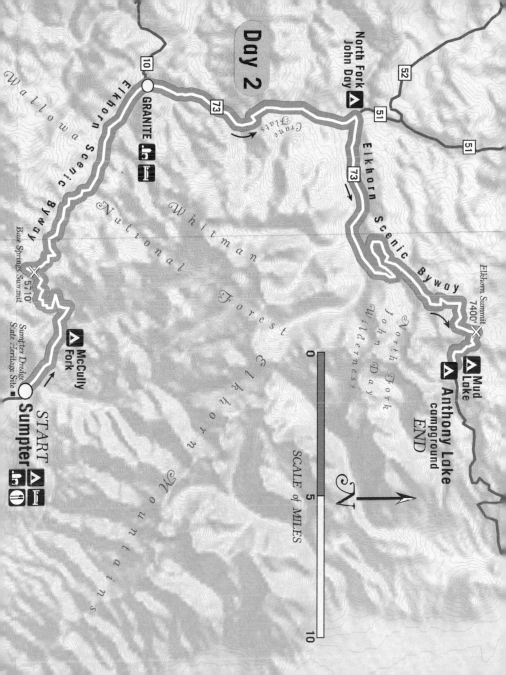

Day 2

North Fork
John Day

Wallowa

Elkhorn Scenic Byway

GRANITE

10

73

Crane Flats

73

52

51

51

Elkhorn Scenic Byway

Whitman

National

Forest

Elkhorn

Mountains

North Fork John Day Wilderness

North Fork John Day

Bald Springs Summit

5510

Sumpter Dredge State Heritage Site

McCully Fork

Elkhorn Summit
7400'

Mud Lake

Anthony Lake
campground
END

START
Sumpter

N

SCALE of MILES

0   5   10

Day Two
Sumpter to Anthony Lake Campground

0	•	From Sumpter Stockade, head North on Mill St
2.9	•	McCully Fork Campground
16.3	•	Turnoff to Granite
24.9	☞	Hwy 73, to 'Anthony Lake'
	•	North Fork John Day Campground
40.2	•	Mud Lake Campground
41.1	•	Anthony Lake Campground

Elkhorn

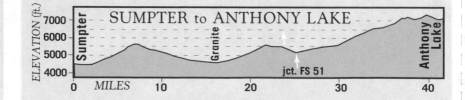

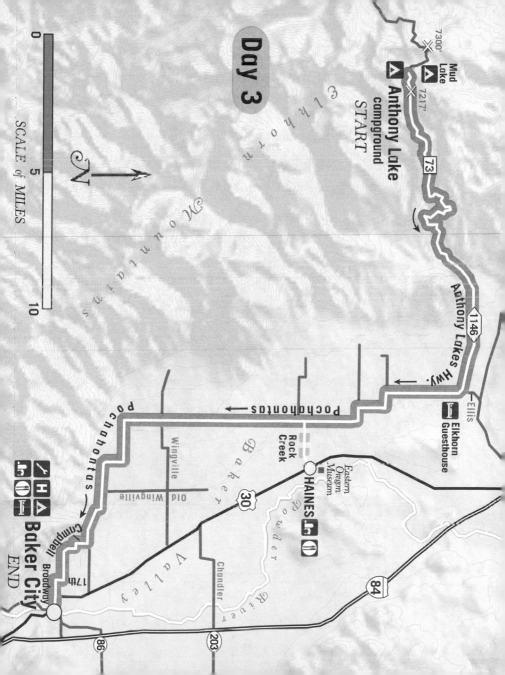

Day Three
Anthony Lake to Baker City

0   •   From Anthony Lake Campground continue East on Hwy 73

15.3   ☞   Continuing towards 'Haines'

     or ☜   To head northeast to North Powder

21.6   ☜ / ☞ Onto Pocahontas Rd/following Pocahontas Rd at stop sign

     or ☜   To go two miles to visit Haines

33.2   ☞   W Campbell Loop

35.6   ☞   17th St

35.8   ☜   Broadway St

37.8   •   Bella Main Street Market (Main St and Broadway)

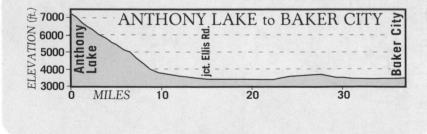

Elkhorn

clean, were tempting, though. There are showers and laundry available to folks in the bunks or those who camp on the lawn.

CAMPING
Sumpter Pines RV Park
(www.sumpterpinesrvpark.com, 541-894-2328, 640 S Sumpter Hwy, tent site $18, cabin $75) A little more than a mile before you hit Sumpter, you'll come to this RV Park nuzzled up to the forest. The people who run it are sweethearts. They also rent one cabin.

Gold Rush RV Park
(goldrushrvpark@questoffice.net, 541-894-2217, 680 Cracker Creek Road, tent site $13) Situated on a stream, this RV park is less than a mile from the center of Sumpter.

McCully Fork Campground (mile 2.9 of Day 2, www.fs.usda.gov, 541-523-6391, Hwy 220, tent site $6) Seven sites. If you are going super-budget, or if you just want to stay out in the woods, this is a good option. You can grab food on your way through Sumpter. Vault toilets. No potable water, but located on a stream.

CHOW DOWN
Scoop-N-Steamer
(www.scoop-n-steamer.com, 541-894-2236, 363 S Mill St, Mon-Thurs 7am-2 pm, Fri-Sun 7am-7 pm) This is my choice in town because you can eat on the deck, the building has good light and the service is sweet as the scoop-ice cream.

Breakfast Club (see Events of Note, page 202).

Borello's (541-894-2480175, 175 S Mill St, restaurant Fri-Sat 5-8:30, dinner in lounge Sun 3-7:30pm, lounge open daily

3pm-close) and the **Elkhorn Restaurant and Saloon** (541-894-2244, 180 S. Mill St, lunch and dinner) are similar in that their dark bars are their life-blood. They both have simple menus, but Borello's is Italian-themed and a bit more expensive.

You can pick up basic groceries at the **Stage Stop Gas Station** and the **Sumpter Gold Post** in town. Both are open daily.

DAY TWO
Sumpter to Anthony Lake
41.1 miles
Elevation Climbed 5,000 ft.

When Barbara and I rode this route, just a couple of miles out of town, a truck on steroids full of camouflaged hunters (with camo face paint) pulled up next to us and drove as slowly as we biked (if that gives you an idea how little traffic there is). They asked where we were going then whistled when we said Anthony Lake.

We declined their offer to throw our bikes in back for a ride up the mountain. The friendly hunters knew that Anthony Lake is only about 40 miles from Sumpter, but that the majority of the way is spent climbing two passes, and not all the grades are cordial. The climb on the first pass, Blue Springs Summit (5,800 ft) begins soon after you leave Sumpter, but the majority of the ascending takes place after you turn onto Hwy 73, which leads you to the Elkhorn Summit pass (7,400 ft).

At mile 16.3, you pass the one-horse town of Granite (pop. 19), which busted after it boomed during the Oregon Gold

Elkhorn

Rush. Many describe this enclave as a ghost town, though there is one store, the Outback, which is open sometimes in summer and fall.

Today is the most spectacular day of the tour. The route is laden with mountain vistas and pin-drop quiet forest roads. The day ends with Anthony Lake as a finale; this high-elevation lake nestled into the forest and mountains is as peaceful as it is pristine.

RIDING TIPS

• The Outback in Granite (mile 16.3) is your only chance to buy food and drink. But the store has a reputation for opening and closing when the owners please, so it's best to be prepared without relying on the Outback. We certainly enjoyed our hot cocoa stop there, though.

EXTRACURRICULAR ACTIVITIES

If you get to Anthony Lake with enough daylight, you can fish, hike or take a dip.

CAMPING AND LODGING ON ROUTE

North Fork John Day Campground (mile 24.9, www.publiclands.org, intersection NFDR 52 and 73, tent site $8) 14 sites. In the Umatilla National Forest. Vault toilets. No potable water.

Fremont Powerhouse Cabins (www.friendsofthedredge.com, www.recreation.gov, 877-444-6777, FSR 10, $65-80) From Granite (mile 16.3), go west on CR 24 for about six miles then veer right on FSR 10, following signs to Fremont Powerhouse. These fully-equipped (except bed linens) cabins are located on the antique Fremont Powerhouse site, a nationally registered Historic District.

Lodge at Granite (mile 16.3, www.lodgeatgranite.com, 541-755-5200, $55) In Granite, this log building houses 9 simple rooms.

The Outback wall tents (mile 16.3, www.lazyvadventures.com, 541-755-5300, 1844 Center St, Granite, per person $25) The Outback rents these structures and provides a separate restroom and shower house. Linens not provided.

Anthony Lakes

Anthony Lake Campground

(www.fs.usda.gov, 541-523-6391, Hwy 73, tent site $12) 37 sites. No reservations. The awesome tent-only sites are nestled into the forest and accessed by dirt trail. We had a nice fire with the wood we bought from the camp host. The same camp host chased us down the mountain in his truck on the way to town with a pile of laundry that he thought we might have left. Dear heart. The grounds have potable water and vault toilets.

Mud Lake Campground (mile 40.2, www.fs.usda.gov, 541-523-6391, Hwy 73, tent site $5, entire grounds $50) Seven sites. This primarily group campsite can be reserved online (www.reserveamerica.com), but if it's not reserved, individuals can use it on a first-come, first-serve basis. No potable water on site. Vault toilets.

Elkhorn

DAY THREE
Anthony Lake to Baker City
37.8 miles
Elevation Climbed 800 ft.

Well, you've earned today. I hope you like to go downhill.

The scenery for your bug-splat-against-sunglasses descent is brought to you by the Wallowa-Whitman National Forest, and this particular section is a slice taken straight from cyclist heaven with sweet smelling pines and magnanimous vistas of Baker Valley.

Once you finally touch down onto flat ground, you'll find yourself in a pastoral watercolor that epitomizes rural Eastern Oregon. Dilapidated, splintering barns oversee wide-open plains that unfurl to the horizon, and the occasional house is decorated with wagon wheels and troughs of unruly wildflowers.

If you have the time, need a cold drink or want to check out a museum about the area (see page 197), take a detour at mile 21.6 to the tiny town of Haines. With some historical character intact, and a couple of historic structures scattered around, it's an interesting, off-the-beaten path stop. Plus, the people are awfully nice.

The last stretch into Baker City is flat and surrounded by wide-open, straw-colored expanses. If a good frothy brew is your ideal way to end a ride, choose from Baker City's two breweries (Chow Down, page 199). Alternatively, I love Bella

Main Street Market where you can grab a lavender soda or coffee drink and peruse the cycling mural in the back. Cheers to you. Nice work.

RIDING TIPS
• The last half of the ride is exposed and without places to refill water, unless you take a short side trip to Haines (mile 21.6).

EXTRACURRICULAR ACTIVITIES
There is the Eastern Oregon Museum in Haines and a couple of museums in Baker City (see page 197).

LODGING ON ROUTE
Elkhorn Guest House
(Near the intersection at mile 15.3, www.elkhornguesthouse.com, 208-861-2749, 47759 Anthony Lakes Hwy, North Powder, $150) This is one of the nicer places to stay in the area. However, there is a two-night minimum stay (which may or may not be negotiable during the off season).

North Powder Motel (turnoff at mile 15.3, 541-898-2829, 850 2nd St, $45-50) Locally owned. Simple rooms.

Elkhorn

～GRAVEL GRINDING～
...around Steens Mountain

**Four days and three nights
Begin and end at The Narrows
198.6 miles total**

THE SKINNY

PRICE POINT: You can do this tour with a **small to medium-small purse.** Prices are very reasonable out here, and there isn't anything in the way of fancy. There are modest lodging opportunities along the way, so that ups the ante over camping.

DIFFICULTY RATING: 9 Despite the moderate mileages, this tour gets a high rating for the challenging conditions, remoteness and lack of services. The first day might be the hardest. If you tack on the Steens Mountain Loop (See Steens Mountain Loop Option, page 229), well, that makes it even harder.

JAW-DROP FACTOR: 9 Steens Mountain, Alvord Desert, steaming hot springs, canyons, plains and wide-open sky.

STAND OUT CAMPING: Mann Lake Recreation Area (page 222) wins, not because it's posh or lovely—though it is hyper-scenic—but because it's without pity, rugged and in the middle of absolutely nowhere.

STAND OUT LODGING: The **Frenchglen Hotel** (page 218) gives you a taste of the stagecoach days.

AVERAGE TEMP IN FEBRUARY: Low 23, high 43 degrees
AVERAGE TEMP IN AUGUST: Low 52, high 91 degrees

Fist Bump!
• **Leaving The Narrows** and the trappings of civilization (Day 1, page 220)
• Pedaling by **Steens Mountain** (Day 1 & 2, pages 220 & 222)
• The **Alvord Desert's sizzled playa and hot springs** (Day 2, page 222)
• **Fields**, which is comprised of one-quarter good folks, one-quarter liquor shop and one-half famous burger joint (Day 2, page 218)
• **Frenchglen's historic hotel** (Day 3, page 218)
• The **loop out to Diamond** past lava beds (Day 4, page 230)
• **Round Barn Visitor Center's book selection** and museum (Day 4, page 230)

When planning this tour, I felt like reenacting dance scenes from "Flashdance" in my living room. I attribute that urge to the fact the route presents a mighty challenge on many levels (like being a female welder in a steel mill in the 80s, as well as aspiring professional dancer—see the movie). The tour is super remote, water is scarce, there's lots of gravel, you need to carry more gear and water than normal and the first day has long mileage.

The prospect of cycling through Southeastern Oregon also made me feel like running in place as fast as I could to the beat of exuberant 80s music. I love pure country, and that's what this part of Oregon is all about. Men and women dressed in dusty Wranglers, cowboy hats, checked button down shirts and buckle belts saunter around Harney County herding cattle (and shaking their heads when tourists don't know how to drive their Subaru through a bunch of cows).

And I'll admit it. I love cowboys.

Plus, Southeastern Oregon's nature is unfathomable in its hugeness and sublime in its unforgiving and harsh beauty. The high-desert plains, buttes and canyons (which hover around 4,000 ft in elevation) surround the freakishly solitary Steens Mountain (almost 10,000 ft), which has its own frigid weather system and relentlessly holds your gaze.

This journey into Southeastern Oregon opens up to you only when you accept gravel in your life. If you are a fan of solitude, challenge and adventure, you too should consider embracing dirt roads. Donnie Kolb, gravel fanatic, speaks well to this (see Off Road Touring in Oregon, page 213).

I accepted gravel into my life, but sadly enough, I was unable to cycle this tour in its entirety before the season turned. But Southeastern Oregon and I have a date in the future, and I hope it meets me at the saloon wearing a tight pair of Wranglers.

Off-road Touring in Oregon
by Donnie Kolb, founder of VeloDirt.com and gravel evangelist

I first got into off-road riding several years ago purely by happenstance. The combination of a few wrong turns with a bad map landed us on one of my all-time favorite rides, Dalles Mountain, just outside The Dalles, Oregon. I was immediately hooked on off-road riding, and I began seeking out routes that maximized the dirt and gravel.

Finding little to no reliable information online about off-road riding in Oregon, I decided to create VeloDirt.com. The primary purpose of VeloDirt is to be a resource to off-road riding and touring in the Pacific Northwest. We also organize informal and unsupported endurance rides on several of our favorite routes in Oregon and review gear from the perspective of an off-road tourist.

I'll be the first to admit that bike tours that leave the pavement are not for everyone. It takes extra effort, extra planning and extra gear compared to traditional touring where there are services and road signs. However, the rewards more than compensate if you are interested in exploring places you simply cannot reach without getting off the beaten path. Steens Mountain is a great example. The route around the mountain rewards you with amazing views, interesting people and unique places; but it's fully accessible only by gravel roads.

One common misconception about off-road riding is that you need a specialized bike or a mountain bike; that's simply not true. In most cases, as long as your bike will accommodate wider tires, you'll be perfectly fine on your road or cross bike. For example, on the Steens Mountain ride, a traditional touring setup with 35c tires would be perfect. While it's not ideal for the gravely sections, this setup makes for a nice compromise when you're mixing pavement with off-roading. Other than extremely remote riding in the mountains, most off-road routes in Oregon will include a fair amount of pavement. So don't let your current bike limit you if you're interested in this type of riding.

Oregon is a great place for off-road touring because the state's terrain is so diverse. Routes like Gravel Grinding around Steens Mountain are relatively straightforward, well-marked routes that make for a great introduction into off-road touring. But you can also push things further into more remote and generally inaccessible areas like the mountains of the Coast and Cascade Ranges, with their networks of logging, state and national forest roads. You can get as remote as you please, but come prepared to ride multiple days without any type of commercial services and spend considerable time navigating the maze of unmarked dirt roads. If you do, you'll be rewarded with some of the best riding anywhere, into places no guidebook or website will take you.

HISTORY TIDBITS

If you really want to geek out on Steens Mountain and Harney County history and geology, read "Steens Mountain in Oregon's High Desert Country" by Edwin Russel Jackman and John Scharff (see John Scharff, page 215).

The Paiute Native American tribe inhabited this area when the settlers began to arrive in the 1800s. The subsequent cattle industry destroyed the ability of the Paiute to continue their traditional lifestyle. The game animals they hunted diminished as did their ability to gather food.

This tour navigates a land with a century's worth of pioneer and cattle country history. One of the remnants can be seen on the Diamond Lollipop side trip (page 230). You pass the French Round Barn, which was not actually a barn but a sheltered corral designed to create a space to break horses during the winter. This creative structure—made from local juniper wood in the 1880s—has stood the test of time.

The building was contracted by Peter French, a famous cattle baron who owned the largest Oregon cattle empire of the time. French's time was short though. He was known for conducting shady business and was murdered by an angry settler. Because he seems to have ticked off many folks, everyone looked the other way. French was only trying to run his cattle empire while squatters and Native Americans constantly hampered operations. What's a cattle baron to do?

Florence and John Scharff Brought the Birds Back to Southeastern Oregon

When Florence and John Scharff first arrived at the newly appointed Malheur Wildlife Refuge in 1935, the area was a dusty wasteland that had been devastated by overgrazing and other cattle industry practices. John became the first Refuge manager and had the monolithic task of restoring the wetlands to a prime wildlife habitat. Though John gets much of the credit for success, it's important to recognize that Florence also played a huge part in the advocacy and work.

John criss-crossed the area on horseback to figure out how to revitalize the land, and he used the Civilian Conservation Corps (CCC) to create lots of the infrastructure—dams, canals and marshes—that you see today. By the time John retired in 1971, geese, trumpeter swans, marsh hawk and meadowlark were just some of the hundreds of species attracted to the newfangled wetland habitat. Today, 320 species of birds and 58 mammals frequent the area, and fish are coming back, too. John has said rebuilding the habitat was "the best thing I've ever done."

In the spring, the annual John Scharff Migratory Bird Festival (www.migratorybirdfestival.com) celebrates the refuge, the migration and the Scharffs' contribution to this natural area and community. And, if you stop by the refuge headquarters, which used to be the couple's home, notice the huge trees out front. They were planted by the Scharffs.

Advocacy for the refuge continues today. For more info go to the Friends of Malheur website (www.malheurfriends.org).

ENVIRONMENT

Get this: the Steens Mountain was born roughly 23 million years ago as a part of the "red, principally rhyolitic and tuffaceous Pike Creek Volcanic Series" (thanks, Donald Mansfield, author of "The Unique Botany of Steens Mountain"). Dang. I hope I have another opportunity to use the word "tuffaceous" in a sentence; it sounds like how I'd describe my hair first thing in the morning.

During the subsequent Ice Age, glaciers trenched out deep gorges, which are now named the Kiger, Little Blitzen, Big Indian and Wildhorse gorges. Due to later glacial forces and subterranean pressure, the east face of the mountain rises sharply and is one vertical mile above the Alvord Desert.

Steens Mountain is physiographically freaky in two respects. For one, Steens is a sole mountain surrounded by high-desert as opposed to being a part of a range. Second, for being such a loner, the mountain has an extensive contiguous alpine (above 8,000 ft) environment. It

Gravel Grinding

creates its own personal weather system and blocks much of the precipitation coming from the west; thus the parched Alvord Desert to the east.

There are some really neat animals out here: elk, mule deer, wild horses, mountain lions, bighorn sheep, pronghorn antelope and coyotes, not to mention interesting snake and reptile species. The famous spring bird migration to Malheur National Wildlife Refuge draws the birding crowd (see John Scharff, page 215).

The area supports hundreds of species of wildflowers, including the Steens Mountain Paintbrush, which doesn't exist anywhere else in the world. Most of what you'll see is scablands and desert sagebrush. On the Steens Mountain Loop (page 229), you'll come across alpine meadows, aspen groves and other types of woodlands.

RIDING SEASON

This tour would work best between April and October. The Steens Mountain Loop Day Ride (page 229) option opens sometime in July. Summer can be super hot, so spring would be the best time to ride the majority of the tour (due to cooler weather and fuller water sources). Fall is also a great time for cooler temps, but water sources may be lower. However, I was there during a strange October that had lots of water, so it's always worth it to check with the BLM (page 219). Crowds will rarely be big; holiday weekends will be more crowded.

WEATHER

Contradicting the common perception of Oregon, the Alvord Desert (Day 2, page 222) gets only about six inches of rain per year. This part of Oregon, in general, gets way more sun than the soggy western part of the state. The route sticks to the high-desert valleys and plains (4,000-5,000 ft of elevation) at the base of Steens Mountain, which tops out at 9,733 ft. So, while the mountain has snowy winter weather that attracts cross country skiers, the surrounding plains have a milder climate that can experience a number of 100-degree days in the summer.

ARRIVING / LEAVING
Car

Having your own vehicle is going to be the easiest way to get all the way out here, but there are feasible bus options. Drive to Burns (pop. 2,700) then head south on Hwy 205 for 25 miles to The Narrows. It's about a six-hour drive from Portland or a three-hour drive from Bend. As there are no rental car outlets with drop-off service until Bend, renting could get pretty expensive. **U-Haul** (www.uhaul.com, 800-468-4285, from Portland $288-300) has a drop-off location in Burns, which is a flat 25 miles from The Narrows.

Bus

From Bend, **Eastern Point Buses** (www.highdesert-point.com, 541-382-2151, $29-31) connect once per day to Burns leaving at 3pm from Lava Lanes

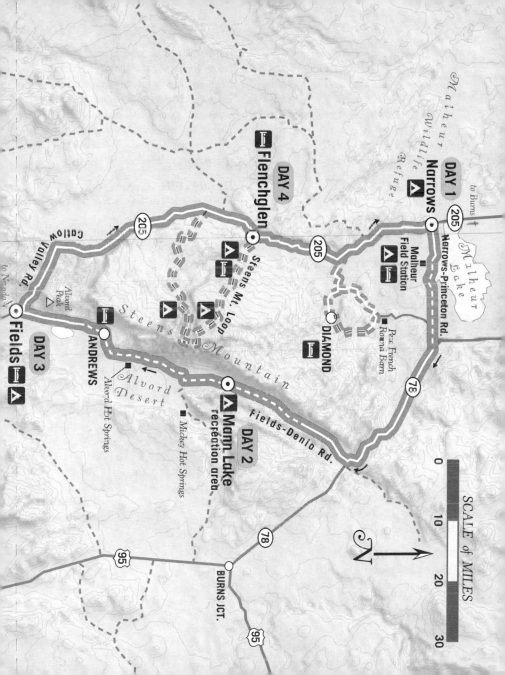

Bowling Alley and arriving around 5:30pm at Figaro's Pizza in Burns. From Burns, the bus leaves at 11:50am and arrives around 2:30pm. Uniquely, there is no extra cost for bikes, and they don't have to be boxed (N/A to other Greyhound connections). See the Bus section of the True West tour (page 138) for info on buses to Bend.

USEFUL WEBSITES
Harney County's website
www.harneycounty.com
BLM information
www.blm.gov/or/districts/burns/recreation/steens-mtn.php

LODGING
Other than the few options on the tour, you'll find lodging 25 miles north of The Narrows in Burns. Lodging choices tend to be historic or quirky; there's nothing fancy out here.

CAMPING
The majority of the land you'll be riding through is BLM or private. The many long sections of road fenced off with barbed wire give you a good clue as to which is which. You are allowed to camp on any BLM land, but unless you want to dry camp and haul in water, your choices are very limited. There are camping options at the end of each day.

FOOD AND DRINK
You're way out there, so food choices are limited. The Narrows has a simple restaurant and mercantile. The cafe in Fields is famous for milkshakes and hamburgers. The Frenchglen Hotel does a hearty breakfast, and the communal dinner surprised me with a salad and steamed veggie component. Sometimes Hotel Diamond (see Diamond Lollipop box, page 230) has monthly regionally-themed wine pairing dinners. Gluten-free folks and vegetarians will have to be creative.

HYDRATION
Well, this is an important little section, now isn't it? Basically, "stay hydrated" is the thesis statement of this tour and the axis from which you make your decisions. The first day is the real doozy with 70 miles before you reach a silty lake. You can purify the billy bob out of this water or drag a couple of gallons from The Narrows to last through the next day to Fields. On all days, it's super important to not be wuss about carrying water weight and to be prepared with extra water just in case.

MAPS
The **Benchmark Oregon Atlas** (www.benchmarkmaps.com, 541-772-6965, atlas $22.95) shows the whole route. Alternately, you could get the **Steens High Desert Country Map** (www.blm.gov, 541-573-4400, 28910 Hwy 20 W, at BLM office $3, online $8), which covers the route and is more detailed. Better for map geeks.

GENERAL RIDING TIPS AND HEADS UP

• Why did the snake cross the road? Because they do that all the time in Harney County. And rattle snakes aren't petite reptiles.

• Call the Burns District BLM (541-573-4400) to check on water levels, road construction or anything else pertinent to your adventure. While you're at it, might as well let them (and someone else in the front country) know your route and exit date.

• When taking a break, try to avoid rolling your tires off the road. Prickly things are everywhere.

• Because of the gravel and the uber remoteness, bring extra tubes, an extra tire, lube and a nice supply of tools.

• Watch for cattle grates in the road.

• See the Moo-ve Over box (right) for tips on negotiating herds crossing the road.

• Water is queen out here. I'm a freak about having enough water, and you should be too on this tour, especially during a dry year.

• Purify the crap out of your water! Literally. This is cattle country.

• I hear there are periods when the mosquitoes can be gnarly. Bring repellent.

• There are strong winds in the high-desert. Hope they are tailwinds.

CELL COVERAGE

Don't count on cell reception except near some of the little towns. Outside those towns, reception can be spotty to zilch.

HOSPITALS

The nearest medical facilities are 25 miles north of The Narrows in Burns.

Harney District Hospital

(www.harneydh.com, 541-573-7281, 557 W Washington St, Burns) 24/7 emergency care.

EXTRACURRICULAR ACTIVITIES

You can visit a number of hot springs. The **Alvord Hot Springs** (Day 2, page 222) is right on the route. The more developed **Crystal Crane Hot Springs** (Day 1, page 221) is a side trip.

Harney County attracts birders in the spring when waterfowl are making their northern migration over the area. **Malheur National Wildlife Refuge** (see John Scharff box, page 215), which is just north of this tour, is supposed to be spectacular.

There are some hiking trails off of the Steens Mountain Loop (page 229), if you have the energy.

Moo-ve Over: How to negotiate cattle on a bike

My dad, in a very unfatherly manner, laughed when we came across a small group of cows in the road on one of our bike tours and I got skittish and a tad scared. Cattle might be gentle and submissive, but they can weigh well over 1,000 pounds, are susceptible to spooking and have a herd mentality. Not cool when you're about 200-pounds of collective bike, bags and person.

Bovine negotiation is relevant to a number of tours in this guide, but this one in particular. I consulted

Gravel Grinding

with some long-time locals and the Burns BLM to glean some tips for cyclists who must navigate a road full of ambling cows. They gave the sage advice to not try to bust through the herd or yell at the animals. Usually, there is a cowhand moving the cows along. Step out of the way of the herd and get the cowhand's attention. That cowboy or cowgirl will probably make a space for you to continue down the road or escort you through.

MORE TOUR!

From Burns (which is 25 miles north of The Narrows) you can take scenic Hwy 395 north for 70 miles to John Day to hook up with the **True West** (page 133) tour. That's good stuff.

COST OPTIONS

It would be hard to spend a lot of money out here. The few hotel or cabins on route are simple establishments. There are no high falootin' options.

The Narrows

Pop. > 50
Elevation Climbed 4,100 ft.

LODGING, CAMPING AND CHOW

Basically, the only thing in this unincorporated "town" is the kooky **Narrows RV Park** (www.narrowsrvpark.com, 541-495-2006, 33468 Sod House Lane, yurt $38.35, tent site $12.12) which has tent sites,

five-person rental yurts and bathroom and shower facilities. Onsite there's a saloon, restaurant (9am-7pm), small store, a pool table and the only gas pump for many miles. Linda, one of the owners, was so darned nice with all of my question-asking about the area. Your car can stay here while you're on tour. For me it was free; I've heard others were charged $5. I guess it depends on whom you ask.

DAY ONE
The Narrows to Mann Lake Recreation Area
71.8 miles
Elevation Climbed 2,200 ft.

This first day doesn't allow for dabbling your toe in the Southeastern Oregon environs to get a feel for the riding. The ride to Mann Lake is the hardest (you're carrying water for two days if you don't purify, plus backcountry camping gear) and longest, with the overnight camping at Mann Lake being the most rugged of the tour. Of the 71.8 miles today, 20 are gravel and all of them subjugate you to the desert's whim and plunk you down in pure, unadulterated solitude.

The desolate landscape is austere—like a wizened, grief-stricken monk who only eats crusts of bread once per day. Crack-your-lips wind whips over the desiccated miles of rock, sand and snakes.

Simultaneously, this barren expanse is ostentatious like a drag queen with a

$1,000 gift card to Filene's Basement. After you head south, Steen Mountain cuts the enormous horizon with a jagged and sheer outline to the west, and to the east, miles of rusty, worn leather-colored buttes and canyons line the valley floor. But the sky is the lord of all things, choosing to be either retina-scorching diamond bright, furrowed with bruised, billowing clouds or akin to watercolors splashed onto an enormous vaulted canvas.

I won't lie. You will have to work today climbing Baker Pass with a booty-load of water weight while negotiating some chunky, apathetic gravel in the middle of a desert. But, in the end, there's a chance you'll start to fall in love with the purity, harshness and silence.

RIDING TIPS AND HEADS UP

• If you don't want to purify silty Mann Lake water, fill up water at The Narrows that will last until you hit Fields on the second day. If you are purifying, still bring plenty of water. If you're lucky, you might be able to find water at Ten Cent Lake (mile 57.4) or Juniper Lake (mile 61).

Call the Burns District BLM (541-573-4400) to check water status before you go.

CAMPING AND LODGING ON ROUTE

Malheur Field Station (mile 3.1, www.malheurfieldstation.org, 541-493-2629, 34848 Sodhouse Ln, room with kitchenette $55, three-room house $150) Open seasonally. In Malheur National Wildlife Refuge, 1.3 miles off the route. Bookstore, natural history museum and food service on the campus.

When I was here during a particularly water-rich October, **Ten Cent Lake** (mile 57.4) and **Juniper Lake** (mile 61) both had water and reasonable places to pitch a tent. These lakes could be options if you want to camp earlier than Mann Lake; they don't have a vault toilet or picnic bench, but that's the only difference in amenities from Mann Lake.

If you turn north on Hwy 78 towards Crane at mile 19.4 instead of heading straight, you'll hit **Crystal Crane Hot Springs** (www.cranehotsprings.com, 541-493-2312, 59315 Hwy 78, cabin $45-60, tent $15) in about 14 miles. It has a

Gravel Grinding

large hot springs pool, sleeping cabins and camping. Access to pools is included with accommodation.

MANN LAKE RECREATION AREA

(Burns District BLM, www.blm.gov, 541-573-4400, free) There is very little to this recreation area besides a vault toilet and a picnic bench. There are tent spots near the coffee-and-cream-colored water. There is no shade, unless you cop a squat in the shade of the pooper. The mountain and desert views are pretty spectacular though. Enjoy the coyote cacophony.

DAY TWO
Mann Lake Recreation Area to Fields
40.8 miles
Elevation Climbed 850 ft.

Today's ride is more chilled out compared with yesterday, but the spectacular vistas don't turn down the volume. The first 28.4 miles are gravel, yet you have less food and water weight and a shorter, flat route.

As you continue your circumnavigation of the Steens Mountain, you pedal past the glittering salt flats of the Alvord Desert to the east, while to the west the Steens Mountain heaves its precipitous, snow-capped peak heavenward. The Alvord Desert is a beacon for land sailors who consider the desert "playa" to be one of the best places in the world to sail. Just pray to the wind gods that the famous gusts are at your back.

At mile 17.7, you'll see a corrugated metal, lean-to and naked people lounging about the rusty shack. No worries, it's just the Alvord Hot Springs: unsigned, privately-owned and free to all. As rustic

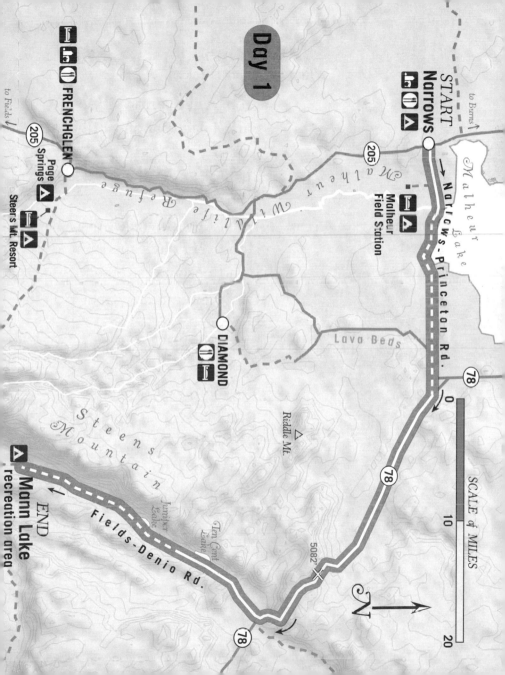

Day 1

START
Narrows

FRENCHGLEN

205 Page Springs

Steers Mt. Resort

Malheur Wildlife Refuge

Malheur Field Station

205

Narrows-Princeton Rd.

Malheur Lake

to Burns

to Fields

DIAMOND

Lava Beds

Riddle Mt.

78

0

78

Steens Mountain

Juniper Lake

Ten Cent Lake

5082'

Fields-Denio Rd.

78

END
Mann Lake
recreation area

N

SCALE of MILES

0   10   20

Day One
Narrows to Mann Lake

0	•	From The Narrows RV Park, head east on Sodhouse Ln
3.1	•	Turn off to Malheur Field Station
6	☝	Road turn to gravel
6.5	☞	Road veers unsigned
19.4	☝	Road become pavement
21	☞	Unsigned Princeton Spur Rd, becomes gravel
22.5	☞	Hwy 78, nice pavement begins
43.4	•	Top of Baker Pass
48.1	☞	To 'Fields,' unsigned Fields-Denio Rd
57.4	•	Ten Cent Lake
59.1	•	Gravel begins
61	•	Juniper Lake
71.8	•	Mann Lake Recreation Area

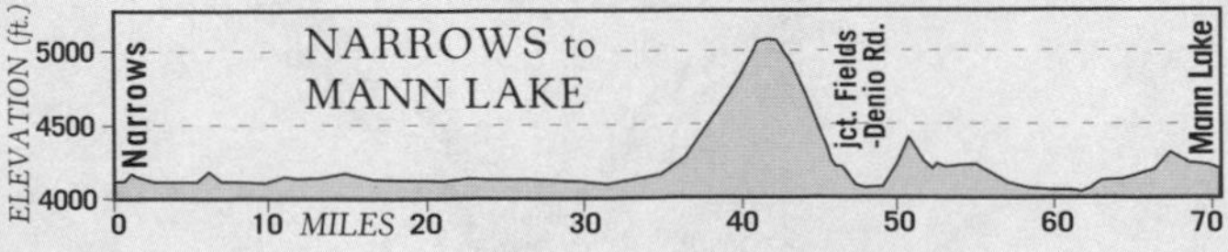

ELEVATION (ft.)

NARROWS to MANN LAKE

Narrows

Jct. Fields -Denio Rd.

Mann Lake

5000

4500

4000

0   10 *MILES* 20   30   40   50   60   70

hot springs are not on my Midwest-born husband's priority list, we passed by. But I hear it's lovely. I suggest an early arrival for more privacy.

On the subject of hot springs, I mention Mickey Hot Springs (mile 7.2) on the cue sheet. The bizarre springs are about six miles off route via a gnarly, exquisitely beautiful road. Signs at the springs warned us that people and animals have broken through the land's crust into steaming water to meet unsavory consequences. Slimy bottoms of the pools weren't that appealing anyway. Gulp.

The day ends in the sleepy little one-tractor town of Fields, a place with one cafe that's known near and far for its hamburgers and milkshakes. If you're a hot springs fiend, ask folks about the Willow Creek (or Wildhorse) Hot Springs, which is about a 33-mile ride from town.

RIDING TIPS AND HEADS UP

• There is no water or shade, and when a car comes, you might exclaim, "Well, I'll be."

EXTRACURRICULAR ACTIVITIES

The **Alvord Hot Springs** (mile 17.7) will be an interesting, if not therapeutic, endeavor.

LODGING ON ROUTE

Steens Country Cabin

(www.steenscountrycabin.com, 541-495-2344, $8-125) The Williams family rents out a two-bedroom cabin with AC, heat, a full kitchen and a DVD player.

Fields

Pop. 86
Elevation 4,236 ft.

LODGING, CAMPING AND CHOW

Alvord Inn (www.alvordinn.com, 541-589-0575, 22308 Fields Dr, $60-80) is a simple two-unit B&B owned by locals. I've heard good things about their cinnamon rolls.

Fields General Store and Motel (541-495-2275, 22276 Fields Dr, room $50-65, per tent $5) With a cafe (8am-4:30pm, Sun from 9am) known widely for delicious milkshakes and hamburgers, this all-in-one stop also has a small grocery store, liquor selection and small adjoining motel with modest rooms. The store owns a patch of land with a grove of trees, which you can sometimes camp on if there aren't too many of you. You can use their outhouse and water spigot.

Gravel Grinding

DAY THREE
Fields to Frenchglen
51.7 miles
Elevation Climbed 2,375 ft.

"Uncountable years to come,
I wish to be left to the desert's peace
And the warmth of the desert's sun,

For I know the soul that I once possessed,
Turned loose on a sagebrush sea,
Would hug spooky knees to a spectral chest
In ghostly ecstasy."

Around half a century ago, John Scharff, historian and advocate of Southeastern Oregon (see John Scharff, page 215), walked up to a creaky, abandoned cabin near your ride today and found this dusty poem tacked to the splintering wall. The anonymous pioneer poet, so taken with these harsh and magnificent environs, yearned to spend his afterlife right where he passed his mortal days.

Around now, you may have cultivated an understanding of why the author would write such a poem. Maybe the silence has revealed something or the wide-open spaces and the sky have shifted your perspective. Or maybe you just have chapped lips and a hankering for a hot bath and double Americano. Who knows.

As you round your way near the southern aspect of Steens Mountain, you'll pedal through more pristine, empty high-desert. Expect a couple of climbs and well-maintained pavement.

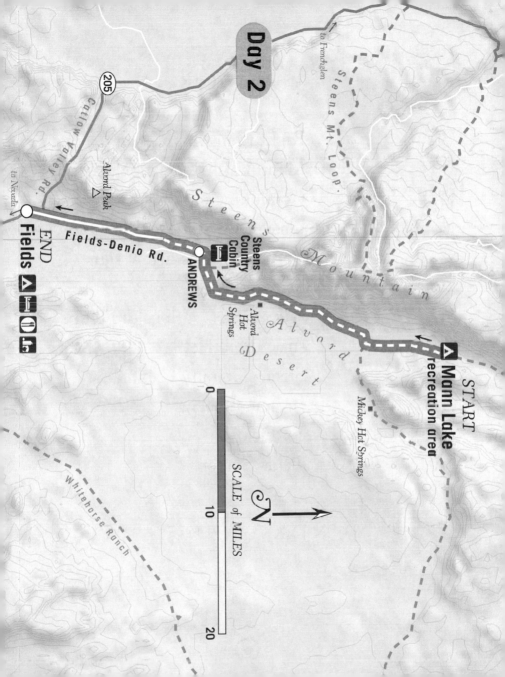

Day Two
Mann Lake to Fields

0	•	Right from Mann Lake Mann Lake Recreation Area
7.2	☞	Continuing on road
	or ☞	Unsigned road to Mickey Hot Springs, orange arrow sign points right
17.7	•	Alvord Hot Springs (little tin structure on left)
25.3	•	Steens Country Cabin
28.4	•	Pavement begins
38.9	☞	To 'Fields'
40.8	•	Fields Station

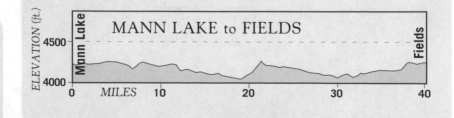

Gravel Grinding

I love Frenchglen, where your day ends, because I'm a sucker for a historical hotel, which is basically the only thing in "town." Now a state heritage site, the Frenchglen Hotel has been restored since its stagecoach stop days in the 1920s, but significant aspects of its architectural character are still intact. The tiny quarters that share a bathroom are simple and to the point, and the communal meals downstairs help create a community of travelers, just like days of old.

Frenchglen
Pop. 60
Elevation 4,200 ft.

CAMPING AND LODGING
Frenchglen Hotel State Heritage Site
(www.oregonstateparks.org, 541-493-2825, Hwy 205, shared bath $70-75) I love this place with its shade trees in the middle of the desert, screened in porch, 1920s-sized rooms and communal meals. You really get a sense of what it might have been like to overnight at a stagecoach stop.
Steens Mountain Resort
(www.steensmountainresort, 541-493-2415, 35678 Resort Lane, cabin $75, one-time bedding fee $5, tent site for two $15, each additional person $5) About three miles from the restaurant at the Frenchglen Hotel, this simple compound has cabins and tents sites. Though the cabins have equipped kitchens, there is no restaurant or store. They have showers and restrooms for campers.

Paige Springs Campground
(www.blm.gov, 541-573-4400, Steens Loop Rd, tent site $8) 36 sites. Up by Steens Mountain Resort, this is a convenient camping option with potable water and shade trees.

CHOW DOWN
Frenchglen Hotel (see previous column) has the only grub in town. They serve breakfast, will make you a bag lunch and serve dinner on long, communal tables (by reservation only). Also, the **Frenchglen Mercentile** (541-493-2738, Hwy 205) is a tiny store that is open daily April-October, with varying hours.

The Steens Mountain Loop: It might just hand you your booty
65.4 miles
Cycling this epic 65.4-mile route packs a lot of scenery in one day: gorges, lakes, meadows, a river view, desert vistas that would make even Edward Abbey gawk and a scenic overlook where you can check out wild horses. But you do work for it, friend. The summit of the pass comes uncomfortably close to 10,000 ft, and portions of the road seem like they got gnawed up by a rock monster then beaten by a steep sick. To boot, Steens Mountain has a weather system unto itself, which is characteristically fickle and makes the road impassable due to snow until July.

Some of the campgrounds along the way have potable water, but come

Gravel Grinding

prepared with all you need for riding all day. Some folks preach that you need a mountain bike on this track, but I'm sure that a number of cyclocross people and fully-rigid fanatics would disagree.

DAY FOUR
Frenchglen to The Narrows
34.3 miles
Elevation Climbed 1,350 ft.

I saw a cowgirl and cowboy wrangling heads of cattle on the road you ride today. It was all I could do to not go up and introduce myself and ask for a picture of us together. No, I played it cucumber-cool and took sneaky photos of them while pretending to do something else.

I love cowpeople. Not to romanticize hyperbolically (and putting aside my qualms with the cattle industry), but they are in touch with their environment in ways I could only dream to be. And I love them Wranglers.

On this homestretch desert ramble, you'll pedal along the gently undulating high-desert valley floor. You pass fascinating rock outcroppings and miles of ornery sage brush as the serrated outline of Steens Mountain shrinks into the distance.

When departing this corner of Oregon, my husband Joe noted that Burns seemed like a mad and hectic place after spending days in what seemed like a universe of silence punctuated with unhurried conversation and coyote

symphonies. In my heart, I felt I had visited a place whose raw, muscular nature shifted me around on the inside and made me more sinewy on the outside. Now, that's a vacation.

The Diamond Lollipop
41.5 miles

Driblet spires, fissures, cinder cones, spatter cones, craters, lave tubes, vents and a graben (sounds exciting like a Cracken!). Though these terms might sound like depictions of a distant planet in a sci-fi novel, they describe real features at **Diamond Craters Outstanding Natural Area**. The Diamond Lollipop transverses this 17,000-acre area, which is completely unique in North America with some of the most diverse basaltic volcano features in the country.

A highlight of this ride was the **Round Barn Visitor Center** (www.roundbarn.net, 541-493-2070). While the actual Round Barn—built by sheisty cattle king Pete French in the 1870s—is pretty cool and unique, I

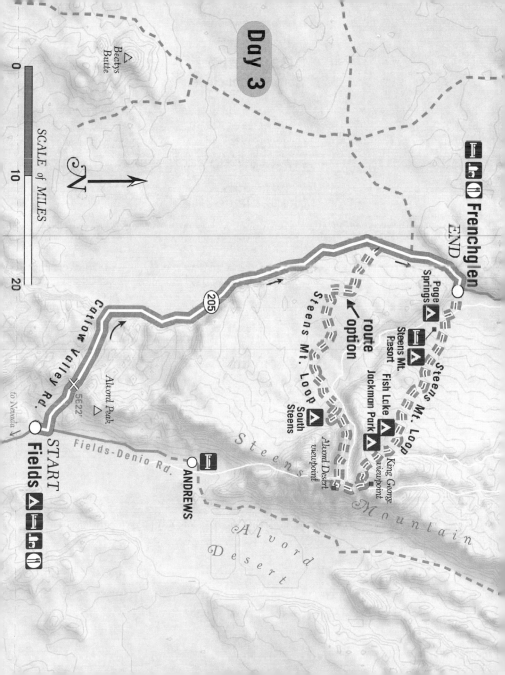

Day 3

Beatys Butte

SCALE of MILES
0
10
20

N

Frenchglen
END

Page Springs

Steens Mt. Resort

route option

Steens Mt. Loop

Steens Mt. Loop

Fish Lake

Jackman Park

205

Catlow Valley Rd.

to Nevada

5622'

Alvord Peak

South Steens

King George viewpoint

Alvord Desert viewpoint

START
Fields

Fields–Denio Rd.

ANDREWS

Steens

Mountain

Alvord

Desert

Day Three
Fields to Frenchglen

0   •   From Fields Station, head north on Fields-Denio Rd

1.3   ☞   Catlow Valley Rd

6.7   •   Top of climb

51.7   •   Frenchglen Hotel

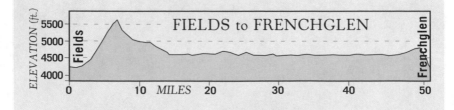

Gravel Grinding

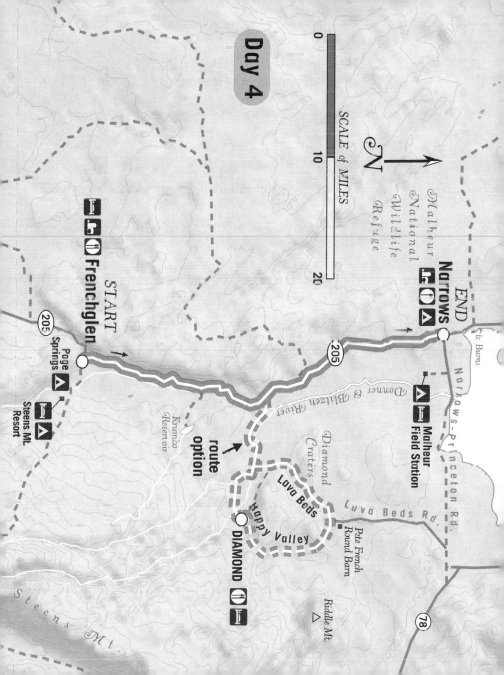

Day Four
Frenchglen to Narrows

0 • From Frenchglen Hotel, head north on Hwy 205

17.5 • Turnoff to the Diamond Lollipop Loop

34.7 • The Narrows RV Park

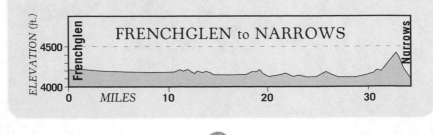

Gravel Grinding

LOVED the book selection in the gift shop of the visitor's center. It has every conceivable book about the region in stock, even nichey self-published titles. Not to mention, one side of the center is a wonky museum section filled with the Jenkins family memorabilia. Dick Jenkins, the owner and a tour guide, is a hoot. PS, you can get snacks and a cold drink here.

Halfway into the ride, you'll come to Diamond (pop. 101) where there is an adorable and historic hotel run by equally adorable ladies. When we popped into the **Hotel Diamond** (541-493-1898, 10 Main St, $55-90), they were having their monthly wine-pairing dinner with a Portuguese theme, I believe. We had to continue riding to beat nightfall or else we would have stayed. Slightly more updated and polished than the Frenchglen Hotel, this place still exudes the same outback stagecoach inn, community vibe.

The route is darn scenic in a deserty, Eastern Oregon way.

Really good idea: add an extra day to your tour by heading from Frenchglen to Hotel Diamond then back to The Narrows the next day. Or mileage fiends can just add this lollipop route into their ride to The Narrows.

Gravel Grinding

SUGGESTED PACKING LIST
(Cut or embellish to your specific tour needs)

Bike gear
- Panniers or trailer
- Handlebar bag
- Water bottles
- Saddle bag for repair kit
- Frame pump
- Front and rear lights
- Fenders

Clothes
- Bike shorts with chamois (2)
- T-shirts or jerseys
- Light weight, long-sleeved sun shirt
- Wool or synthetic base layer (could sub with arm and leg warmers)
- Wool or synthetic mid-layer
- Down vest or jacket (my preferred material, but fleece is fine)
- Rain gear
- Warm hat
- Cycling gloves (no-fingers and fingered pair)
- Socks
- Bandana
- Something for swimming
- Non-synthetic civilian clothes for out of the saddle
- Non-cycling shoes
- Compression stuff sack

Cold weather
- Warm jacket
- Extra pair of warm gloves
- 2 extra pairs of warm socks
- Neoprene booties
- Chemical hand and toe warmers
- Bike leggings with chamois
- Neck warmer

Your gear
- Helmet
- Cycling shoes
- Hydration system or extra water bottle for pannier
- Map in waterproof holder
- This book. Woot.
- Sunglasses
- Sunblock
- Lip balm with SPF
- Bug juice, when necessary
- Camera
- Cell phone and charger
- Extra Ziplocs (to protect, separate and for trash)
- Sarong
- Travel size baby wipes
- Dr. Bronner's soap or equivalent for washing clothes in sinks
- Tupperware (for leftovers/snacks)
- ID, credit cards, cash
- Keys to vehicle, if applicable
- Whistle (or whatever you use) for dog management
- Toiletries
- Wine key/beer opener
- Snacks and/or calorie powder
- Emergency iodine tablets
- Bungee cords
- Thermos (for hot tea en-route or extra water)
- Compass (depending on tour)
- U-lock (if you are traveling alone or in a city where you want to make stops, they are nice)

Repair kit
- Extra tubes and patch kit
- Tire levers
- Pump (frame or otherwise)
- Multi-tool with Allen wrenches, chain tool, Phillips and flat head screwdrivers
- Extra spokes and spoke wrench
- Extra tire (light weight and cheap to get you to the next shop, unless your tour is remote)
- Tire boot
- Chain link
- Rag for chain or other icky parts
- Zip ties
- Duct tape
- Lube
- Pocket knife

Camping gear
- Tent or bivvy
- Sleeping bag
- Sleeping pad
- Food
- Utensils
- MSR camp pot (can be used as Tupperware and bowl as well)
- Stove
- Fuel
- Lighter
- Water filter
- Waterproof matches
- Headlamp

Med kit
If your tour is remote and/or in back country, like on the Gravel Grinding tour, you'll need a more in-depth kit with meds. If you are touring, say, in wine country, the kit can be less intense. I always have a pair of rubber gloves and a CPR mouth barrier in an easily accessible place. A good itemized med kit list can be found at bicycling101.com, or a medium-sized, pre-packaged backcountry first aid kit can work. A couple of things I like to have in remote places that aren't usually included:
- Travel-sized backcountry first aid guide
- Irrigation syringe and Betadine tincture for wound management
- Thermometer
- Sam splint
- Ace bandage
- Lady kit: Urinary tract infection treatment (ciprofloxacin and over-the-counter UTI pain meds) and over-the-counter yeast infection treatment. (Good to have even if you've never experienced one of these. On tour = bad first-time experience.) *Taking the Lane #5, Our Bodies, Our Bikes* (www.takingthelane.com, $3), has great musings and info about women's bodies and cycling.

Luxury items
- Light-weight, nylon hammock
- Yerba mate accoutrements
- Novel
- If you have to work, computer device (not suggested)
- Technology: bike computer, GPS, iPhone handlebar mount

INDEX